LOVE Letters

MADELEINE L'Engle

Harold Shaw Publishers
Wheaton, Illinois

Library of Congress Cataloging-in-Publication Date

L'Engle, Madeleine.
    Love letters / Madeleine L'Engle.
      p. cm.
      1. Americans—Travel—Portugal—Fiction. 2. Married women—Portugal—Fiction.
    I. Title.
    PS3523.E55L6 1997
    813'.54—dc20

                                                            95-51555
                                                            CIP

03 02 01 00 99 98 97 96

10 9 8 7 6 5 4 3 2 1

Love Letters

By Madeleine L'Engle

An Acceptable Time
And Both Were Young
And It Was Good
The Anti-Muffins
Anytime Prayers
The Arm of the Starfish
Camilla
Certain Women
A Circle of Quiet
A Cry Like a Bell
Dance in the Desert
Dragons in the Waters
Everyday Prayers
The Glorious Impossible
A House Like a Lotus
Ilsa
The Irrational Season
The Journey with Jonah
Ladder of Angels
Lines Scribbled on an Envelope
Many Waters
Meet the Austins
The Moon by Night
The Other Side of the Sun

Penguins and Golden
    Calves
Prayers for Sunday
A Ring of Endless Light
The Rock That Is Higher
A Severed Wasp
The Small Rain
Sold into Egypt
The Sphinx at Dawn
A Stone for a Pillow
The Summer of the
    Great-grandmother
A Swiftly Tilting Planet
Trailing Clouds of Glory
Troubling a Star
The Twenty-four Days
    before Christmas
Two-Part Invention
Walking on Water
The Weather of the Heart
A Wind in the Door
A Winter's Love
A Wrinkle in Time
The Young Unicorns

Love is a revolt against the finitude of the finite, the transience of the transient, the relativity of the relative.

George Tyrell

It was an old moon, late in rising, and lopsided, shining wetly through the gathering clouds. Its cold light barely touched Charlotte Napier, sitting hunched into her coat on a marble bench; the surrounding pattern of mosaic on the plaza by the Convento de Nossa Senhora da Conceição was lost in shadow. It was three o'clock in the morning in this unknown town of Beja, Portugal: cold, raw, the dead of winter. In New York, so variable a thing is time, it would be barely bedtime, and Patrick, her husband . . .

What would Patrick be doing? Getting ready for bed as though nothing had happened? as though Charlotte had not fled across an ocean to escape him? Or, rather, to escape not Patrick, but his words:

"Raped you? . . . A child conceived in hate? . . . The hell with you. Leave me alone . . ."

The old moon was dying. Would Patrick notice it between the tall buildings of the city? The death of the moon; the death of a child; the death of a marriage . . .

She said aloud, "But I didn't kill him!" and then, silently, clasping her arms about herself as though to contain her anguish, —It wasn't anybody's fault, not even mine. It was an accident—

"Mrs. Napier—"

She sat upright, rigid. Had her cry, her private, inviolable grief, been revealed?

"Mrs. Napier." The voice came again, and with it the young man, Antonio de Tieve, who had sat at the table with her at dinner in the pensão.

She crouched there in silence and looked at him, his silhouette dark against the white walls of the convent. A cloud obscured the moon so that she could not see his features, only the shadow of his face between black hair and black jacket.

"Let me take you back to the pensão," he said. "It is much too cold for you to be sitting out here. And at this time of night it is not good for you to be out alone."

At least he did not ask her why she was there, and this was such a relief to her that she did not think to ask him what he himself was doing up and on the convent plaza in the small hours of the morning. Not moving from the marble bench she said, "The pensão is too cold. I couldn't sleep."

"I will get you some more covers."

"No. There are plenty of covers. They're just heavy . . ."

He sat down beside her. "I will stay with you, then, until you are ready to go back."

"No. Please don't bother. I'm all right."

"You are in trouble."

"I'm all right," she repeated. "When my mother-in-law gets back from Paris tomorrow and I can talk to her . . ."

"But your mother-in-law didn't know you were coming. You didn't let anybody know."

—Because I didn't know, she thought. —I hardly knew even when I was on the plane. "I came rather unexpectedly," she said.

He turned as though to try to make out her features in the darkness; his face came closer to hers, and then he was kissing her, roughly, passionately.

She pulled away and stood up. Her voice cut icily through the cold of the night. "Stop."

"But I thought you—"

She cut across the words she would not hear. "Go. Now."

"Mrs. Napier, I am terribly sorry," he said. "I only wanted to help."

"You're not helping. You're only proving Patrick was right. Please go. Now."

He bowed with precision, turned, and crossed the plaza. He moved with grace, despite the impediment of a slight limp. At dinner he had told her that he had been hurt in a duel while he was a student at the University of Coimbra, "one of the three oldest universities in Europe—did you know that?"

No, Charlotte didn't.

"We still keep the old traditions, a notch in our gowns for each of our love affairs. Many of our gowns are rather frayed, as you might imagine. And so, of course, we have duels, though these are frowned upon. And fado, you should hear us sing fado."

Exhausted from the plane trip and lack of sleep, she had not asked him what fado was. She did not want to know; not that, not anything else about him. His very being here in Beja, his presence at her table in the pensão for dinner, his coming to her here at the convent in the middle of the night, were outward and visible signs of the depravity of which Patrick had accused her.

—But wrongly. It is not true. I did not send Andrew to his death. There was nothing between me and Gus, or between me and anybody else, except Patrick.

The moon was lost behind the clouds. A chill, misting rain began to fall. She pulled the collar of her coat up about her pale hair. The rain beaded her face, cold, clear, unlike the hot, salt tears which might have helped if only she were still able to cry. But she had not cried for a long time. She could not cry now.

He had been helpful, the young man. That was all she had thought when she saw him in the lobby of the pensão, that he could help. She had arrived at the pensão at dusk after driving from Lisbon in a rented Volkswagen; the door was opened to her by a dark child, a boy, perhaps twelve years old. But all she could see was the blaze of his smile, the dark tangle of lashes shading enormous eyes. Her heart began to thump so painfully that she was hardly aware of his stream of Portuguese, soft *sshh*s and *jjhh*s with a few Teutonic *ch*s. He was at least twice as old as Andrew; his hair was black and curly instead of pale silk; there was no real resemblance; it was nothing but fatigue superimposing image upon image.

And there was no way to communicate with this image until the young man came into the lobby, holding a book, his finger marking the place, and, speaking fluent French, asked if he could help. Senhora Vieira, the child's mother, the proprietress, was out for a few minutes.

"I have a reservation, made this morning from Lisbon. I am Mrs. Patrick Napier."

His smile was almost as brilliant as the grubby Portuguese child's, as Andrew's. He switched to English, more heavily accented than his French. "But Mrs. Napier, we've been waiting for you! Ever since we heard your name—I stay here at the pensão, too, you see— are you coming because of our glorious Dame Violet?"

Charlotte sighed. Yes, of course she had come because of the glorious Dame Violet; but she could not under any circumstances go crawling to her, though she had crossed the ocean to see her. One did not drop in, unannounced, on Violet Napier; therefore the pensão reservation; even in her present desperation Charlotte would preserve protocol. If Violet was to help her, Charlotte would have to go to her on her own two feet, figuratively as well as literally. Violet had no patience with people who went limp under strain like boiled spaghetti.

"She is my mother-in-law," she said. "If you would help me put a call through to her—"

The call was as much a nightmare as the whole flight from New York. Violet was not in Beja. Violet had been in Paris to do a concert and would return the next evening.

Trying not to show shock and disappointment, she let Antonio de Tieve register for her; she let the child take her to her room. She ate dinner, hardly knowing that Antonio was sitting across from her, talking charmingly. After dinner she went immediately to bed and plunged into an exhausted sleep. And slept two hours. Two hours and she was awake and cold and the blankets were only a damp weight on her tired limbs. Around two o'clock she got up and dressed, as she had done so often that winter in New York, and let herself out. She did at least remember to adjust the lock on the door so that she could get back in.

The pensão was on a large square. Directly across the square was a barracks-like building; in the yellow circles of light from the lamps it seemed foreboding, frightening. She remembered a time when she was a small girl and she and her father had been held for several hours in Antwerp, because, for some never explained reason, the customs officer had thought her father's typewriter was a bomb. When they were finally released, they were down in the Antwerp police records forever as Mr. and Miss Blue-Blonde, the investigating officer having transcribed the color of eyes and hair from the passports in place of their names. There was something about this barracks in Portugal that reminded Charlotte of the one in Belgium and that sent her hurrying in the opposite direction.

She turned up a cobblestoned street with narrow sidewalks that were an intricate design of black and pale grey mosaic. Mosaic at her feet; the colors luminous in the street lamps; ceramic tile on the white houses to her right and left; everywhere a sense of order, of design. But in Charlotte's own chaos she was unable to comprehend order, and she found that her sense of smell was less blunted than her sight. The air was sharp not only with impending rain but with the acrid stink of drains and of rancid oil and damp cold; the smell seemed to seep through her coat along with the night wind.

She went along a street of small shops, dark now for the night, so that their windows were blind expanses of glass, turned down a street of private houses, and then saw on her right a great white building gleaming softly in the dark. As she reached the top of the street, she could see a plaque on the corner of the building. She crossed and peered at the lettering in the dim light of the street lamp: CONVENTO DE NOSSA SENHORA DA CONCEIÇÃO. The convent building faced a large mosaic terrace with marble benches and a life-sized statue of a woman. The building was entirely dark. Of course it would be, at this hour of the night—or morning. It would be time for the nuns to be up, soon. Where was the chapel? There would always be a light in the chapel. But she could see no glimmer of light anywhere, could sense only an empty darkness hanging about the convent. Or was she projecting her own desolation on her surroundings?

Beja.

She was in Beja to see Violet Napier—Dame Violet Napier, the harpsichordist—Patrick's mother, Charlotte's mother-in-law. And it was not for nothing that Violet had been nicknamed the Violent.

—When Violet comes back tomorrow—no, today—and I can talk—

What made her think she could talk to Violet, Violet, of all people, Violet who was Patrick's mother?

Antonio de Tieve knew Violet, and this was only logical in a small town, not horrid coincidence. What would Violet think of Antonio's coming to the convent plaza, of his arrogant, blasphemous kiss?

The rain began to fall more heavily. Her pale hair, her coat were soggy. She could not stay here any longer. Would the nuns let her in?

Without thinking she crossed to the arched entrance of the convent. There did not seem to be any bell to the door, so she began to knock. She knocked and no one came, and it was the very lack of response that broke through her unthinking pounding and she withdrew her hand quickly.

If she was this tired, so tired that she could think of trying to rouse the nuns in an unknown convent in the middle of the night— and she was this tired—she might as well accept the fact that she was not thinking coherently, that she was really incapable of thinking at all. She had better return to the pensão and get back into the damp bed that was at least drier than the rain.

But when she had undressed and slid, shivering, under the comfortless weight of the blankets, she could not sleep. There had been wine with dinner, and then too much coffee, and alcohol and caffein warred in her blood. She turned on the dim lamp and sat up in bed, her arms circling her knees, and looked around as though seeking reassurance, as though she might see something the room had not revealed before; but no revelation was forthcoming in this dark, chill rectangle, only a foreboding sense of past time, of lost time, of things sought for and not found. Behind her the heavy carved wood of the bedstead loomed up almost to the ceiling; its very massiveness seemed menacing; there was no comfort to be found in the bed, nor in the great, cumbersome wardrobe that matched it. In the spring of the year, with sunlight brightening the dark chintz of the curtains, the spidery pattern of the wallpaper, the room might have seemed full of Old World charm and atmosphere; the feeling of the past pervading the present might have been a delight. In the dead of winter and the small hours of the night, it filled her with a sense of oppression that was suffocating.

She got out of bed and took her coat down from the wardrobe, pushed into it, though it was still matted with rain, and pulled the collar up. The floor was icy under her bare feet. She crouched and opened the door to the night stand: on the bottom shelf was a chamber pot; above it were three books, which she pulled out. Despite the inadequate light, she would try to read herself to sleep. The first book was a Gideon Bible: even in Beja, Portugal? Essie, her father's housekeeper, beloved Essie, in all times of stress had reached for her Bible, opened it, and pointed a finger at a verse. There she was supposed to find the answer. Charlotte, with the certainty of youth, had told Essie that this was superstition if not sin, but, as she thrust the Bible aside now, she wondered: —But suppose it *could* answer me . . .

She pulled it back across the covers, opened it, and put her finger down on the page. The psalms. *My flesh trembleth for fear of thee; and I am afraid of thy judgments.*

—Well, Charlotte, what did you expect? Serves you right.

She turned to the other two books, both paperbound. The first was French, *Lettres d'une Réligieuse Portugaise*. The second was Portuguese, something about Soror Mariana; another nun, then. There seemed no escaping them, though nuns were not what Charlotte was fleeing from; more like to: —get thee to a nunnery. (Her father had sent her to convent schools not for religion but to learn manners. Or so he had said.) She opened the Portuguese book and her smattering of Spanish helped her to pick out a few words, but at the end of the page she had made no sense of them, so she turned to the French book. At least it would hold a reasonable safety, because from this distance the years in the convent schools seemed to be haloed with an aura of comfort, if only the comfort of time past, passed through; but at least she had learned what to expect from nuns, so even a Portuguese nun would not offer many surprises, would give a kind of familiar childhood reassurance.

She began leafing through the book at random. *You made me completely yours with your violence; it was your love that made mine burst into flame; your tenderness melted me, and then your promises completely reassured me. My own awakening passion undid me, and the result of what started with such happiness is tears, and deathly despair, and I see no help anywhere.*

Certainly there was no help here! She sighed. The language of the Religious, particularly the Latin Religious, in describing the reaction of the human to the divine love, frequently makes use of the language of secular love, of sexual love; there was nothing really new or startling here, so Charlotte, cold, tired, groping, read on: *It's true that in loving you I felt a joy I hadn't known was possible, but I'm paying for it with a pain I didn't know was possible, either. If I had tried to resist your love, or held back out of false modesty; if I'd let my reason be stronger than my love, then you'd have a right to punish me now, and to use your power over me. But it seemed to me that you loved me even before you told me that you did; you made me believe that yours was a great passion. You carried me away and I gave myself entirely to love . . .*

She sighed again. This stuff was useless as a soporific. When she was twelve she had memorized large quantities of St. John of the Cross, wallowing in a romanticism far from that austere saint's intention. She still remembered much of it. Closing her eyes, she whispered,

Whither hast thou hidden thyself, And hast left me, O
  Belovèd, to my sighing?
Thou didst flee like the hart, having wounded me: I went
  out after thee, calling, and thou wert gone.
Shepherds, ye that go yonder, through the sheepcotes, to the
  hill,
If perchance ye see him that I most love, Tell ye him that I
  languish, suffer and die.

Since thou hast wounded this heart, wherefore didst thou not
  heal it?
And wherefore, having robbed me of it, hast thou left it thus
And takest not the prey that thou hast spoiled?

Well, St. John of the Cross was not only a great mystic, he was a great poet, which this Portuguese nun was not.

She turned wearily back to the first of the letters. *Oh, my darling, if only you had known when you first came to me what was going to happen! Poor love, you betrayed me, and you betrayed yourself by hoping for the impossible. You expected so much joy from our love, and all that is left is the pain of our parting.*

She rejected the nun's letters with the same revulsion with which she had thrown down the Gideon Bible. What kind of answer was this? . . . *the result of what started with such happiness is tears, and deathly despair, and I see no help anywhere . . .*

—What would you have made of *that*, Essie?

She put the three books down on the night stand, turned out the light, and, still in the damp coat, plunged under the covers.

The strange words of the Portuguese nun, the mystical words of St. John of the Cross, the searing words of Patrick whirled in discordant counterpoint in her head. She slid in and out of a half sleep, a sleep riddled with dreams that left her exhausted instead of refreshed. As soon as it was daylight she got up and dressed. Her throat felt raw and hot.

As she went down the pink marble stairs she heard a high, clear whistling: Bach: a theme from Bach. Bach, here, in this smelly pensão?

In the cold of the lobby the dark child was sitting behind the table, whistling. He looked up and saw her and the radiance of his smile still whipped across her like a blast of wind. Why was he here, with his strange, dark echo of Andrew? Why was he whistling Bach? Bach belonged to Violet, and she would not see Violet until she had worked through time to evening, when Violet would be back from Paris.

She walked to the dining room, moving slowly, heavily, as though time were tangible, as though she had to push through it like a swimmer against the tide.

She had forgotten Antonio de Tieve.

In the dining room he rose to greet her. His face was anxious; he was full of apologies.

She said, "Forget it."

He pulled out her chair, then sat down across from her. He smiled at her, tentatively. "If I forget it, will you also? It was unpardonable of me, but if we could start again . . ."

"There is nothing to start," she said. "And we will certainly forget it."

The waiter who had served them the evening before appeared, beaming paternally over the rimless spectacles that slid down his nose. He spoke nothing but Portuguese, and Antonio had ordered dinner for her. Now he asked her what she wanted for breakfast.

It hurt her throat to speak. She said, "Coffee, please, and some rolls."

"Nothing else?"

"No. Thank you."

He spoke swiftly to the waiter, then smiled at Charlotte, speaking in his careful English, "He will bring it right away. One second."

Her tired mind repeated the last two words. —One second. One second. One second. Most peculiar to term our smallest fragment of clocked time a second. Is it because it was not the first?

Antonio had coffee before him, and a plate of some kind of meat with fried eggs. "I need a heavy breakfast," he said, "to get me through the rigors of the day. Although today is a holiday and I do not work. Madame Napier has visited Dame Violet before?"

Charlotte shook her head. Violet was in Beja only in winter, and she and Patrick took their vacations in summer, when Violet was in England. They had never seen Violet's treasured villa in Beja, given her by an admirer before Patrick was born. It was a strange gift, perhaps all the giver had to give, but Violet liked it because of its very inaccessibility, because it was the last place on earth one would expect Dame Violet Napier to have a villa.

"You do not mind if I exercise my English? It fatigues more easily than my French." He had such an air of vitality, sitting here across from her, that she found it difficult, in her own exhaustion, to believe that he could fatigue easily in anything. He asked, "Did madame perhaps find some books in her room?"

"Yes," she said. "There were some books in the night stand."

He smiled his charming smile; yes, it was charming, if a little too deliberately so; he was doing his best to erase the night before. "When the front bedroom is not being used, I sleep there," he said. "Of course I am in it with the understanding that any time she—the old Vieira—can rent it, I move out; she is charging me only for a much smaller room. There are very few tourists in winter, so I move seldom."

"The books are yours, then?"

"Yes. But madame is more than welcome to read them."

She made the effort of smiling back.

"Out of curiosity, tell me: how did a Gideon Bible get to Beja, Portugal?"

He laughed. "The Bible is part of my research. An American college student gave it to me when I was up north skiing during the holidays. He said he lifted it from a Y in Boston. A Y is a youth hostel?"

"Something like. Where did you learn your languages?"

"In school, to start with. We have five years of French and three of English. At Coimbra I continued my studies. Then I completed my time in the army, returned to Coimbra for my graduate work, and here I am."

At last the waiter came with her pitchers of hot milk and coffee, two rolls, a dish of jam, a tiny curl of butter. She poured coffee and sipped at it gratefully; it warmed her, and the hot milk was soothing to her throat.

He sat looking at her; she did not like the expression deep in his eyes; but all he asked her when he spoke was, "Did you look at the books?"

"I glanced at them."

"The letters of Soror Mariana?"

"Yes."

"And?" His smile held a questioning that seemed to her to be disproportionate.

She looked at him and shrugged, not smiling back.

"You have never heard of Mariana Alcoforado?" he asked. She shook her head. For a moment he seemed to ponder, and when he spoke again, he returned to French. "She was from Beja. A noblewoman. And a nun."

He paused for so long that Charlotte finally said, "Well, many noblewomen have become nuns. That's not extraordinary."

"But she was an extraordinary nun. In Beja, of course, we all believe in her."

"Believe?"

"That she wrote the letters. That it all happened."

"That what happened?"

"But you read the letters!"

She was beginning to be angry. "I glanced at them."

"Well?" He was still somehow challenging.

She shrugged again, and picked up her coffee cup, warming her hands against it. "Many Religious have written about Christ as lover. What's so odd about that?"

"She was not writing about Christ."

Now she looked at him sharply. "Who, then?"

"She was writing to her love, but it was not Christ, it was the French soldier who seduced her."

Why was she shocked? She had been surrounded by nuns for long enough to view the Religious with detachment, with no illusions of glamour. There wasn't much in the way of human fault or foible one could not find in a nun.

She did not like his smile.

But now he was quoting poetry.

If I could have my love
Would my love go?
If I could know my love
What would I know?

Is what I have
All that I lose?

Is what I lose
All that I keep?
If my heart could
How would it choose?
And must it choose,
Poor heart, to weep?

It struck too close to home; she did not like it.

He waited for her to comment on the verses, but she was silent. He said, "Mariana had her love. Therefore she lost him. Of course for some a nun cannot commit a sin, must preserve a kind of super-natural piosity. They, like the others who are shocked, forget that it was three hundred years ago, that things were different."

"You think, then," Charlotte asked, "that basic values change? that there are no absolutes?" This was the kind of absurd, intense question that got her into trouble. ("It's an invitation," Patrick said, "loud and clear.") She turned to her coffee, wishing, even with her sore throat, that she smoked. It might be one way to keep her mouth shut. There was an ashtray on the table between them, but he had not used it either. They both talked too much.

"I say that I believe that Mariana had her love," he said. "This is necessary for me for my work. There should be some integrity in these things. Aside from that I see no particular reason to believe in anything."

His brow furrowed, but smoothed as she asked, "Just what is your work?"

"You will forgive me if for a moment I talk about myself?" He looked at her anxiously.

"Please do."

He told his story fluently, as though it were one he enjoyed re-counting, as though it had become by now a small performance. Only a slight tightening of the lines that ran from his nostrils to the corners of his mouth betrayed tension. "My father was an older man, a respected man, a judge on the bench. He married a young and beautiful wife, and he was to have his first child, and all was very well with them. Then it was the usual story of a colleague lying and cheating and destroying his reputation and from the sorrow and shame of this he dies. In her grief my mother came to term early and died of a broken heart—and of having me, puny infant though I was. It was thought of course that I, too, would die, but I did not. So what to do with me? There were no relatives. My father had been ruined by his friend. There was no money, so I was sent to the fathers at the monastery of São Sebastian. They saw to it that I received my education. And discipline. One of their disciplines was beating. One of their disciplines was a kick that sent me rolling down the stairs and broke my hip, so that my limping gait reminds me of their disciplines to this day."

He did not see as she looked at him, startled. What about the duel at Coimbra? He continued, "It is because of their cold care that I went to University, so for this I must thank them." He shrugged. "Of course as a result of my years with them I am an atheist."

She gave a small laugh. "Does it follow?"

"As the rains of winter follow the drought of summer. But I am grateful to them for this. I have my spiritual independence as well as my physical."

"But you haven't told me what your work is," she reminded him.

He shrugged again. "In one sense it is that I am teacher of Latin here in the school in Beja. But even though I am atheist I know that man does not live by bread alone, and in any event I prefer cake. The teaching is a necessary means to an end, that I may live at all. As for the rest of it, I am a poet."

"Was that your lyric, the one you said just a little while ago?"

"Yes. Did you like it?" Again the quick look, the vulnerable look.

"Very much. But I would have to hear it again, so that I could really listen. And—it wasn't in Portuguese!"

"No. I try to write my poems in several languages, because in one I may find a nuance that is not available in another. It is in the music of languages that I have my gift, and sometimes I think that what I write in English or French is better than the Portuguese that is too easy for me; I am too fluent."

She asked, "What about Latin?"

He scowled ferociously. "After a day of school I have already had more Latin than my stomach can tolerate."

She said, "Say your poem again."

His expression could change as quickly as a sky with clouds racing across the moon. "I will say another. Listen: it is not my voice that you must hear, but the voice of Soror Mariana."

> My love is lost
> And so it stays.
> I count not cost
> Nor look for ways
> To love again
> For I love still
> And love is pain
> and pain is naught
> and love, like light,
> Cannot be caught
> And sun and rain
> And nights and days
> My heart have tossed
> A thousand ways.
> For love, like light,
> Cannot be caught.
> Fingers closed tight
> Hold naught.

20

She did not look at him but down at her clenched hands on her lap. "It's lovely." The words seared her throat.

"It moves you?" he asked.

She did not raise her head. "Very much." She tried to open her fingers.

"I am writing Mariana," he said. "Writing her, not about her, you understand. Writing her and her lover. It is my magnum opus. Their love. I am not concerned, basically, with historicity. Others have gone into that before me. It is not for us a new subject. There have been many books on Soror Mariana, good, bad, indifferent, romantic, cynical, shocking. I want my book to look at Soror Mariana from all aspects, beginning with her childhood. How, for instance, would you feel if you had been thrust into a convent as a small child when your mother died?"

"I was," Charlotte said softly.

But he didn't even hear. He was listening only to his own words.

"She must have had some of the same feelings I had with the fathers at São Sebastian."

Charlotte stood up. "I'm sorry," she said. "You will have to excuse me. I have things I must do." She left him and went upstairs to her room.

She lay down on the lumpy, unmade bed. The sun shone through moving clouds, but even this watery light hurt her eyes and she closed them against it. From somewhere downstairs in the pensão came several shrill, sweet chords. For a moment she thought it was a harpsichord . . .

Violet . . .

But even if a harpsichord, unlikely instrument, could be in this cold pensão, it could not be Violet, still on her way back from Paris, hurrying back to her loved Beja (not knowing that Charlotte was waiting).

From the way Violet talked you'd think Beja was made in heaven.

A heaven that was raw and cold, that smelled of mustiness and exhaustion and drains.

The music stopped.

She did not know what the unknown instrument had been.

—Oh, Violet, hurry, hurry, I need you.

She ached with the need for her mother-in-law, who could be so frighteningly violent, yet never when she was contained in the discipline of music; in music her violence was controlled, could be muted, transmuted, into infinite gentleness.

—Oh, Violet, be gentle with me now.

Her father had once told Charlotte that only the truly strong can afford to be gentle. He had continued and used the word *meek;* meek, he said, as in the Beatitudes, and in French meek was translated as *debonaire;* or it could be translated as chivalrous.

Ought one to expect so much of anybody?

It was cold. It was too cold. She tried to pull the blankets about her, but there was no warmth in them. She reached for the book of Soror Mariana's letters. Antonio had wakened a faint curiosity in her. She opened the book, then let it drop onto the covers.

"How, for instance," Antonio had asked, "would you feel if you'd been thrust into a convent as a small child when your mother died?"

Convent after convent . . .

The first one had been in England, and her father, stunned with the shock of her mother's death, had taken her there. It was summer, and they had gone into a garden where the Mother Superior was sitting in a carved wooden chair, a superb chair, not garden furniture at all, under an ancient pear tree. That was a long time ago, and she could not remember the face of the nun. The features she saw in her mind's eye under the magnificently starched coif were Violet's. Why Violet's? Her father had left Charlotte in the garden with the nun. Her mother had gone somewhere—

. . . "To heaven," the nun who looked like Dame Violet Napier told her, "where she can pray for you even better than she did on earth."

"I don't think she ever prayed for me," the child Charlotte said.

"But you say your prayers at night, and grace before meals?"

"No."

The nun's face tightened briefly. Then she smiled at the child. "These, then, are things you will learn. Do you think you will like that?"

"I would like to know where my mother has gone," Charlotte said, "and where my father is going."

Violet—no, the nun—studied her. "Your speech is harsh and American, Charlotte dear. We will have to do something about that."

"Yes'm."

"Yes, Reverend Mother."

"Yes,

. . . Aunt Brites."

"Yes, your Reverence."

The child looked at the nun. "But you are my aunt."

"While you are here in my convent I am the abbess and you call me your Reverence. Because I am Dona Brites Alcoforado you may also call me your Grace."

"Yes, Aunt Br—yes, your Reverence—Grace."

"It is not wholly your fault, Mariana," the nun said, smiling down at the child. The wind stirring the branches of the pear tree made a moving pattern on her serene and austere face, on her hands resting on the arms of the carved chair. "Your father is not willing to accept that I am a Religious first, and an Alcoforado and his sister second, that I am indeed both. You will have to learn to think of me as a sister, but not *his* sister. You have, indeed, much to learn."

"Yes, Aunt Brites—your Reverence."

. . . Charlotte stood in the superior's large and airy office. The windows were open, although the day was cool, and starched white curtains blew in the breeze. Behind the superior's chair, and high on the wall, was a large dark cross with an overrealistically carved corpus.

"Where is my father?" Charlotte asked.

"He is in Paris. He sent you a postcard."

"How do you know?"

"All the mail must go through my hands, Charlotte."

"I want to see my father."

"You will see him when he comes back to England."

"But when will that be?"

"I am sure he will inform us when he knows his plans."

"I want Reuben and Essie."

"Who are Reuben and Essie?"

"Reuben is the butler and Essie is the housekeeper."

"Where are they?"

"In New York. In our house in New York."

"Then it is not possible for you to see them, is it, dear?"

"I want my mother."

"Charlotte."

"Where do you think my mother is?"

"That does not matter."

"It matters to me. She never prayed for me. Reuben and Essie did. They went to church but we never went. When I ate with them— my mother and father—we just started to eat. She wore beautiful clothes and painted her eyes. I liked to look at her, but she didn't like me to touch her, in case I messed her up, you know. But I just liked to look at her. Sister Mary of the Ascension says that people like that are damned."

"It is only God who has the power to damn people, Charlotte, not Sister Ascension."

"Yes, but what do *you* think?"

"Your mother loved your father, didn't she?"

"Yes."

"And she loved you?"

"Yes . . ."

"I do not think God will forget that,

. . . nor must we forget, Mariana, that she is in eternity now, whereas we are still in time, and cannot fully understand these things."

"But if papa gave more money so that we could say more masses for her soul, Sister Maria da Assunção said she would get to heaven sooner."

"It is not Sister Maria da Assunção who is judge of these things, is it, Mariana? However, if and when Francisco deigns to pay us another visit I shall certainly ask him for more money."

"For masses?"

"We will say the masses in any case. You have been listening to too much indiscreet chattering. For food, child. Food for you and Peregrina. And food for my sisters. Most of what there is goes to the children, while the sisters are hungry. So I must not be harsh with Sister Maria da Assunção. It does me little good to feed my sisters' souls if I must starve their bodies. A hungry nun is not a good one."

The abbess looked at the blazing sapphire on her finger; her pale eyes seemed to hold and reflect its blue. "It is incongruous," she said, "but I could not sell it. There is a great deal for you to learn, child. But it will have to wait. Meanwhile, do not worry about your mother. God will do that."

"God worries about my mother?"

"Not now. But there were many times during her life when he must have done so."

. . . Charlotte woke up. Her legs ached from the cramped position in which she had been huddled under the blankets. Her hands and feet were icy cold, her throat a pillar of fire. She could not stay in this room.

She rose, stiffly, and walked over to the window. Pallid sunlight touched the square, although the prisonlike building across the way was dark in the shadow of a cloud. But at least it was not raining, so she could go for a walk.

Her coat still felt damp from the night before, and she pulled it tightly around her, and tied a scarf over her fair hair. Outside the pensão the ground was puddled, and the damp seeped through the soles of her high-heeled pumps. The beautiful, uncomfortable shoes were for Patrick because in them she walked like a lady; she could not move with the swinging stride that was more comfortable for her long limbs. It wasn't only Patrick: the sisters had always been at her to walk properly too, but they hadn't bought her expensive shoes to do it in. They had expected her to move gracefully in the horrible school boots.

The cobblestones hurt her feet. Buying a pair of practical shoes would give her something to do; it wouldn't matter if she walked like an English schoolgirl as long as her feet warmed up. She looked in the shop windows, then saw the convent up the hill ahead of her. Would the nuns speak nothing but Portuguese? There would surely be someone who spoke French. She could buy the shoes later.

She hurried up the hill to the convent. There was no sign of life. The windows were blind and black. She crossed the terrace to the marble bench where she had sat the night before. From there she could see the barred door under the arches, could see a broken window.

The convent was empty, was dead, though she had a lingering sensation of dark-habited presences; she would not have been surprised to hear the high, light voices of the young sisters, or to see the swing of skirt and rosary moving along the arched cloister. She sat down on the bench, turning to look at the statue behind her. QUEEN LEONOR, the plaque said.

"Well after Soror Mariana's day," came a voice, and Antonio limped across the plaza to her, followed by a large man with a mop of brown-grey hair and beard, and a black mourning band on the sleeve of his brown tweed suit.

"Mrs. Napier, this is Dr. Ferreira, a friend of Dame Violet's—and of mine."

The doctor bowed courteously over her hand, speaking in impeccable Oxonian. "I'm dining with Dame Violet tonight," he said. "Perhaps I shall have the pleasure of seeing you then."

Not to be able to see Violet alone: it seemed that one unexpected and unpleasant event followed upon another. "Perhaps. I—I haven't made any plans yet. Do you—do you know what time she'll be back from Paris?"

"If she makes her usual connections it should be before sundown. Her chauffeur drives like a madman. You'll be staying with her?"

Charlotte said again, "I haven't made any plans."

"She was not expecting you?" The inflection was barely a question; it was almost a statement.

"I was hardly expecting myself," Charlotte said flatly. He was Violet's age, this doctor, he was old enough to be her father; there was something about him that made her feel no need for pretense.

"Your husband is not with you?" There was no prying in his voice, only courtesy. If he really did know Violet well he would know about Patrick, too, at least that Patrick existed; he might even know that Charlotte existed.

"No. He stayed in New York."

For a moment the doctor looked at her sharply, but he said only, "In any event, I will see you at lunch. Since my wife's death I take most of my meals at the pensão. Senhora Vieira has the best kitchen in Beja. Now I must be off to my surgery."

As he left, lumbering heavily across the plaza, Antonio said, "Do forgive me; I am really not following you; I had already planned to meet Dr. Ferreira here."

She stared at him. "How did you know I was here last night?"

He sat down beside her. "Last night I did follow you. I was working late, and I heard you leave. And we have made a bargain to forget it, have we not?"

She looked at him bleakly. "I wish things *could* be forgotten."

He put his hand down near hers on the bench, but did not touch her. "You are so strange, Mrs. Napier," he said. "Not like an American at all."

She sighed. "I'm tired of this American business. I got it all the time when I was a child. *Oh, what a nice little girl. Not at all like an American child.* I am an American, and I'm exactly like an American, because that's what I am."

He said, gently, "But there is no need to get so excited. You are yourself. And you are a lady. That is obvious. One always knows what to expect from the bourgeoisie, but not from either the lower or the upper classes."

At this snobbery she smiled, "Another generalization, Mr. de Tieve."

"Please call me Tonio. All my friends do."

"All right," she said, but called him nothing. "What was the music I heard?"

"It disturbed you?"

"No. Not at all. I enjoyed it. But I couldn't tell what the instrument was. At first I thought it was a harpsichord. Then I realized it couldn't be that, but must be more like a guitar."

"It is a guitar. A Portuguese guitar. It is usually played with the Spanish guitar as accompaniment. For once Portugal has the melody and Spain is in the background. Joaquim—the little Vieira—and I play together. I the Spanish guitar, and he the Portuguese. He is the musician. Some time we will play for you. Your mother-in-law likes to hear us. She has even made arrangements for us of some of the Alentejo—that is Beja's province—folk songs, and then she has arranged our *pièce de résistance,* a Bach Two Part Invention. She does it for Joaquim, you understand, because she says he is a born musician." He made a face. "I am jealous of my little friend." Then he smiled, looking away from Charlotte and towards the white arches, the ornamented terraces and towers of the convent. "It is in its own way very beautiful, is it not?"

She nodded, following his gaze. "What were your wicked Sister Mariana's dates?"

"She was a young woman in the mid-seventeenth century. And do not call her wicked until you know more about her. We should not judge—"

She cut him off. "I would not presume to judge anybody." And, more vehemently, "Not anybody." Then, realizing the disproportion of her response, she asked, "It isn't a convent now?"

"No. Nor has it been for a long time. What we see is only a small part of what was here in Soror Mariana's time. The street has cut through it, is paved with its stones. But there were two hundred nuns here once."

"And now?"

"Now it is a national monument. A regional museum."

Charlotte shifted her position on the cold marble of the bench. Her legs ached. She was irrationally sad that there were no nuns in the convent, that there was no one there to recite the Divine Office, that the lovely white building was dark and desolate.

"Odd," Antonio said, "that she seems so alive, that despite the decay I can feel her here. I can sense her presence, through my pores, as it were, even more than in the letters. There are only five of them, you know; at least there are only five that are considered authentic. I'm inclined to think that the others are without question a fraud, some literary hack trying to batten on the success of the first and legitimate ones. Everything we need is in those five wild letters. I say wild. But I imagine that there were times when she, too, could have been marble," he looked over at the statue, "times when her life, too, was suspended. Your Thoreau— you know him?"

She did not smile. "Yes."

"He said," Antonio closed his eyes, wrinkling his face in an effort of memory, *"Time is but the stream I go a-fishing in. I drink at it; but while I drink I see the sandy bottom and detect how shallow it is. Its thin current slides away, but eternity remains. I would drink deeper; fish in the sky whose bottom is pebbly with stars."*

He switched back to French. "What I would really like to do is write about Mariana in eternity, in her fullest meaning, instead of having to pin her like a butterfly against the finiteness of history." He broke off. "You have made your plans for the day?"

Again she felt trapped. She spoke carefully. "I have no plans until I have seen my mother-in-law. I'm still very tired, so I'll spend the day quietly. I thought I'd walk around a little and look at the town and buy a pair of shoes. Who *is* Dr. Ferreira?"

His smile held spontaneous and genuine affection. "He is the best doctor in Beja. A very important man here. And he is the intimate of your mother-in-law."

But Charlotte did not want to discuss Violet for fear her need for Violet would become too acute. Violet would not be back until evening, and evening was lost in the far reaches of time. Evening, not having been yet, was further away than the three hundred years past when Sister Mariana and the other nuns had filled this convent with life. She looked about her at the whiteness of the building, these walls meant to hold a community but which now gleamed emptily in the thin light that filtered through the clouds. She, too, would fish in the strange river. "So what about your nun?" she asked.

He sighed, not the deep unconscious sigh that can be so expressive, but a deliberate, slightly theatrical sigh. "She is not my nun. She should not, of course, have been anybody's nun, except her supernatural bridegroom's. What an extraordinary study in love she is proving to be for me. Profane love, you understand. Eros. I am not interested in theological implications."

"Even profane love is rather an enormous subject."

"Yes, but with Sister Mariana as the focus I may speak specifically rather than generally."

"With a nun as the focus of a study on profane love I don't see how you can avoid the theological implications."

He put his hand lightly over her gloved one. "I've managed to avoid them for over a quarter of a century."

Quietly she moved her hand. "What hours is the museum open?"

This was a mistake. He said, too quickly, "You would like to visit it?"

"Yes. Why not? I'm here, and your nun rather intrigues me." She kept her voice light, impersonal.

He turned on the bench so that he could face her. "How charming this is! Mariana and her Frenchman must have spoken together just as we are doing. She was educated. She would have spoken French easily. It is obvious from the letters that she and her lover had no trouble communicating with each other. How quickly she understood him, as you, too, so quickly understand me."

She gave him no response, so he said, "You won't find much of her in the museum officially, you know. It is chiefly a regional museum. Pottery. Examples of our beautiful tile, going back to the very early centuries. Roman remains. Things like that. However, for me there is still a feeling to the cloister; I am aware of her presence when I am there. It is very strong. And the chapel is in good repair and must be very much as it was in her day. I could arrange for you to pay a visit this afternoon."

"But isn't it open? I mean, aren't there regular hours?"

"Technically at the moment the museum is closed for repair and renovation. But I can procure the key. The present curator is a retired professor of mine from Coimbra. He has already written one of the definitive books on Soror Mariana and is giving me much help. And I will tell him that you are Dame Violet Napier's daughter-in-law; he is a great lover of music, particularly ancient music. As well, of course, of Dame Violet herself. We could perhaps plan to come directly after lunch, if that would be convenient to you."

She sighed, the deep, unconscious sigh—she had let herself in for this one—and said, "Yes, that would be fine. Thank you."

The smile lit his face again, the Portuguese smile that was so piercing in the small Joaquim, but that in Antonio was faintly demonic. "Then I will be off to get the key. Professor Nunez is not always easy to find. He is now on what you would call a 'jag' about the Roman ruins, so he may be off anywhere, though with his arthritis he should not be wandering about in this weather. Never fear, I will run him to earth and will see you at the midday meal."

She remained seated on the bench until she was sure that he would be safely away. Then she walked to a shoe store she remembered passing the evening before and bought a pair of shoes. They were quite hideous, of stiff orangey leather, but they had thick soles and were, she hoped, waterproof. The proprietor of the store spoke just enough French to make the transaction possible, though in the end she had no idea how much she had paid for her purchase, whether the shoes were a bargain or an extravagance.

When she left the store a watery sunlight was sliding through the clouds. She looked at her watch. Not quite ten o'clock. In New York it would not be daylight.

She went from the shoe store back to the convent (why? because it was the only place she knew except the pensão?) and sat on the bench near the statue of Queen Leonora, hoping that the sunlight would strengthen, for it felt warmer out here on the convent plaza than in her room at the pensão, and if it did not rain she could stay until time for lunch.

In her first convent, the one in England (there had been one in France and two in the United States), there had been a terrace too, but of flagstones instead of mosaic, and the convent buildings were of grey stone instead of this brilliant expanse of whitewash. But that was only a superficial difference, and even the passing of centuries should make no more than surface changes. She had been to Roman Catholic convent schools and Anglican convent schools, and despite differences in language and rules and regulations they had not been unalike. There were still too many females herded together, living without privacy, and under enforced rules.

It was in the earliest of her convent experiences, the convent where she had stayed the longest, the convent she had in the end loved best, that she had first witnessed violence outside herself, outside the rhythm of her own small experience. Strange to see violence in a convent where habit and rule clothed and curbed passionate emotion. She had seen anger in which her father had shaken her mother, though never struck her; she had seen the excitement in which her mother would hit out at her father, would scream strange, incoherent words. There were tears and then great laughters of reconciliation, but this storminess was the familiar weather in which the child Charlotte moved. Its very changeableness was predictable, and therefore part of her security. She had been a happy child, full of laughter and gaiety, and old Essie's great lap was always there for her to climb on, and Reuben's thin and wiry shoulders.

But after her mother's unpredictable death, met alone in an open car on one of the winding mountain roads above Monte Carlo, the security was snatched away. Charlotte had a stunned feeling of walking on thin air, that the ground had gone from under her feet as it must have for her mother when the car skidded off the narrow road and hurtled into empty space.

In the convent school Charlotte held with anxious desperation to the reliability of regulations. The strictness of the Rule under which the sisters lived made a structure to which she could cling. She knew when they would be in chapel, in the classrooms, in the refectory. Their very silence could be counted on. As the violence of her parents' behavior had made it calculable, so, conversely, did the control of the sisters. Therefore, to see them break from the beauty of their ordered pattern was to the child an almost unendurable shock.

She had been in the convent garden, as far away from the children's dormitories as possible, for she had been squabbling with her roommates and had run to the lily pond to nurse and to enjoy hurt feelings. Her mother without warning had gone to wherever death thrusts people and her father was wandering about the continent with his typewriter and his charm, and he no longer played lion to Charlotte's unicorn, down on all fours and roaring fearfully at her, and therefore it was unutterably unfair that Perry should shout at Charlotte for fumbling the ball when it was Perry herself . . .

Two of the novices, their white veils like clouds against the blue of the English sky, had come down the path towards the lily pond. They did not see her. The children were all supposed to be back in their quarters changing for tea. Charlotte sat still, looking at them confidently, waiting for them to notice her, to ask her, perhaps, what was wrong.

But they were isolated in a frightening fragment of anger. "No!" one of them cried out in violent protest, and a hand flashed out and slapped against a white face.

The novice who had been slapped was the one to turn and run. She brushed by the child, not even seeing her, and Charlotte heard her whisper, half sobbing, "Through my fault, Lord, through *my* most grievous fault . . ."

. . . She ran, white veil flying, along the mosaic path from the lily pond, back towards the white buildings of the convent blazing in the sun. Nerves and tempers were at the breaking point. Even the abbess was short with them. If it were not for the violence of the sun, Sister Joaquina would not have been angered, would not, could not have struck her . . .

She ran, without looking, into a group of blue-aproned children playing ball in the rose garden. The roses were brown and dry from the heat. Sister Maria da Assunção grieved over them, but there was no longer any point in keeping the children from playing there. One of the little ones ran up to the novice and flung her arms about her.

"My *own* darling sister!"

The novice picked up the ball which had been thrown onto the dry grass near them and tossed it back into the center of the group. "No, Peregrina, I'm not your sister any more than anyone else's. Not since I put on this habit."

The child stamped jealously, possessively. "You are, too, Mariana! You are, too! We have the same blood in our veins, you know how papa's always talking about blood. You are, *too,* my sister!"

Mariana spoke automatically, smoothing back the child's dark hair which was curling moistly from the heat. "Yes, my sweeting, I'm your sister, and I'm Sofia's sister, and Ampara's sister . . ."

The child pulled at the deep sleeve of the habit. "I don't want you to be *their* sister. I just want you to be mine. Mariana! What's the matter with your cheek? It's all red!"

Swiftly the novice put her hand up to the still tingling skin. There would be a small bruise where the wedding ring had struck. "Nothing." She reached out and caught the ball which one of the children had tossed to her. "Here, Teresa. Catch."

But Peregrina was unwilling to have anyone else take her place as the center of Mariana's attention. "How different you look since your Clothing. I can't get used to you in a veil. I'm not always even sure when it *is* you. And I can't tell whether you look older or younger."

"Older, I hope."

Peregrina studied the novice judiciously. "Well, you don't *look* old, anyhow. Now Sister Joaquina looks much older than you."

"She's not," Mariana said shortly. "And the ages of the sisters is nothing for you to discuss."

Peregrina giggled, butting her head affectionately against the nun. "You know we're always guessing at it. It's one of our favorite games. But we *can't* guess the Most Reverend Mother Abbess Brites's age. Even papa won't tell me. I think he's scared of her, even if she's his sister. He will tell me that she's his older sister, but since I don't know papa's age that really isn't much help."

Mariana smiled down into the little girl's eyes. "You're an awful little gossip."

"Oh, I'll confess it," Peregrina agreed glibly. "But I really don't see what's wrong with wanting to know people's ages." She looked at the novice, an old and almost wizened look of shrewdness coming over her child's face. "Are you happy, Mariana?"

"Sister," the novice corrected.

"Yes, but are you?"

"Very."

A roly-poly little girl who could not have been more than three or four stumbled and tumbled onto the dry, stubbly grass. Bellowing, she ran to Mariana to be comforted. The girl picked the child up, kissed her eyes dry, put her down, and gave her a little shove back towards the group.

"Your Clothing—" Peregrina said, "it's like a wedding day for you, isn't it?"

"It *is* a wedding day."

"Of all of you who were clothed together Sister Michaela's my favorite—next to you, of course. I'm scared of Sister Beatriz. We all are, but we respect her, you know. And Sister Joaquina's an old crab, even if she isn't old."

Mariana put her hand up to her cheek. "You're impossible," she said, absently. "How's your embroidery going?"

Peregrina shrugged. "The stitches in my dove's foot were too big. At least Sister Isabella said they were, and she made me take them out and do them again. She's half blind so I really don't know how she knew. And she made me miss ten whole minutes of our playtime. I don't see why I should have to waste so much time on dove's feet and never get to the interesting part of the pattern."

One of the littler children threw the ball at Mariana, deliberately hitting her with it, and then ran up to her to retrieve it, shouting, "Sister! Sister! Pay attention to *me!*"

Mariana bent down and looked into the flushed face. It was no wonder the children tended to get out of hand in this heat made more unbearable by the searing winds that blew across the Alentejo plains. "You're getting very good at catching the ball. Now see if you can throw it to Maria da Gloria."

The little girl threw the ball wildly so that it went back over her head and into the withered rosebushes.

Mariana pushed through the dead flowers, catching her unfamiliar habit on thorns that had lost none of their sharpness. "Oh, Delores, you just won't aim . . ."

Peregrina followed, pulling at Mariana's skirts. "I'll get it. You'll tear your habit. Move." She pushed into the thicket and grabbed the ball. "There, Dolores. Run along, now. I scratched myself. Look, Mariana." She licked the long rough mark that ran across her wrist, then sat back on her heels. "Mariana, does papa expect me to stay in the convent, like you? Or am I to be married? He simply won't say."

Mariana dropped down onto the grass beside the child, rubbing the palm of her hand softly over the stubble. "It's too early to be thinking about such things."

Peregrina glowered at her. "If I'm to be married I'll have to have a bigger dowry than if I just become the Bride of Christ."

"Peregrina!"

"It's true."

"Peregrina, I shall have to send you to her Reverence."

Peregrina scowled blackly. "I don't care. And it's true, anyhow. I heard papa say so."

"Papa's a man of the world. He can't be expected to understand the things we've grown up with here at the convent. You can."

With one of her lightning changes of mood Peregrina grinned impishly. "But I'm only a child. Anyhow, I think papa's right. All I hope is that he'll be willing to spend the money on me. I don't want to be wasted on Christ."

Mariana rose, turning on the child in real anger. "Go. Go at once. I don't know what to say to you."

. . . "I don't know what to say to you, Charlotte," the superior said. "I realize that it is disappointing to you to have to stay with us over the holidays, but that is no excuse for you to be blasphemous."

"My father promised—"

"You saw his letter. I showed it to you. He will not be able to get back to England until after the first of the year."

"But he promised about Christmas. He said—"

"Charlotte, stop crying and go look in the mirror. I want you to see how you look with your face all red and mottled."

The rain on her face seemed to have the salt taste of remembered tears. Why should she think of such a stupid childish disappointment when there were instead all the holidays they *had* spent together? In England, in France, in Belgium, in New York in the house on Seventy-fourth Street. . . . So why remember the one time he had failed her, the one time he had not come to pick her up at school or at least meet her train or plane? Or why remember the opposite side of the coin, the time he had failed her precisely by bringing her home to the dark, high brownstone on Seventy-fourth Street for Christmas? Aunt Ada, who was her father's sister, was there, Aunt Ada who stayed with the house, not with her father. Where were Reuben and Essie? They were not in that memory. Well, they wouldn't be. It was Christmas Eve, so they would have been in church . . .

Her father sat at his desk in the library, writing, an ashtray and a glass of whiskey and soda beside him. The light from the desk lamp illuminated his bent head, and Aunt Ada, mending Charlotte's school uniforms ("What do you do to get them in this condition, Charlotte?"), said, "James, your hair's getting thin."

"It is not," Charlotte started to say, but didn't, because she looked, and it was.

No. No. No.

She got up and left the library and sat on the bottom step of the stairs where she could see her father through the open doors, but not Aunt Ada; she could, therefore, pretend that Aunt Ada did not exist.

But she could not shut out her aunt's voice saying, "James. When are we going to trim the tree?"

Her father continued to write. "I don't care."

"Are you going to wait until Charlotte is in bed? It's time she went to bed now, if you're ready."

"Let her stay up as long as she likes. She has enough rules and regulations at school. Why can't she help trim the tree? She's old enough."

Aunt Ada sounded aggrieved. "Charlotte is twelve. She's been old enough for years. It's been your idea to keep the tree trimming for yourself."

At last James Clement raised the pen from the paper. "Hardly for myself, Ada. The whole point has been to give her at least a little of the magic of childhood. We've taken most of it away."

"All right, then, what do you want to do about it this evening? James? Am I disturbing you? You're not writing, are you?"

"Obviously," her father said.

"But you're not at the typewriter, it's not—"

"It's only a letter, if that's what you mean, Ada, but even a letter does have to—" He flung down his pen, took a drink. "Tell Charlotte to come help trim the tree. Let's get it over with."

Charlotte stood up, backed two steps up the stairs. Her knees felt weak. She thought —I won't do it. I'll go upstairs. I'll hide.

But her aunt was standing in the library doorway. "Charlotte. Your father wants you to help trim the Christmas tree."

"I still have another Christmas present to tie up . . ."

"That can wait," her aunt said. "Your father can't."

Charlotte followed her aunt into the library. The tree was in the corner where a large potted plant of her aunt's usually stood. Her father got up from his desk and poured more whiskey into his glass from the bottom-heavy sea captain's decanter.

Aunt Ada pursed her lips. "Haven't you had enough, James?"

He looked at her darkly, but did not speak until she went to the cupboard where he kept his liquor bottles. Then he barked, "What are you doing in there?"

Her voice came muffled from the cupboard. "I am simply getting the decorations for the Christmas tree." She emerged, her arms filled with white cardboard boxes which she spread out on the black leather couch.

Charlotte asked, "Do you really want me to help trim the tree, Father?"

"I wouldn't have sent for you if I hadn't wanted you to."

"Because I really don't mind not—I mean—"

He did not respond. Instead he left the library and Charlotte simply stood, waiting, not listening to her aunt urging her to start putting on the decorations, until her father came back with the kitchen ladder. "Hand me the star, Charlotte," he said. "Please."

They worked in a terrible, empty silence. Charlotte broke it, her voice babbling too rapidly. "Honestly, Father, that bookstore is awful. I ordered a book for you at the beginning of November and it hadn't come when I had to leave for vacation. They said they'd send it to me, that I'd be sure to have it in time for Christmas, but it never got here. It'll probably come some time in March. With luck I'll get it in time for your birthday."

Her father made an effort to respond. "What is it?"

"Oh, I'm not going to tell you, Father. It's going to be a present no matter when you get it." Then her voice trailed off. She spoke again only when the decoration of the tree was complete. "There!" She stepped critically away from the tree in a twelve-year-old imitation of her father. "I think we're about finished. It does look gorgeous." As there was no response from either her father or her aunt she said, "Well . . . Do you want me to do anything more? . . . You don't want me to be here while you put the presents out or anything, do you?"

"No, child," Aunt Ada said. "Run along to bed now."

"Aren't we—going to sing Christmas carols?"

"It's too late," her father said shortly, then, softening his voice, "I'm coming up to bed in a few minutes myself."

"Oh. I guess we did take rather a long time trimming the tree, didn't we? Will you come in and say good night to me, Father?"

"Yes. Of course."

"I'm going to tie up that last present and take a bath. I didn't have time this morning, but I won't be long."

"It's too late for you to take a bath," Aunt Ada said.

"Please, Aunt Ada, would you really mind? At school we only have baths when they're assigned and we only have fifteen minutes and—and I won't have time tomorrow morning. You know how things always are on Christmas morning."

"Let the child take a bath if she wants to," her father said.

She ran up the stairs quickly, but when she reached the third floor she stopped and walked to her bathroom slowly, her hands trembling a little as she turned on the water. Then she went back to her room and stood looking at the small pile of carefully wrapped presents on her bed. She picked up the last present for her father that remained untied, a little bottle of his favorite and very expensive shaving lotion; it had taken her several weeks of saving her pocket money to accumulate enough to buy it. She wrapped it, slowly, carefully, and put the presents in a cardboard box on her closet floor, presents for her father, very carefully the same number of presents for Aunt Ada, for Reuben, for Essie. Her mind was numb as she undressed. She simply looked at her room as though she had never seen it before, and something inside her—it seemed to have nothing to do with her thinking—repeated over and over again, "But he always trims the tree. Even when we're in a hotel. Anywhere. He always trims the tree. We always sing Christmas carols."

She expected to cry in the bath, but didn't. She lay back in the hot water and relaxed and felt sleepy and thought that everything would be all right the next day, when Christmas day actually came, everything would be as it always had been, Christmas itself would make everything all right.

She heard Aunt Ada come upstairs, to the third floor, then her father, his footsteps slow, to his room on the floor below. She washed, then, and dried, quickly, and got into bed and lay there waiting.

Her father came up the stairs to her floor; she listened to each footstep, counting the stairs. He came into her room and opened the window, stood there, looking out onto the street.

"How soon can I wake you?" she asked. She had asked him that question every Christmas eve. She was afraid either to ask or not to ask it now.

"Try to wait until a reasonable hour," he said. From one of the houses across the street a radio was on, too loud, blaring *Silent Night, Holy Night*. "Why can't they turn the damned thing down?" he said. "How is anyone expected to sleep?" Then he said, "God damn God, Cotty. Damn him."

She lay silently, her pale hair spread damply on the pillow, watching his back as he stood looking out the window. Yes, his fair, still ungreyed hair was thin, and this was as wrong as his asking her to trim the Christmas tree.

She noticed now that he carried a glass in his hand. He drank, then put the empty glass on the small table between the windows. He still did not turn to her bed. She lay there, breathing very carefully, counting each breath. Thirty-one. Thirty-two. Thirty-three.

She thought of the words of the carol that they had sung every year but this year, that was one of his most favorite. *Of the Father's love begotten, Ere the worlds began to be.*

"You still pray, Cotty?" her father asked her. "You still say your prayers at night? The nuns see to that?"

"Yes, Father."

"You don't forget? Even when you're away from the convent?"

"No, Father."

"And what do you pray for, hah? Now that you're too old to ask for dolls and toys."

Her voice was low. "That we may be together for Christmas. That we may be happy."

"But that's not in it, Cotty. That's not part of the bargain. Pray all you like, ask anything you want, but don't forget that he never promised he'd say yes. He never guaranteed us anything. Not anything at all. Except one thing. Just one thing."

After a moment she asked, "What one thing, Father?"

"That he cares. Never forget that, Cotty. That is all. Nothing else. But it is enough. It is why I write what I write . . ." His voice faded. Then, "It is enough. Isn't it, Cotty?"

When she did not reply he suddenly shouted, "Why don't you answer? Haven't those nuns taught you any manners? Why do I send you to a convent school if they aren't going to teach you anything?"

Without kissing her, without saying good night, he stalked out of the room and slammed the door behind him.

She waited a long while for him to come back, but he did not come. She began to writhe as though she were in pain, pressing her feet against the foot of the bed until it creaked, beating her hands softly against the wall (Aunt Ada must not hear), feeling every muscle tense, trying to press against something she could not resist. She got out of bed and looked at the pile of presents on the floor of her closet, then walked over to the window and stood looking out, as her father had stood.

The floorboards were so cold that her feet ached up on her ankles, and she pressed them even harder against the cold floor as though the physical pain were welcome. The lights across the street were still on, the radio still blaring; now it was *Santa Claus Is Coming to Town*. Her father would loathe that. She loathed it. As though in response to her disapproval the nasal singing stopped in the middle of a note; the light was extinguished.

She turned back to her bed, not getting in, standing there, the warmth of the rug kind to the cold soles of her bare feet. She knelt, finally.

—Of the Father's love begotten, Ere the worlds began to be, she thought numbly. —I don't understand. Don't be mad at him, God, please. Don't strike him down. Let him be all right in the morning. Let him be Father again. Let it be Christmas. Not presents. That's not what I mean. I don't care if there aren't any presents. Just don't strike him down. Just don't be angry with him . . .

. . . if you're not angry with my father, or if you'll make your anger cease, I'll— dear Lord, what can I do, because I'm already promised to you! He blasphemes, but he doesn't mean anything by it. You know that. He is so much in the world that he forgets whose business it is he ought to be about. But it's only because he wants Portugal free from Spain. When I'm grown up I'll know more. Now I only know what I'm told. . . . Is this lack of humility, to think I'll know more, myself? I don't think I understand about humility. This afternoon Mother Escolastica said that humility is the secret of power. How can that be? It can't be the secret of the kind of power my father wants. She told us that it is very difficult to learn humility. If we think we're humble we probably aren't. She asked us, Do you want to *be* humble, or do you want to be *considered* humble? I don't know. I've never thought about it very much. Mother Escolastica says I'm old enough now to start thinking. I cannot stay a child forever.

On her knees she slept.

There were happier times.

. . . When her father was half dead with unhappiness then she was half dead, too. But when he was happy it was with a kind of happiness that most people could never dream of knowing and that spread out in rippling circles until Charlotte was caught in the joy. There was one night when they rode the Métro all night. And one time, during a vacation in the house on Seventy-fourth Street when they sat in the library after Aunt Ada had gone to bed and her father read to her, things that excited him, and they excited Charlotte, too, and he was so happy when he found out that she was truly aflame that he ended up leaving the floor spread with open books and going into the drawing room where they played (of all things) Chaminade's *Scarf Dance* as a duet, and then Charlotte danced to it in her bare feet, waving her father's woolen muffler about, and then they sang *The British Grenadiers* at the top of their lungs and waked up Reuben and Essie who came down in their nightclothes to see what was wrong, and after just the smallest time of scolding and trying to send Charlotte and her father to bed they began to sing, too, Essie raised up her voice alone and sang *He Shall Feed His Flock,* and then Reuben went down to the kitchen to make hot chocolate, and Charlotte sat in Essie's lap, as though she were four instead of fourteen, and Essie sang lullabies. . . .

Soaring, bird-high happiness.

It was worth everything.

It was before and after. It was evermore and evermore.

There was rain on her face.

Where had the sun gone? The marble of the bench was cold and damp. The white walls of the convent became streaked with grey as the rain started to fall more heavily. There was nothing for her to do except go back to the pensão and wait there until lunch.

She sat again on the edge of the bed and opened the French book, the *Lettres d'une Réligieuse Portugaise.*

. . . it was from this very balcony that I first saw you ride by and could not help noticing you, and I was standing on the balcony on the fatal day when I first felt the stirrings of my unhappy passion. It seemed to me that you were trying to please me, even though you didn't know me. I was sure that you had noticed me particularly among all the other nuns. I took a secret interest in everything you did, and I was sure that you knew about it, and that you were as aware of me as I was of you . . .

How could Charlotte have thought that this was about Christ? What she had read the night before had perhaps been more ambiguous.

What was he, this man who could turn a nun from the most sacred of vows?

Charlotte flipped the pages, skimming, unable to concentrate enough to read slowly or consecutively. . . . *I despise myself when I realize what has happened to me: I've lost my reputation and angered my father and broken the rules of the convent, and I've earned only ingratitude from you, which is the worst misfortune of all* . . . She turned the pages, shivering. *A French officer was kind enough to talk to me about you for three hours this morning. He told me that now the peace with France has been concluded. If this is true, couldn't you come to me, and take me back to France with you?* . . .

—What would a French soldier have been doing in Beja, Portugal, three hundred years ago? If you go back and read the preface you could probably find out . . .

But she sat there, the book open on her lap, not reading, not thinking, because what was there for her to learn in these strange letters from a Portuguese nun? What was there in them that might explain something to Charlotte about Patrick? Or even about love, for it did not seem that this nun knew much about love . . .

When she went down to lunch Charlotte learned the Frenchman's name: Noël Bouton Saint-Leger, Count of Saint-Leger, later to become the Marquis of Chamilly and Marshal of France. And she learned what he was doing in Portugal.

The doctor and Antonio were sitting together at the doctor's table, their plates pushed aside, a bottle of Mateus between them, fighting a battle on the tablecloth. Like little boys with their toy soldiers, Charlotte thought. Like my father with his drinking companions, male and female, in hotels all over the world, marking tablecloths with burnt matches or fork tines which made as much of a mess as if he'd gone ahead and used a pencil.

She ate her soup and listened to Antonio and the doctor. The two men were using small pieces of bread for soldiers, and after a while Antonio, openly acknowledging his audience, began to explain what they were doing.

"I sometimes get impatient with Dr. Ferreira's mathematical insistence on historical accuracy," he added. "He allows me no poetic license."

"Scratch a Portuguese and you find a poet. We have them on every street corner. We need good teachers far more." But the doctor's voice was affectionate.

"We're fighting a battle," Antonio said, "not personal, not present, you understand, but a reenactment of a battle three hundred years ago. Dr. Ferreira knows more about military tactics, ancient and modern, than any man in Portugal. So he teaches me this way. We have a system. It is something like chess. This battle, our battle today, is an imaginary one, but it is also one which actually took place although there is no historical record of it. It was not just *a* battle, it is the specific battle after which the triumphant Portuguese soldiers marched through Beja and Soror Mariana saw, for the first time, the French soldier, Noël Saint-Leger, to whom she later wrote the famous letters."

The doctor, sitting back tolerantly, toyed with his pipe. Antonio, empty-fingered, flexible hands illustrating his words, talked on, his dark eyes focused partly on Charlotte, partly on the world of his words. "It was a battle fought with a kind of guerilla warfare, because, although John of Braganza was already on the throne in Lisbon, the southern provinces had not yet thrown off the yoke of Spain and were still fighting for freedom. They were led by a German general, Schomberg, an excellent soldier."

This seemed odd to Charlotte, but she did not ask for an explanation, fearing that Antonio would give her too complete a one.

"His army was made up largely of mercenaries," Antonio continued, "Frenchmen, Dutchmen, Englishmen, all of whom were helping the Portuguese patriots. The oppressing Spaniards were led by Don Juan of Austria."

—Not *the* Don Juan, Charlotte thought vaguely, —couldn't be, wrong century. But some Don Juan.

"Picture it, Mrs. Napier. They must have made a blare of color against the rocky hills with all the different national costumes. It would have been easy enough for one of the mercenaries on either side to get confused about who he was fighting."

She looked at the doctor, who was placidly eating, occasionally giving a shrewd look at Antonio. Once his eyes rested on Charlotte, kindly, without curiosity.

There were foot soldiers and cavalry, Antonio explained, and of course Noël Saint-Leger rode on a coal-black charger. He had a sense of the dramatic in war as in love. There were cannoniers and har-busquiers and oxcarts with food and ammunition; there were water carts filled with the same red earthenware wine and water jugs which Charlotte must have seen on the drive down from Lisbon and which during Soror Mariana's day had already been in use for centuries; wine at that time was cheaper than water, Antonio informed her. There were flags, tents, bugles, banners: Antonio painted the picture for Charlotte, waving his hands as though holding a brush.

The doctor wiped up the last of his gravy with a piece of bread, then pushed his plate aside again, and sat back benevolently, his gravy-spotted napkin still tucked in his collar. After a while he began moving his breadcrumb soldiers, pulling Antonio back into the game, playing with cool deliberation. He was manipulating the Spanish soldiers, and Antonio, struggling with the Portuguese, was no match for him.

"But you forget that Schomberg's troops won the battle!" Antonio expostulated, and scattered the breadcrumbs with his hand like a thwarted child.

The doctor reached out and rearranged them. "They had to work for it, Tonio. It was not given to them. Come, now. What's your next move?"

Antonio looked sulky for a moment, as though he would refuse to play, then, glancing at Charlotte under his silky lashes, he set his men up. "All right. We're at the top of the hill, here. We've appro-priated this house. There's a cemetery behind the house and its white wall is battered from yesterday's fighting, but it still affords excellent cover. The stream is here, so we have water. There are cypress trees in the cemetery. Eucalyptus trees. Cork trees. So we have shade and protection for the wounded."

He turned again to Charlotte. "At night they'd be roasting kids out in the open, turning them on the spit, and there would be camp followers and dogs and color and noise and *sturm und drang.*" He gave her a sidelong glance to make sure she appreciated his multi-lingualism. "There was one battle described in an English history of Portugal that was won by our side because our men wanted to take the yellow coats from Don Juan's guards. Sometimes this kind of thing can be a more useful motivation than honor and nobility.

Then—I don't know which of the forays it was—but anyhow things weren't going well for the Spanish and one of the officers rode at Baltazar Alcoforado—he was Soror Mariana's brother, and Noël Saint-Leger's friend—in a fury, knocked Baltazar off his horse and would have run him through if Noël hadn't come along and knocked the Spanish officer off *his* horse, and run *him* through. Of course this is partly speculation. I don't know if that's how they became friends, or if Noël saved Baltazar's life because he already was his friend. Most of it is conjecture. Dr. Ferreira knows more than I do."

The doctor shrugged. "It is not that I know more. It is only that I am more dispassionate."

The waiter took away Charlotte's fish. "Please tell him," Charlotte said, "that soup and fish is already more than I am accustomed to eating for lunch. If it would not hurt his feelings I should like just to go up to my room and rest, and I'll let him know about dinner after I've spoken to my mother-in-law."

She felt the doctor's shrewd brown eyes on her. Perhaps his concern was, as he said, dispassionate. It was also, at this moment, comforting. He said only, "You should be careful not to take cold. This is inclement weather. We are not used to such extremes of cold."

Antonio looked at Charlotte in distress. "But I've made arrangements to take you through the museum this afternoon—"

She had completely forgotten, but she said, "Yes. Thank you very much. I only want to rest for half an hour."

Antonio's face radiated relief, far too great relief; he was indeed an actor. "I will be waiting, then."

"Not half an hour," the doctor said. "An hour. Mrs. Napier is tired."

"Yes," Charlotte said. "Thank you. An hour, then." She left them to their battle.

The "inclement weather" permeated the walls of the pensão, filled the small space of her room. There was nothing to do except get back into bed. She lay there, wrapped in her coat and weighted down by the mound of blankets. She stared up at the mottled ceiling; its sickly splotches made her shudder, and she picked up the book of letters again, though her hands, outside the covers, were quickly cold.

You knew you weren't going to be in Portugal forever, so why did you take me, only to make me so desperately unhappy? I'm sure you could have found another woman in our country who would have been more beautiful and with whom you could have found just as much pleasure, since pleasure was all you were looking for, someone who would have loved you while she was with you, but who would have been able to forget you quickly, someone you could have left without cruelty, without betrayal. You've acted more like a conquering hero than . . .

Charlotte sighed, let the book drop, drew her cold hands under the covers. She closed her eyes, but though the glass of wine she had had with her lunch made her lids heavy and her mind fuzzy, she could not sleep. She thought of the two men, the old bear and the young black panther—yes, that was what Tonio was like—reenacting battles as her father had done. Those hotel dining-room games had always seemed distant and unreal to her, far removed from life; however, as she lay there, the minor skirmish which had so animated Antonio seemed closer to her than the playing out of attacks and retreats through which her father had actually lived. Perhaps it was because she could not visualize his battlegrounds, whereas she had only that morning walked along the streets through which Noël and Baltazar had ridden.

Before the triumphal march they might have assembled in the Square of the Dove so that anyone standing in her pensão window could look down on them as Mariana, standing on the terrace-balcony of the convent must have looked, laughing and clapping with the other nuns, cheering and waving as the procession wound its way up the hill to the convent.

. . . first the foot soldiers and then the cavalry, led by a Portuguese major, Alipio de Vasconcelos, father of Sister Joaquina, the nun who as a novice had slapped Sister Mariana. . . .

At the rear of the procession were Noël Saint-Leger and Baltazar Alcoforado, side by side as usual, Baltazar on his white charger, Noël on the black (a deliberate piece of drama on the part of the

two flamboyant young men). The parade wound all the way uphill,
over the many-arched Roman bridges beneath which women were
doing laundry in the gently flowing water and spreading the clean
linen on the banks to dry. Among them were lay sisters from the
Convent of Nossa Senhora da Conceição, and all stood to cheer,
waving their wash like flags, the soldiers cheering back, blowing
kisses indiscriminately to shawled girls and black-habited nuns.

(Women had washed in this way in the river when the Romans
built the bridge. Charlotte had seen them in the January cold when
she drove to Beja.)

The procession moved across the bridge, in through the gates of
the city, clattering over the cobblestones of the street: donkeys, mules,
horses, braying, whinnying, dropping steaming loads of manure. In
the doorways, to get the breeze and yet remain in the shade, to re-
move themselves from the overlavish embrace of the sun, sat burned-
out old women making lace, which they waved at the soldiers,
cackling approval.

As the procession reached the square a group of boys and girls
was waiting to start a dance of welcome around a maypole that was
carried by the biggest boys. They wove the ribbons in and out with
delicate intricacy, punctuating the rhythm with castanet-like clapping.
Some of the soldiers joined in the dance, the procession was slowed
down, and Alipio de Vasconcelos cantered up, waving a careless whip
and shouting angry commands until the untidy line started moving
again. The dancers skipped alongside, children ran up and down,
assorted mongrels yapped and barked, and a bewildered rooster
flapped his wings and let out a crow that ended in a defeated squawk.

As the procession approached the convent, the men could see the
dark habits of the nuns and the bright clothes of the children as they
stood pressed against the elaborately wrought-iron balustrade on the
balcony. The sun beat against the white walls, was reflected in a
scorching glare, was held, quivering, on the red tiled roofs. The sisters hovered behind the children, quieting the little ones who were
jumping up and down and screaming with excitement as the blare
of trumpets came closer. Almost all of them there on the balcony,
children and sisters alike, had relatives among the soldiers, and the

nuns were almost as open in their joy as the children, especially when they caught sight of someone they knew.

Near Mariana stood Joaquina, watching the parade with intensity. Her face, always white with a smattering of freckles that betrayed the fact that the hair under her wimple must be red, was even paler than usual. As she saw a fox-faced man with red beard and mustache, wearing an ornate officer's uniform, she cried out joyously, "Papa!"

Alipio de Vasconcelos looked around indifferently, not stopping to try to find her among the nuns, took a pinch of snuff, and rode on. Directly behind him an officer waved and called to a little shriveled nun who was old enough to be his grandmother, "Mother Escolastica! Here! Look here!" He waved exuberantly and the old woman jumped and clapped her hands like a child.

Sister Joaquina turned her shocked, hurt face away from the others, closing her eyes for a moment as though against the sun. One of the children near her squealed. She snapped, "Be quiet, Dolores," and slapped the fat little girl's hand. The child burst into startled and noisy sobs, and Joaquina withdrew against the wall, her face stiffening with resentment as she watched the joy of reunion from which she had been excluded. The child's eyes reflected Joaquina's own hurt as she moved away and stood nearer Mariana and Peregrina.

At the end of the procession the two young men rode on their black and white chargers. Peregrina, pressed against the balcony rail, cried out, "Baltazar!" and the young man reined up, laughing and pointing the child out to his companion. Then he saw Mariana, standing just behind the little girl, calling at him, laughing, half crying, and he took his plumed hat and waved it at her in an extravagant gesture of greeting.

Mariana waved back, her face vivid with joy, and it was in this moment of illumination that the Frenchman first saw her. He, too, rose in his stirrups, took off his hat with a sweeping gesture, and bowed.

To Mariana.

Only to Mariana. Their eyes met, and then Mariana turned away as though to speak to the child.

Standing against the wall, Sister Joaquina watched. As Mariana turned from Peregrina and looked after the two soldiers, Joaquina pushed up to her and plucked her sleeve. "What's the matter, Sister?"

Mariana, only half hearing, half feeling, did not turn to see who was pulling at her attention. "Matter? Nothing. How could anything be the matter?"

"You look so strange."

Mariana turned to see who was speaking, and answered impatiently, "Look at the soldiers. Don't look at me."

Joaquina frowned, still holding the sleeve of Mariana's habit. "But I'm not sure it's right, all this excitement. I don't think it's what her Grace meant—"

Sister Beatriz, the young nun of whom Peregrina had said, "We're afraid of her but we respect her," turned her cool gaze to Joaquina. "Sister, what *are* you talking about?"

"All this wild behavior, when this is a convent of the Reform—"

Beatriz said quietly, "Her Grace would be the last to deny us a moment of joy for our men who have fought and suffered for us. This is no time for long faces."

Mariana turned away and watched the procession until the last moment when the consciously colorful figures on the black and white chargers rounded a corner and could no longer be seen from the balcony.

. . . It was on (or would one call it in?) a balcony that Charlotte had first seen Patrick Napier. She had been taken to the opera by a young cousin of her father's. (Why was Jane referred to as Charlotte's father's cousin, rather than Charlotte's, since surely she was both?) Jane was older than Charlotte, married to a medical student, and Patrick was one of their friends. Charlotte was then seventeen and for two years had been living in New York with her father and going to the inevitable convent school, though at last as a day student. For her to sit next to a medical student was to partake, even if for a few hours, of the real world, for neither the world of school nor the world of her father's house had much, she felt, to do with reality. Patrick seemed to know a great deal about music but he did not foist his knowledge on her. When Jane asked him questions, perhaps showing him off, he answered, but briefly, almost unwillingly.

After the opera they had gone to Jane's apartment, where Pete, her husband, was studying for an exam; this was how Charlotte had happened to be given his ticket. Jane had cooked them a superb supper, and then asked Charlotte down for a party the following week. Patrick was at the party, and then, extraordinary joy, had asked to see her again, had made a date. It was perhaps less extraordinary that it was Charlotte's first date.

If Mariana was unprepared for Noël, so was Charlotte for Patrick, though differently, for Charlotte, leaving her father's house, had determined quite consciously that it was the moment for her to enter fully the adult world, to participate at last in reality, no matter what that involved.

("You're so *square*, Charlotte," Ursula, her best friend, told her with heavy patience. "Don't you know the world is different now? You have to break away from the Establishment. It's passé. You've got to find things out for yourself. What do you think we've learned from the little talks Reverend Ma's had Sister Mary Michael give us? What can a *nun* tell us about sex? You seem to think everything Mary Michael tells us comes from a direct line to God. Well let me tell you, it doesn't.")

Properly primed by Ursula, Charlotte had been quite determined to find out for herself.

It was the martinis with the red cherries bobbing in them that saved her virtue. It wasn't just that they tasted vile (Patrick used far too much vermouth); it was that he didn't know about martinis. If he could be wrong about such a basic thing as a martini, then she had misjudged him utterly, no matter how much he knew about music. Or medicine.

She took several large gulps, however, because it was the only way to get it down, like castor oil. And she couldn't leave at once; that would be rude. And then, gulping again, she wondered —Maybe Patrick's testing me to see if I'm just a dumb kid instead of sophisticated, the way I thought he thought I was. Maybe he's doing it deliberately.

She shuddered and tried not to make a face.

"What's the matter, Cotty?" Patrick asked.

"Nothing. I just felt cold for a minute. And please don't call me Cotty." She tried to make her voice cool and aloof. If Patrick didn't know about martinis she couldn't tell him how awful his were, and she was disappointed, in spite of his asking her for dinner, in spite of his looks, in spite of his being a medical student with his own apartment in the village . . .

At least his looks were all right. His looks were more than all right. But she wasn't going to let him know that. She glowered over at him as he sat across from her in an orange canvas sling chair, the sort of chair, Charlotte thought, that used to be smart but that had become almost old-fashioned. But he looked splendid in it, hunched over, wearing tight Levis on his long, thin legs, and a black turtleneck sweater, and above it his thin white face and the lovely mop of thick, silky black hair. And his eyes: his eyes were a startling blue with long, shadowy curtains of lashes. Oh, Patrick was beautiful all right.

Hamlet, exquisite and thin as moonbeams in an inky cape.

Who wrote that? Elinor Wylie? Would Patrick like it if she quoted it to him? No. Yes. Maybe he'd like it too much. She'd save it.

"If you're cold I'll close the window." Patrick leaped to do it, moving with feral grace. "And you told me the other night at Jane and Pete's party that your best friends call you Cotty."

She looked down at the cherry, repulsively red in the pale liquid, and decided that it wasn't a test. "I don't know you well enough to be on best-friend terms yet."

"Things seem to have changed from the way they were when we made this date, Charlotte," Patrick said, sitting down in the orange chair again so that his thin knees in the faded Levis stuck up forlornly.

"You can call me Lottie," she said graciously.

"Nope. If it's not to be Cotty it's Charlotte. Okay, relax for a minute, will you? These chairs aren't for sitting like ramrods in." He slung around in his and draped his long legs over the side.

She didn't lean back against the canvas—hers was scarlet and clashed with the orange—but she took another gulp of martini and looked around Patrick's room. It was his whole apartment, the one room, and it wasn't a particularly large room. There was a pink marble fireplace that didn't go at all with the orange and scarlet chairs; they were as clashing a combination as the cherries in the martinis. But there was a fire of cannel coal burning in the grate, and a dented copper coal scuttle. In one corner of the room was a round electric heater, and she wondered if the fire and the heater were the only things Patrick had to keep his apartment warm. As a matter of fact, it really wasn't very warm. She was glad she'd worn her new cashmere sweater.

She took another sip of martini and looked over at the studio couch, probably his bed, undoubtedly his bed, with a printed Indian throw over it; on the wall above there was an enormous nonobjective painting with angry splashings of blood reds and storm blacks. It was a violent sort of painting and she couldn't decide whether she liked it or not, or whether it was good art or not. There were a lot of paperbound books in unpainted shelves that looked rather rickety; perhaps Patrick had built them.

"A small place, but all mine own," he said, waving one arm constricted by the metal wings of the chair. He finished his drink and sat holding the cherry by the stem, twirling it. "I dote on these things," he said, and popped it into his mouth. "Can't afford 'em very often. Has to be a special occasion. I live a frugal life."

Carefully she removed the cherry from her glass and handed it over to him. "Here. Eat mine."

Patrick raised the dark, silky lines of his eyebrows, and took the cherry. "My budget doesn't include restaurants right now, so I've cooked us a meal. Hope that's all right with you."

"Oh. Sure."

"It needs another few minutes, so let's have another drink."

"Why not?" she asked, very casually. "And why don't you let me make it this time?"

Patrick's eyebrows went up again. "If it would give you pleasure. The kitchen's behind the screen. The refrigerator is under the stove. The liquor's on the shelf with the Worcestershire sauce and the catsup. Things are in kind of a mess. You look too pretty to go splashing about in the kitchen. Do you know you have hair the color of a lemon?"

She went behind the screen. The stove was two gas burners and on one something was bubbling. A basket of greens was hanging over a cracked bowl to dry; there didn't seem to be any sink.

"What did you make the martinis *in?*" she asked.

"You'll probably see a dented saucepan with a few dregs of ice I broke my only pitcher a week ago."

If there was one thing Charlotte felt she knew how to do, it was to make a martini. She was perfectly willing to admit that she was not in the habit of drinking martinis. But she knew how to make them. If she had learned nothing else from her father she had learned how to make a martini. Since she had been living at home with him they had developed an evening ritual. She would go into the library at seven-thirty and make him two martinis. Two. Strictly two. This was why Charlotte made them. If her father made them himself he cheated. So Charlotte made them. And sat with him while he drank them. It was their one real time together. So she knew about martinis. The drink she brought to Patrick was chill and pale and perfect.

"Didn't you see the cherries?" Patrick asked.

She was silent. Patrick was cooking her dinner and he didn't even have a pitcher to mix his martinis in, and she couldn't just out and say, "Patrick, one does not put cherries in martinis. I could put in a touch of lemon peel if you want it." She said with studied casualness, "Just for fun see how you like it without the cherry."

"Whatever you say," Patrick said, and sipped. She couldn't tell whether or not he thought her martini an improvement over his. He reached out and caught her hand. "I don't go in much for entertaining, Cotty—sorry, Charlotte—and I'm not much in the habit of drinking. My mother, who, as you might say, abandoned me in my infancy and only now that I'm on my own and she's sure I'm not going to demand anything of her is beginning to take a maternal interest in me, is continental in her taste in drinking. I know something about wines but nothing about so-called mixed drinks. However, I am aware that a martini's the proper thing before dinner in New York, and I imagine you're used to everything being fairly elegant."

There was something romantic, which was all right, but something pathetic, which was not, in this speech. Charlotte had not come to dinner with Patrick because he was pathetic. Pathetic was the last thing Charlotte wanted Patrick to be. But her father cared even more about courtesy than about martinis, so she said, "I just love your apartment, Patrick. It's—it's unique. But Patrick, Patrick, why did you get an orange chair and a red chair to go with a pink fireplace?" That question was anything but courteous, but it slipped out before she realized it.

"Some people like the combination," he said with an unexpected grin. "As a matter of fact, I bought the chairs for a quarter each. Couldn't afford to be choosy at that price." He looked at her in a speculative sort of way as she sat there in his scarlet chair in her pink dress and sweater. "You know, I have a feeling that this evening isn't going to be quite what I expected, but maybe it will be good for you to see how the other half lives."

She looked at him suspiciously. "What do you mean?"

"I mean maybe it's good for you to go slumming once in a while. The thing I liked about you the other night at Jane and Pete's was that you were different. You stood out like a sore thumb—sorry, that's not a very complimentary metaphor, is it? —The first thing—or maybe it wasn't the first thing—anyhow, it was the way you ate asparagus. You ate it as though it was the first asparagus you'd ever tasted in your life and it was the most wonderful thing in the world. You picked it up in your fingers like the rest of us and dipped it in the lemon butter, and when you'd finished with a stalk you licked your fingers, delicately, elegantly, like a little cat. There wasn't anything messy about it. But what struck me was that you really *enjoyed* it. You were eating asparagus and you were completely alive while you were doing it. And Cotty" (this time he didn't stop to correct himself, and she didn't say anything, either), "have you realized that most people are fully alive only *part* of the time, if that?"

"Yes," she said, and suddenly she was furious, though she didn't know why. Yes. Yes. She did know. But she didn't want to think about it.

"What's the matter?" Patrick asked her.

"Nothing. Nothing you said, anyhow. I couldn't agree with you more."

"You're a funny girl," Patrick said. "How old are you, anyhow?"

"Seventeen."

There was naked shock in Patrick's face. Then he recovered and swooned in the orange chair. "Oh, gawd. What on earth were you doing there, then?"

"Where?"

"At Jane and Pete's."

"Jane's my father's young cousin. At least I suppose she's my cousin, too, but—and she knows what I—what I want to do with my life."

"You mean what you want to do with your life is go to beer parties in cold-water flats and help chip plaster from walls?"

Charlotte stood up with dignity. "Some day I am going to have a cold-water flat of my own, and I am going to invite people in and have a party and knock off all the plaster down to that beautiful pink brick the way Jane and Pete did, only I won't serve beer, I'll serve champagne."

Patrick groaned. "I know you're a minor and I should be shot for letting you have a martini, but have you any idea of the comparative cost of beer and champagne?"

Charlotte could feel herself turning pink with anger and humiliation at her own stupidity.

"Don't take on," Patrick said, gently. "It was blind of me not to realize how much younger you were than the rest of us. We're rather an elderly crowd as medical students go. Most of us have done our time in the army, and most of us are having to pay our own way with odd jobs and time out. Finish your drink. You might as well now that you've started it."

Before she could stop herself she flashed out, "I made a darned sight better martini than you do, Patrick Napier."

"Okay, okay," Patrick said. "Bottoms up, and we'll have a nice hot bowl of stew. Gourmet stew. Where, O Charlotte, do you live?"

"With my father."

"No mother?"

"No."

"Divorced?"

"No."

"I'm sorry, Cotty," he said gently.

She did not want Patrick to be sorry for her. "Oh, I didn't like her very much. Anyhow it was a long time ago."

"So you live with your father. Where?"

She looked around Patrick's apartment. It was an old brownstone on Bleeker Street and the building had smelled of fish and onions when she came in and climbed the three long flights to Patrick's room. "Well, it's an old brownstone," she said.

"Where?"

"East Seventy-fourth."

"What does your father do?"

"He's—he's a writer."

"What does he write?"

"Books," she said.

"Come on, Cotty. What kind of books?"

"You're calling me Cotty," she said sharply. "You'd probably think his books were kind of peculiar."

"Why?"

She looked down at her feet. "You just probably would."

"What name does your father write under?"

"His own name. James Clement. You probably wouldn't have heard of him."

"But my God," Patrick exclaimed, "I didn't know he was still alive—I mean—I'm sorry, Cotty."

"You mean you know who he is?"

"Do I know who he is? I did a paper in college on his books."

"On Father's books?"

"Sure. My mother's crazy about him. The brilliant apocalyptical novels of James Clement. She likes to discover geniuses nobody else knows about. James Clement's one of her particular pets. She introduced me to him. But why hasn't he written anything lately?"

"He has," Charlotte said. "He writes all the time."

"Then why hasn't he published anything?" Patrick asked.

O God, how she hated Patrick. She got up and walked over to his window and looked out into the dark courtyard. She pressed her forehead against the windowpane and cupped her hands about her eyes so that she could cut out the light of the room. She saw a winter-bare tree, and a long laundry line running from one building to another with one lonely pair of long men's underdrawers still hanging out and kicking listlessly in the wind. She swung around and faced Patrick. "You can probably tell me why publishers don't publish books as well as I can."

"Oh," he said softly. "I see."

"I doubt very much if you do," she said acidly. "And what does *your* father do?"

"Fair exchange, eh?" Patrick asked. "He's a missionary doctor in South America. If I'm lucky I'll see him once in five years. Don't think you're the only person in the world with parent troubles."

"Did I say that?" she asked.

"Sorry. No, you didn't, Charlotte. You didn't at all. So there's your father writing brilliant apocalyptical books that practically nobody understands, and there's my father in the middle of the jungle struggling with the bodies and souls of a tribe of people who are still savage and could quite easily turn and kill him for dinner."

"And what about your mother?" she asked, still angry. "The one who abandoned you."

He laughed. "She's the only one. She's a harpsichordist. As a matter of fact she's rather well known. Violet Napier."

But Charlotte could not return Patrick's compliment. At this point there were still enormous gaps in her musical education in spite of— or because of?—years of piano lessons. "Well, what about her? Where is she?"

"In Portugal at the moment, though she lives most of the year in London. She used to do a lot of touring when she was younger, but she's had to cut it down. She manages a lot of recording."

"It's still not a very clear picture," Charlotte said. "With a father in South America and a mother in Portugal or England, I don't see where you come in."

He laughed again, but there was a certain amount of tension in the laugh and in the pose of his body as he said, "Quite a number of years ago she was on an American tour and she was playing with the Boston Symphony and she got a chill that turned into pneumonia. My father was resident at Massachusetts General then, and he pulled her through and fell in love with her while he was doing it. And she fell in love with him. But Violet's not cut out for a permanent union with anyone except her harpsichord. I don't say she's right or wrong. I don't feel in any position to judge Violet. And Dad couldn't have been an easy man to live with."

Echoing Ursula, or the influence of Ursula, Charlotte said, "What man is?"

But Patrick did not hear. "If Violet was in love with music, Dad was in love with medicine. Their hours didn't jibe. He was up at the crack of dawn and she practiced half the night and slept until afternoon. He wanted her to give up playing professionally when she got pregnant. She promised she would. She did. She tried. Then when I was six months old she walked out of the house and went back to England. Dad didn't go after her. He brought his mother to live with us as housekeeper. When she died last year it seemed his chance to go to South America. He's a bug on tropical diseases. Not much chance for field work in that in Boston. He's a great guy, and so was my grandmother. Gave me a great childhood. Okay, Charlotte, let's get off the subject of parents. It seems to be an upsetting one to both of us. I'll feed us now."

"Let me finish my drink." She took a sip and suddenly she was on the verge of tears. Everything was wrong. Everything about the entire evening had gone wrong. She wanted to go home.

"Tell me about yourself," Patrick said. "What do you do all day?"

"I go to school."

"Yeeps, I keep forgetting how young you are."

"I graduate this spring." The easiest thing, the thing she wanted to do, was to walk out of Patrick's apartment and go home. But she'd told her father, she'd told Reuben and Essie, that she was going to Ursula's apartment, and that she would be there late doing homework. So she couldn't go home. Not for a long time yet.

"Patrick," she said, "let's have another martini."

"I think you've had enough." Patrick stood up and went to his cupboardy kitchen.

"I'm old enough to know whether or not I've had enough. I certainly don't *feel* anything. If I'd had enough I'd *feel* something, wouldn't I?"

"We're having wine with dinner," he said. "And I don't want your palate to be too jaded. Nor my dish to burn. Do you want to wash up or something?"

She was curious to see Patrick's bathroom, having learned that people reveal a lot about themselves by their bathrooms. But Patrick didn't really have a bathroom, not of his own, not in his apartment. She had to go out to a dark closet all the way down the hall for which Patrick gave her the key, since it was shared by all the tenants on the floor. In Europe she had stayed with her father in inns where the only bathroom was a semi-protected hole in the ground, but this had not given her nearly the sense of discomfort and dis-hygiene as the idea of a group of people all having keys for one small, dank toilet on Bleeker Street.

Patrick was stirring his stew when she got back and it smelled wonderful. "I'd like to wash my hands, please," she said, and looked around because she couldn't see any place to wash them. In that refrigerator down the hall there had been nothing but the toilet, and she began to think there wasn't any water, except that he'd obviously washed the lettuce hanging in the basket.

He took a red Persian cloth off what she had thought was a table, then lifted up what looked like the tabletop, and there was a big tub. It was big enough to take a bath in, with a certain amount of discomfort. Patrick gave her soap and handed her a beautifully embroidered linen towel. "Made for my mother by some order of nuns in Portugal she gives a benefit concert for every year," he told her.

In some ways perhaps he was even more interesting than she'd expected.

She washed her hands while he ladled out the dinner into two brown willowware bowls. The bowls were slightly chipped, but brown willowware, unlike blue, cannot be bought at Woolworth's. Patrick had the table covered with a brown cloth; all his materials were odd and foreign-looking and went along with the Patrick she thought she'd come to have dinner with instead of the Patrick he was turning out to be.

She did not understand him at all.

The wineglasses were beautiful. There weren't mates, but each one had a delicately shaped bowl and a long, slender stem; the wine was a Chambertin. The knives and forks and spoons, like the wineglasses, didn't match, but they were real silver, even though they needed polishing. And the stew—was it stew?—was superb.

"Cotty—I mean Charlotte," Patrick started.

She finished her glass of wine and looked at him kindly. "You may call me Cotty after all," she said, "even if you're not the way I thought you were."

"How did you think I was?"

She felt herself growing a little pink. "Oh—just different." She changed the subject. "That big picture—who painted it?"

"Oh, that? I needed something huge and splashy for that wall, so I bought a hideous old picture in a junk shop for a quarter for the canvas."

"You mean you painted it yourself?"

He grinned at her. "I spent a couple of afternoons in the Museum of Modern Art and came home and imitated four or five different artists all at once. Miró more than anybody else."

"But—you're a medical student!"

Patrick laughed and absent-mindedly poured her some more wine. "That doesn't mean that I have to close my mind to the rest of life. And painting relaxes me at the same time that my subconscious goes on studying." He got up and went to the kitchen part of his room.

"What are you doing?"

"Making us some coffee. Want some more stew?"

Usually there was nothing wrong with her appetite, but that evening she seemed to have nothing but a terrible thirst. "I don't think so."

"Okay, I'll bring on the salad," Patrick whisked their bowls off the table and put on two plates. These weren't brown willowware. Chippendale, and very good Chippendale, Charlotte thought, then realized a little fuzzily that Chippendale is not china, it is furniture—isn't it?—and how was it that she could be getting china mixed up with furniture, and what kind of furniture was she confusing the china with anyhow? She drank the wine and shook her head to clear it, but that didn't help, so she picked up the plate to look underneath to see what kind of china it was, though she hated using a dictionary rather than being able to think of the word all by herself . . .

She looked at the bottom of the plate and before she could see the faint lettering it slipped through her fingers and she could hear it break as it crashed onto the floor, because of course Patrick had no rugs to cushion anything. And then suddenly she squawked out, "Patrick, I have to have the key, *quick*," and Patrick leaped out from behind the screen and had his arm about her and she was out of the room with him and down the hall and he had the key in the keyhole and was opening the door without a fumble and she could never have found the keyhole at that point and she flung up the lid of the toilet and vomited out all Patrick's martinis and stew and wine and he held her head and stroked her damp pale hair back from her forehead.

She was quite tidy about throwing up and was conscious enough of what was happening to be grateful, although her face was damp with an odd, cold perspiration, and she knew that she must look quite ghastly. For the moment she could not bring herself to care, and she hardly realized it when Patrick took her back to his room where the fire was leaping gaily in the pink marble fireplace, and helped her to lie down on his couch and put a cover over her. She lay there looking up at the ceiling, and the ceiling began to swoop around her in slow, graceful ellipses. Her stomach gave a flipflop but she shut her eyes and things quieted down. Patrick was so full of apologies he was almost cackling in his anxiety like an old mother hen.

Finally she said crossly, "Please do shut up, it wasn't your fault at all. I sneaked a lot of wine you didn't know about. It was entirely my own responsibility. Just fix me some good black coffee and I'll be all right."

She knew that she couldn't go home until she was all right, perfectly all right. Why was it that it would be even worse to go home to her father when she'd helped Reuben and Essie fix black coffee for him many a time, or had ordered it for him herself during vacations in hotels, than it would have been if he never drank anything at all, like (presumably) Patrick's father and grandmother? Now she understood why, if he fixed his own martinis, he was apt to cheat: you just don't realize it until it's too much.

"Your plate," she moaned faintly. "Oh, Patrick, I'm so sorry about the plate."

His voice came quite close to her and she opened her eyes and he was kneeling beside the couch holding out a big, delicate cup of coffee. The china was so thin she could see the lovely dark liquid through it. "It's all right," he said gently. "Just drink the coffee. Don't worry about the plate. I have nothing but dribs and drabs of china anyhow."

"Yes, but everything is beautiful," she wailed, "and the plate was beautiful. What kind of plate was it?"

"Staffordshire," Patrick said. "Drink some more coffee."

She drank, propped up on one elbow, then managed to sit up, though the entire room shuddered before it steadied and settled. She drank all the coffee and Patrick filled her cup again. By the time she had finished she felt almost all right. She thought of her father standing for long minutes under a hot shower if he'd been out late at the club the night before, and then coming out and dressing in clean clothes and smelling all fresh and of soap and after-shave lotion, and then going down to the library and being absolutely silent for a while; then at last she would hear the sound of his typewriter clacking away and know that everything was all right.

"Patrick, my father would murder me, I mean really, if I came home and he thought I was drunk. I think I'd be okay if I could have a bath and then one more cup of coffee. Do you think I could take a bath in your tub?"

"Well, sure, Cotty, it's pretty primitive, but if you think it would help . . ."

"And you wouldn't mind sitting out in the hall? I mean, it's so cold out there and everything, you wouldn't mind too much?"

"No, sweetie, I don't mind a bit sitting out in the hall," Patrick said, and fixed the tub for her, folding the cloth and leaning the board against the wall, and putting in one of those flat rubber things to cover the drain hole. From a drawer he got out a towel and a face cloth and a brand-new cake of soap—how nice of him—and then he took a large kettle from the stove and emptied it into the tub, then ran in some cold water. "Okay, Cotty, yell when you're through." He took a large medical tome and left the room, shutting the door briskly behind him.

She looked after him at the shut door, and noticed that there was rather a large keyhole, so when she took off her skirt and sweater she hung them over the knob, though she didn't think that Patrick was the kind of person who would consider looking through a keyhole.

He had put a chair by the tub and actually she needed it to help her climb in. There wasn't very much water and it wasn't as hot as she would have liked it to be. She had forgotten when she'd asked Patrick if she could have a bath in his tub that he lived in a cold-water flat, and that this meant exactly what it said: cold water. The tub was a bit of a squeeze, too, so that her knees were hunched up under her chin. It wasn't going to be at all like her father standing and steaming himself under the shower, but she thought perhaps she'd feel better if she washed, so she got the face cloth full of lather and began to soap herself all over.

Then she heard the whistle. A long, low wolf-whistle.

She sat rigid in the tub. She'd been so worried about Patrick being in the room or even looking through the keyhole that she hadn't thought about his windows, his two, big, bare painter's windows. She grabbed the towel off the back of the chair and looked out through the window and there, across the court, was a big man in a sweatshirt leaning out his window despite the cold, looking in at her as hard as he could, and grinning from ear to ear.

"Pull down your shades!" she yelled, though he would not hear through Patrick's closed windows. "Stop looking at me!"

He leaned farther out the window and roared with laughter.

"Patrick!" she shrieked. "Patrick!"

Patrick opened the door, his finger marking his place in the heavy medical book. "What's the matter?"

"There's a man in that window! He's looking at me!"

Almost as quickly as he'd put the key in the keyhole of the water closet, Patrick took the screen from his kitchen and put it in front of the tub. Charlotte burst into tears.

"Don't be upset," Patrick said kindly. "He's never seen anyone as beautiful as you are in his life. It will be something lovely for him to remember always. Now finish your bath and call me when you're dressed." And he went out again.

What had she expected him to do? Certainly not to tell her that she'd brought light into that man's life. She'd expected that he'd at least shout at him. Or perhaps go plunging down the stairs and over to the next building and up to the man's apartment and grab him by the scruff of the neck and beat him up.

She managed to get the soap off her in the inch of lukewarm water in the bottom of the tub, deciding to have a proper bath as soon as she got home. When she was dry she realized that she would have to get out from behind the screen to get the clothes that she'd hung over the keyhole. She'd certainly called her shots wrong. She wrapped the towel around her as best she could, darted out from behind the screen, snatched the clothes off the doorknob, dropped her slip, bent down to pick it up, and was rewarded by another wolf whistle from across the way. She slunk behind the screen, dressed, and called Patrick.

"Is it because you paint that you don't have curtains at your windows?" she demanded. "Couldn't you have shades?"

"I'm aiming for them one of these days," he said. "There always seems to be something more important to get instead, like something to eat."

"You bought that canvas for your painting, and you didn't buy ten-cent store china."

Patrick shrugged. "What I pick up at junk stores can't be bought for the same money at the five-and-dime any more. Woolworth is no longer for us of the proletariat. I could take Violet's money but I prefer to do things on my own. You know what, Cotty? I think you should go home now, and we should make another date, a brand-new one, and start all over again. I have a feeling you'd like to forget this evening entirely, and though there are moments of it I'd like to treasure, I'm willing to go along with the gesture. What do you say we pretend you never came here tonight, and that we make a date for—perhaps next Friday evening. Maybe I'll blow us to artichokes and take you to a French movie. In any case I think I ought to call for you properly. Okay? Now I'll take you home."

Didn't she ever think? Why was she surprised when Patrick took her to the subway instead of calling a taxi? Perhaps it was because her father always whistled and waved his cane at a taxi automatically. If Patrick had asked her when her father had last taken a subway she wouldn't have had the faintest idea.

She said goodbye to Patrick at the foot of her street. She didn't want him walking up to the house with her, she explained, not when she'd lied about going to Ursula's house to do homework.

It was only as she was walking up the brownstone steps and fumbling in her bag for her latchkey that she realized that not only had she not sacrificed her innocence on the altar of Patrick's sophistication, but Patrick hadn't seemed in the least interested in her doing so.

Was it because she had sneaked too much of Patrick's wine and thrown up and everything or was she really as much of a failure as she seemed?

I am very unhappy and the result of what started with such happiness is tears and deathly despair and I see no help anywhere

. . . no, Antonio was not coming to the room for her, she was to meet him downstairs. That was what Dr. Ferreira had told her to do. She looked with anxiety at her watch. By the time she had put on make-up and tidied herself, the required hour would have passed and Antonio would take her to the Convento de Nossa Senhora da Conceição—

To her surprise the doctor came with him (was Antonio sulking?) and both men tried to shelter her under huge dark umbrellas, Antonio holding her arm tightly and guiding her as though she were blind. They spoke in French, the doctor's as felicitous as his English, making hers and Antonio's sound like schoolchildren's. In both languages Dr. Ferreira spoke with a perfection not heard in one born to the tongue.

"I am jealous of that brat Joaquim," Antonio was saying, apparently continuing a conversation with Dr. Ferreira. "She doesn't care anything about me. Only about Joaquim."

She?

The doctor asked, "It isn't Jacopo himself, is it? It is his music."

Antonio's face was brooding. "Is there any difference?"

Charlotte realized that "she," then, was Violet.

"No, I suppose not," the doctor answered. "But you are not being very rational."

Antonio burst out, "I am being completely rational!"

The doctor laughed and held his umbrella more carefully over Charlotte's head. "The more rational we think we are, my dear Tonio, the more we open ourselves to the wholly irrational. Our rationality is only a frail and fragile structure keeping the irrational at bay. If we were like Dame Violet, or like Joaquim, we might say that rationality is the form of the fugue keeping the passion of the music within bounds. For me my intellect is the very inadequate leash with which I try to control the enormous wild beast that is life as human consciousness experiences it."

"It *is* a wild beast, isn't it?" Charlotte asked.

"Yes."

"And it can devour us?"

"Oh, yes," Dr. Ferreira said quite calmly. "And frequently does."

They turned the corner, past the plaque saying CONVENTO DE NOSSA SENHORA DA CONCEIÇÃO, and went onto the plaza. Antonio muttered, "And calling him Jacopo, after Dante's son—*I* am the poet—oh, never mind. Here we are."

The convent lay deserted in the rain. Antonio took out a large rusty key and struggled with it, turning it back and forth in the lock. "Don't exercise yourselves," he said. "Professor Nunez told me that it is very difficult to open. One has to give it a special little twist to the left . . . There used to be gardens south of the convent, Mrs. Napier, kitchen gardens and rose gardens and an orchard and, I believe, a pond. Of course at this time of winter there isn't much blooming anywhere in the Alentejo. Geraniums, of course, and the palm trees are in flower. You probably saw them on your way down from Lisbon yesterday. And the cork trees being stripped . . . oh, good, here we are."

The door creaked open and they entered a damp, cold hall, though no damper nor colder than the hall of the pensão, nor more redolent of the past. That was it: the musty odor of decay, the overlushness of the tropical flower that blooms riotously and then rots along with leaves and ferns and tangled vines so that the jungle steams with the odor of death.

The dank and musty hall led into a room that was stripped of all furnishings but that held nevertheless an aura of richness and over-ornamentation. The floor was a complex pattern of many colors, the tesserae tiny and vivid. The walls were faced with the Portuguese tile, again in a complex design, up to the lintel of the doors; above the tile were murals in gaudy colors depicting scenes from the life of Christ. The ceiling was arched and vaulted in rose and blue and gilt, blossoming from ornamented and fluted columns. Charlotte felt smothered with color, with design after involuted design seeming to curve in from ceiling and column, entangling her in lush tendrils.

She stood in the center of the room and turned, slowly. Antonio looked at her expectantly and she said, "It is very different from the convents I have known—"

Again the doctor turned his probing gaze on her, his thick brows drawing together. "You have been to many?"

"For most of my schooling."

"And our Nossa Senhora da Conceição?"

"It's—a little ornate for what I am used to." She looked at him helplessly, feeling that she was being impolite, and yet not knowing what else to say.

But he nodded placidly. "Yes. They were a strange combination of asceticism and luxury, those nuns. Their public rooms were full of gilt and velvet, but, judging from their cells, and we should show you one of these cells for its absolute contrast, they may have had a sense of guilt about the gilt, for the cells were tiny and bare, and the nuns slept on a straw pallet placed on a slab of wood. And when they died they were buried in a common and unmarked grave in the crypt. All except the Infanta Dona Brites, the foundress. This is her sarcophagus here." He patted a cold stone effigy. "She was an ancestress of our Soror Mariana and of the Dona Brites who was abbess in Mariana's day. They like to keep these things in the family, though in their dying they were more democratic than in their living. We don't know which are Mariana's bones, nor which the abbess's, nor which the most menial of the lay sisters. We must show you the cloister because Professor Nunez has some interesting things lying around, but you must see the chapel first. How did the good nuns feel about all this luxury that is strange to you? The chapel was the center of their lives, and perhaps it was logical to them that all the glory of which they were capable should be lavished upon this one particular place . . . I myself find it rather magnificent in its own slightly vulgar way."

Yes, Charlotte thought, it was indeed a magnificent confusion of gold and more gold, of statues and paintings, and an altar against a reredos that soared, gilded tier upon gilded tier, to a statue of the Virgin crowned as Queen of Heaven.

"Remember," the doctor said, "that although it was the chapel on which all the money and lavishness was poured, within it the nuns knelt motionless for hours on cold stone. It is a contradiction of indulgence and denial, and the contradiction is important. What they wished was to indulge God and to deny themselves, to give him everything and themselves nothing." He led the way out of the chapel, saying, "I think, Tonio, that it is this very paradox that appeals to the poet in you."

Antonio spoke with unexpected bitterness. "You keep saying there's a poet on every street corner in Portugal. I understand. You think I'm just one of them. One of too many. We are expendable, but we have nothing but ourselves to spend. You take Joaquim seriously, but I am only a Latin teacher and so—"

The doctor interrupted him, "Be quiet, Tonio. If I did not take you seriously do you think I would put up with you at all? You have the makings of a poet but you have absolutely no discipline. Without discipline all your talent is worthless. Now come."

He led the way with decision into the ruined cloister. Rain was

falling steadily into the garden, where there were a broken
and fragments of statues, a torso, a bodiless head, a hand,
of an arm. Under the arched walk were more bits of statua
ments of columns, and the odor of rain and dust and age.
them, protecting them from the downpour, the vaulted ceili.., was
covered with flaking paint. The inner wall to the convent was again
ornamented with tile.

"We have always been like no other people, like no other country
in the world," the doctor said, "and Portugal must have seemed like
another planet to the soldiers who came from France and England
and Holland to help us break free from Spain."

To Charlotte, too, it seemed like another world. She stood wearily
near a broken marble column, barely out of the rain, half listening to
the doctor and Antonio telling her that John of Braganza was technically
returned to the throne in 1640, but when Soror Mariana met Noël the
war was far from over. The Spanish kept their hold on the southern
provinces (as the dampness held Charlotte, seeming to crush her down
on the marble column) and it was only with the help of mercenaries
and adventurers that they were finally able to break loose.

"Of course," Tonio was saying, "not only was our great period of
exploration and expansion two hundred years behind us—it died more
or less with Henry the Navigator—but we've always battled for libera-
tion, first against the Visigoths, then the Romans, the Moors."

"Yes." The doctor leaned against the moisture-streaked wall and
began to prepare his ancient pipe. "They all occupied us and left
their marks on us. The Romans gave us our bridges, our art, our
irrigation systems that are still in use today, and you cannot look
around this so-called Christian convent without feeling the breath of
the Moor on the back of your neck. Never forget that we are half
African, and, like our young friend here, violent and volatile."

He picked up a corroded piece of iron that seemed to have been
a shallow dish and held it out to Charlotte. "The remains of the kind
of lamp that was used in the convent. A wick floating in olive oil.
It gives out a miserable, smoky sort of light, but candles were expensive and were used only by the wealthy and the church, and even
then only when a display was felt essential. In Mariana's time I fancy
we'd have found candles used in the chapel as part of their offering
of beauty. But the dishes of oil would have served the sisters."

Antonio took the rather dirty piece of metal from Charlotte and put it down on the stump of a column. "Smoky oil lamps, gold and velvet in the chapel, and not enough to eat. People used to bring the nuns all kinds of desserts and sweets, but they often didn't have enough plain food. What miserable complexions those poor girls must have had."

Charlotte started to ask why there was not enough to eat but it seemed too great an effort and she realized that this was partly because her throat was now so sore that it would hurt to talk: the back of her throat felt burned and raw. No wonder, with all this plowing about in the rain and cold. The hideous yellow shoes pinched her feet, and she sat down on the broken pediment that was all that remained of a marble column. An occasional gust of wind sent a splatter of rain through the arches and into her face, and she felt wrapped in a tight cocoon of discomfort.

Was it ever warm in Beja? Probably not. Probably it was either freezing cold, as now, or stiflingly hot. In the winter the nuns' habits must always have been damp. They would all have had colds in winter, and chapped hands. And in the summer the dark robes would cling hotly and they would feel the sweat trickling down their backs and legs, how miserable, how unendurable, how

. . . hot it is," Sister Joaquina said. "My embroidery thread is all damp, and the red is running. It's going to spoil the pattern. What ought I to do?"

Why would Sister Joaquina notice the heat, why would she find something to worry about, on this day of all days when the town was a turmoil of joyful celebration and the convent, where the abbess had relaxed all rules, echoed the noise of the streets? The parade had dispersed and the soldiers were roaming Beja, looking for women, for wine, for any available pleasure after the austerity of battle. The humid air shimmered with laughter and desire. The rough shouting and singing soared over the convent walls, was picked up by the children who romped in and out of the white buildings, tore through the gardens, throwing discipline joyfully to the winds.

Everywhere, in all the silent places, talking and laughter were heard. When Michaela ran, singing, along the covered cloister, out into the garden, down the path to join the young nuns by the frog pond at the bottom of the convent grounds, Sister Maria da Assunção only smiled tightly instead of intoning her usual "A sister does not run," "A sister does not raise her voice," "A sister controls herself at all times."

By the pond Mariana lay, stretched out on the browning grass. She did not even hear Joaquina's complaint. When a group of children came running to the pond in a shrieking game of tag, she leapt up and ran off with them, came laughing back, threw herself down on the grass again, and plunged her hands into the tepid water of the pond, wetting the long, concealing sleeves of her habit.

Joaquina was still struggling with her embroidery, still talking, still complaining, about Sister Michaela now, was it? "We're not out here to *chatter*, Sister. We may have been given special permission to talk because of the victory, but Mother said *quietly*. I'm sure she didn't mean throwing over all the rules this way. Personally, I would have preferred to remain in our usual silence during this hour so that I could pray."

Mariana rolled over onto her back, holding her wet fingers up to the hot and humid breeze. "We *have* prayed, and with joy. All we're doing now is bringing our joy out of the chapel and into the garden with us."

Joaquina, sitting upright on a marble bench, looked somberly at Mariana's relaxed limbs. "You're always talking about enjoying things."

Yawning widely in contented reaction to excitement, to heat, to pleasure, Mariana said, "What's wrong with that?"

"If anybody's brought any gold thread I could work with that," Joaquina said. But nobody had, so she turned her attention again to Mariana. "Maybe there's nothing wrong with it on earth, but we're supposed to have our minds more on heaven than on earth."

Still stretched out, closing her eyes against the blinding glare of the sun, Mariana said, "Now there I think you're quite wrong, Sister. We are on earth, and surely God has put us here to *be* here. If he wanted us to be in heaven we'd be there."

Joaquina rubbed her red-stained fingers against her handkerchief. "You have to earn heaven, Sister, and I hardly think you care." '

Mariana sat up. "Is loving earth not caring about heaven? You think just because the sight of the soldiers who spent so much of themselves fighting for us filled us with such joy—" But her voice trailed off. She stood up, murmuring, "I'll be back," and moved down the path as a group of little girls called to her, "Sister Mariana! Come play with us!"

The abbess was not at supper; rumor had it that she was seeing the governor, something about the battle, something about politics; the abbess knew everybody; her opinion was respected, and requested. She had left word that rules were still lifted, and the refectory rang with unaccustomed laughter.

Sister Joaquina, unable to share the pleasure, was saying, "I'm not sure it's a good idea."

Beatriz directed her clear gaze at Joaquina. "What? Being free of Spain?"

"Counting buttons."

—What? Mother Escolastica, sitting across from the younger nuns, focused her dark old eyes, still bright as beads, on Joaquina's pasty face. Did the young nun, like Sister Maria da Assunção, suffer from dyspepsia? Her diet should be checked. Why should a casual remark from silly little Michaela on the brightness of the buttons on the French soldiers' jackets be made an issue?

Joaquina, overly fond of mortifications, took the driest, hardest crust from the bread tray. "It keeps our minds from the contemplation of inward visions."

Mariana burst into such a peal of laughter that all heads in the refectory turned in her direction.

Joaquina flushed. "What's so funny?"

"Forgive me," Mariana said quickly as she reached for an orange and began to peel it. "I wasn't laughing at you. You're quite right. I should spend more time, as you do, worrying about saving my soul, but I can't seem to do it, because surely *I* cannot save my soul. Only God can do that. And when I see—" she looked out the long, open windows to the garden, "—the way the evening sun is touching the flowers right now—or when I look at this orange, look at the brilliance of its color and smell the sharpness of its scent—isn't that as much a vision of God as anything we see inwardly?"

"I don't know," Joaquina said flatly. She looked across the table at Mother Escolastica. "I don't mean to criticize, Mother, but there's something wrong with it."

"With what, child?"

"The way Sister Mariana looks out the window at the flowers, and the way she enjoys that orange."

"Well?"

"She enjoys it too much."

Mariana's mouth was full of juicy pulp. "Aren't we supposed to?"

"You get up at night to watch the moon rise. Sometimes I wonder how seriously you take our rule."

Beatriz intervened. "As seriously as you do, I think."

Mother Escolastica's voice was reprimanding. "Beatriz."

"Mother," Beatriz said quietly, "there was nothing even remotely wrong in our rushing to the balcony to see the soldiers march by. Even an order as strict as ours would have been sliding into scrupulosity to have forbidden that."

"And we were not forbidden," the old nun replied.

Joaquina eyed the bowl of oranges but did not take one.

The talking among the children and nuns reached a peak before Compline, after which Silence was to be resumed. Groups of sisters strolled up and down the arched walk of the cloister, their laughter high, sweet, and profoundly innocent against the guffawing and shouting in the street. The long last rays of light reached over the walls and caught the high spray of the fountain. Michaela, still bemused by the sight of the soldiers, the resplendent clothes of the Frenchmen and the Englishmen, stopped, leaning dreamily against one of the soaring columns. "If I had to choose, if I absolutely had to choose which one was the most gorgeous, I couldn't possibly."

Joaquina strolled past. "Mariana could."

"Oh? Could I?" Mariana laughed.

Beatriz allowed herself unusual enthusiasm. "That was Mariana's brother, the one who stopped right where we could see him best, and took off his hat and bowed to us, standing up in his stirrups."

Now Joaquina turned in the deepening shadow of the arched walk and looked directly at Beatriz. "We all know Sister Mariana's brother. I didn't mean him. I meant one of the Frenchmen."

Beatriz moved to Joaquina. "Why were you so busy watching Mariana instead of the parade?"

Joaquina's voice trembled. "Maybe I was afraid, which is something you and Mariana never seem to be."

"Afraid of what? That they'd come leaping over the convent wall to drag us off with them?"

"Stop it," Joaquina cried, all control broken by anger. "It was obvious that Sister Mariana was looking at one French soldier in particular."

Mariana moved to the fountain and raised her hand to catch the spray. "Oh, Sisters, you all know that I always look at one person or one thing in particular. Joaquina's quite right. I look at one blossom on the bough. One little lizard sunning itself on the wall. One orange. One drop of rain as it slides down the windowpane. When I look at one more carefully, then I know all the better."

Joaquina stepped out of the shadows towards the silver of the fountain. "Does eating rain make you understand it better?"

Beatriz was amused. "What are you talking about?"

"I've seen Mariana *eat* rain. I saw her stand out on the balcony one afternoon during a shower, and I saw her holding out her hand and catching rain and tasting it."

Mariana laughed. "It was wonderful."

"And I've seen her taking the petal of a flower and sucking it."

"I just wanted to see what the bees were after."

Beatriz looked affectionately at Mariana's laughing face. "We'd all like to get as much pleasure out of things as she does."

Joaquina tightened her lips. The happiness of the other sisters seemed to choke her. "I didn't think our lives were supposed to be spent in the pursuit of pleasure."

Mariana spoke earnestly and with joy. "Surely, Sister, we aren't meant to deny the wonderful things around us that are just asking to be marveled at."

The bell for Compline rang. They turned and hurried towards the chapel. "It's so hot," Joaquina murmured to herself. "I feel as though

I had fever—" She put her hands up to her burning cheeks.

was strange to feel her face flushed and hot this way when her hands
and feet were so cold.

The doctor stopped in the middle of a sentence. "Mrs. Napier, you
have fever."

"Yes. I think I must have taken cold."

"Then you mustn't stand around in this wet place any more." He
pulled out his heavy, old-fashioned gold watch, appeared to consult
it, then looked at her again. "Four o'clock. If you have fever you
really should be in bed."

Charlotte felt a surge of panic. In that terrible room at the pensão
she would die. "I must see my mother-in-law tonight. It is imperative."

Dr. Ferreira looked at her gravely. "I understand. But she will not
take it kindly of me if I let you come down with pneumonia. Is there
a heater in your room?"

"No," Antonio said. "The only heaters are in the dining room and
the lounge."

"Let us go back to the pensão and see what is best to be done,
then, until Dame Violet returns. I imagine she will want you to stay
with her?"

"No," Charlotte said frantically. "Not if I'm not well. I can't bother
her. It was bad enough my coming at all."

"But you have come. And since you are here she will want to see
that you are properly cared for."

—Do you really know Violet? Charlotte wondered. —She won't
care. This is not the kind of thing that concerns Violet.

"I will take care of her at the pensão," Antonio said.

Dr. Ferreira brushed this aside. "Let us make no plans until Dame
Violet returns. Meanwhile take Mrs. Napier back to her room, Tonio,
and I will stop off and get my bag."

He held his hand out to Charlotte and she rose from the broken
column, her hem ripping as it caught on a jagged piece of stone.
The cloister swirled for a moment and she was suddenly more willing

to let the doctor do anything he wanted with her.

He hurried off, bent under his umbrella, as Antonio closed and locked the heavy door to the convent—no, museum, but it seemed still to be a convent to Charlotte; she still half expected to see the dark figures, almost indistinguishable one from the other, moving across the plaza, rosaries clicking. Oh, the safety of it, the comfort of the familiar pattern . . .

"Why wasn't there enough food?" she asked. Her voice sounded tight and croaky.

"There's never enough food during wartimes," Antonio said. "Don't you remember that?"

Under his big dark umbrella she nodded.

"The convents felt the pinch more than most places because they were crowded. Fathers couldn't marry off their daughters because there weren't enough men. We'd lost them first in our explorations and settling of the colonies, then in the wars. So what was there to do with the poor girls but make nuns of them? They say they came with all their family jewels that they'd have had if they'd married, and dressed up their habits with them. Sounds weird, a nun's habit festooned with necklaces and brooches, doesn't it?"

"Rather," she murmured, only half listening. Antonio was protecting her from the rain with his huge black umbrella, but beneath it his words fell on her like a shower, and slid off her as easily. She thought only of putting one foot in the ugly shoes in front of the other, of getting back to the cold comfort of the damp bed in the pensão.

"But it's insupportable in here," he said as he helped her into her room. "We're not used to this kind of weather, you understand; we're unprepared for it. It's the first bulletin on the radio now, this cold wave. We've forgotten world crises."

She sat hunched over on the edge of the bed. "I think I do have fever."

He listened, finally, to her instead of himself. "Wait. I'll bring you some hot coffee with brandy. That will help. And you can trust Ferreira. His reputation reaches all Europe . . ." His voice trailed down the corridor.

Hot coffee with brandy. Yes. That might help.

She sat there, humped like an old woman, feeling suffocatingly hot, and yet shivering so that she huddled more deeply into her coat, and he did not return. He had gone to South America for the coffee beans, or Africa; he was in a vineyard growing the grapes; he had forgotten, because there was not enough food, and the nuns went visiting, and danced to the music of the orchestra

. . . which wafted up the stairs of the Alcoforado villa where Peregrina sat on the landing waiting for Baltazar.

As he climbed the stairs with a plate of food and a glass of wine in his hands she whispered down to him, "I thought you'd never come. I thought you'd forgotten."

"I promised, didn't I?" Baltazar asked. "But I got trapped a couple of times. Why couldn't Mariana come home with you tonight?"

"Ever since she was professed, Aunt Brites hasn't wanted her to leave. Not only Mariana. All of them. Me, she knows I have no vocation. She couldn't care less."

"That's not true."

"Oh, she cares about *me,* Peregrina. But not whether I come home or not." She led him down a long gallery hung with portraits, up a narrower, longer flight of stairs, down a hall lighted dimly by a smoky torch, and into her room. It was a large room, as large as her dormitory at the convent that slept twenty. She jumped like a small child up onto her high, huge bed. The tall windows were open, the heavy drapes pulled back to let in all the air possible. "I'm so glad you're in one piece and nobody killed you. Did you kill lots of Spaniards?"

Baltazar handed her the plate and the wine. "Thousands. Seven with my musket, three with my sword, fourteen I stabbed with a knife, twenty-nine I strangled with my bare hands, eleven I decapitated with my Turkish scimitar, over thirty-two I poured boiling oil, and the rest I simply talked to death."

Peregrina laughed with such abandon that she almost knocked her plate onto the floor. Baltazar rescued it, and she said, "Note that it's *before* I've had my wine," took a generous draught, and began to eat avidly.

"Don't they feed you at that convent of yours?"

"Oh, they feed us all right. Better than most convents, they keep telling us as we sit down to another dinner of codfish. Aunt's always after papa to send food. But nobody ever seems to give us anything but codfish. Dom Alipio is always sending enormous quantities of codfish." She giggled. "Maybe that's why Sister Joaquina looks like one. In the spring we have lots of vegetables from the garden. But it's hardly what you'd call *cuisine qui peut me plonger dans l'estase!*" She rolled her eyes at him. "Did I say it right?"

"Superbly. So you *are* learning something."

"Mariana teaches us French. And our aunt, the most august abbess herself, taught Mariana. I suppose it will be a useful language if I ever have a chance to talk about any kind of food except codfish."

"You're getting something besides codfish tonight."

"One of the best reasons I know for coming home. May I have some more wine later? I come whenever papa can be bothered with me. He always seems to be dashing off to court. But when he's home he likes to have me around. I amuse him. I do manage to get lots of gossip out of him. It makes me very popular with the other girls. Aunt would die if she knew some of the things we know about the sisters."

"Papa has no business to—"

"Oh, Baltazar, we have to have *some*thing to make life bearable. Don't *you* start treating me like a child."

"Which is exactly what you—"

She interrupted him again. "I'm centuries older than Mariana, if you want to know! She practically never comes home and she doesn't know anything about life."

"And you do, I suppose?"

"One can't be around papa, or my dear sister Ana and her husband for long, and not pick up *some* information. And I think I'm old enough to be told now whether or not papa intends to have me marry."

The door to the bedroom was pushed ajar and the wrinkled, impudent face of a monkey peered in, and the little beast, on all fours, scurried over to the bed and leaped up onto it. With a soulful look he gazed at the plate of food and Peregrina popped a tidbit into his greedy mouth. "Papa tells him things he won't tell me—or Ana or Rui, for that matter. How I wish Pinto could talk! I'm sure papa has told him what he intends to do about me."

"Why don't you ask papa yourself?" Baltazar suggested.

"I have. And he says there's time enough to think about it. But I know papa, and I know he's already made up his mind, and if he won't tell me I'm afraid it means he wants me to stay in the convent and be a nun, like Mariana. Baltazar, I don't want to be a nun."

"Have you told him that?"

"Of course. But you know perfectly well that what I think isn't even going to enter into it. He had to give Ana a big dowry when she married Rui, and he doesn't want to break up the property, you know that, he wants to keep it together so it all can go to you, and I just know he's not going to want to—"

"Now, look here, Peregrina, I don't come into it."

"In papa's mind you do."

"You overestimate his affection for me."

"Oh, it's not out of affection for anybody except himself. You're an extension of papa, and he only wants you to have all the property because it's all his and in that way he manages, somehow or other, to keep it."

Baltazar looked at her unhappily. She sat there on the bed, the monkey curled up like a baby in her lap, reaching his little fingers out to her food which she absentmindedly put into his mouth. She looked at her brother with candid, wide-open brown eyes, but about her lips there was an expression of tension and almost of cynicism that was out of place with her openness. The monkey, in thanks for a bit of food, reached up and stroked her cheek, still childishly rounded.

"You shouldn't—" Baltazar started, then sighed. His dark eyes, his full lips, slightly florid complexion, his very helplessness before her made him seem younger than she. He finished, inadequately, "I don't want papa's property. I can take care of myself, and who knows, I may be killed."

"Stop!" Peregrina shoved plate and monkey aside, and flung herself into Baltazar's arms, almost strangling him with the intensity of her hug. The monkey grabbed the plate and began stuffing food into his mouth.

Baltazar extricated himself, saying with a half smile, "But that would make everything fine for you. There wouldn't be any problem about your dowry, and—"

Peregrina clapped her hand over his mouth, shaking her head violently.

"What, then?" he asked.

"Everybody knows you're the only person papa listens to—"

"All right. I'll try. God knows I wouldn't want you there against your will, and especially because of me. Let me go, now, and I'll bring you some more to eat—Pinto's had most of it—and one more glass of wine."

"Don't be long," she called after him. "And don't forget the wine."

He paused in the doorway. "Is it that important?"

"After convent food? It's *desperately* important. It's the only thing I have to remind me that there's a *real* world."

"But which is the real world?" Baltazar asked the empty corridor as he left Peregrina's room. "And don't look for reality in wine. Or importance."

"Why not?" Peregrina called after him, her face wrinkling up with a kind of anguish so that she looked like Pinto.

Is anything important?

If we could get the different worlds into their relative places, into
proportion

then we would know what is important

if anything

and then perhaps Mariana would never

then perhaps Charlotte

No, Cotty, don't flatter yourself, you are not like Mariana; you are like Peregrina, the way you went to Patrick's that first night (that almost only night) and drank so wildly, so (in Peregrina's sense) innocently. It could never be that innocent again.

...After Patrick had left her to go back to Bleeker Street, after she had climbed the steps to the brownstone on East Seventy-fourth and let herself in, she stood leaning against the door for a moment, trying to acclimate herself. Reuben and Essie must already have gone to bed, because only the night light was on in the hall, and the stairs leading down to the kitchen and dining room were pitch dark. But her father was still up, because a thin line of light was coming from under the double doors that led to the library. She knew that he was waiting up for her, and that he had told Reuben and Essie to go to bed. Someone always waited up for her, but it was usually her father, because Reuben and Essie were getting old and needed their rest.

She knocked on the door of the library. Her father did not answer. She knocked again. Finally she slid the door open. The light was lit on his desk. Within the past hour he had turned the hour glass, because the sand was trickling down in a fine stream. No matter how upset Charlotte was she always found a kind of peace in her father's library, and it must have been that way for him, too, for it was to the library he always turned for refuge, not to Charlotte, not to Reuben and Essie, not to any human being in the world.

There had been a fire in the fireplace earlier in the evening, but it had died. The only light came from the student lamp on the desk and at first she didn't see her father; then she realized that he was lying on the black leather couch. He was lying very still with one thin hand over his eyes, and she knew that he had not fallen asleep. He was lying there, not asleep, but somehow not there.

This was something that happened, that was not totally unexpected, but that always frightened her. It occurred usually when he was particularly depressed. He would lie down, and then he would seem to go away, much further away than if he had been asleep. She had read about holy men in the East who could lie down and appear to go to sleep, and then they would leave their bodies and wander out among the galaxies. This was the closest analogy she could make to what her father did when he lay down on the black couch and went not to sleep, but away. Did it help? Did he, in his own way, wander about among the galaxies until eventually he could bear to come back to himself again, to his brownstone house, to his typewriter?

She wondered if anything particular had happened to upset him. Perhaps another cold letter from a publisher. She was not supposed to know about these letters. She was supposed to be too young. She was supposed to see only the image of her father that Aunt Ada had held up for the world to see, for Charlotte to see, for James Clement himself to see, the image of the great, misunderstood genius. And perhaps it was the true image.

Charlotte looked down at him. His lying there, gone wherever it was that he went to, was all part of the strangeness of the evening, of Patrick knowing about James Clement, and being excited, but at the same time surprised that he was alive. It was all part of the strangeness of her feelings about her father, of other people never having heard of him, of the curt letters from the publishers or from his agent.

All she knew was that she loved him. The love became a pain that was physical when he lay down on the black leather couch and retreated. Or when she did not make his martinis and he cheated. Or, worst of all, once when she had slipped quietly into the library, and had seen him sitting leaning forward at the desk with his head in his hands and tears falling slowly from his shaded eyes and dropping quietly onto the manuscript in front of him. She had left as quickly as she could without making a sound, and he had never known that she had seen him that way. And she had never known what was making those slow, terrible tears. People used to say how deeply he grieved over his wife. But Charlotte did not think it was that kind of grief.

She went over to him now and sat beside him on the black leather couch and very gently moved his hand from in front of his eyes. His eyes, as they were at times like this, were completely unfocused. They were open, but they were not looking at anything. Their blue, an almost purple-blue, like Charlotte's, seemed veiled, greyed. He was not, she was certain, seeing anything at all, at least not anything that can be seen with the physical eye.

"Father. Come on, Father, please."

A small tremor went through his body. She knew that when he went off in this manner it was difficult for him to return. And if she had thought that he was really out among the galaxies, if she had thought he was any place that made him at all happy, she would not have tried to make him come back, no matter how much it frightened her to see him lying there. But the most frightening thing was that now she did not think that he was really anywhere at all. He was just gone.

"Come on, Father," she said again. "It's Cotty. I'm home. Let's go down to the kitchen and make ourselves something to eat."

Slowly perception moved from the clouded depths and he was looking at her. He rolled over and stretched as though he had been asleep. She knew that he wanted her to think that he had only been asleep.

"Hello, my darling," he said, and held his arms out to her and she gave him a hug.

"Father, I'm hungry. Let's go down to the kitchen and make something."

He gave her one of his big, beautiful smiles. "Hungry, Cotty? As a matter of fact, so am I, now. Essie's losing her hand at cooking, I'm afraid. Dinner tasted like plasticene. Shall I make you an omelette?"

"That would be lovely." She hadn't been in the least hungry when she suggested food, but suddenly there was a great gap in her stomach where all Patrick's dinner had been, and the sound of an omelette, one of her father's omelettes, was beautiful.

They sneaked down the back stairs as though fearful that Reuben and Essie would hear them, which of course they couldn't possibly because their rooms were up on the fourth floor. Her father had tried to get the old couple to move downstairs after Aunt Ada's death so that they wouldn't have to do so much climbing, but they refused. They loved their rooms and they would not, Charlotte knew, move unless they had to, or unless her father ordered them to, and her father seldom ordered them to do anything. Orders were the other way around.

They turned on the light in the kitchen. It was Charlotte's favorite room in the house, large, warm, with polished copper pots and pans hanging, and a copper hood to the stove. Essie and Reuben were very fond of copper. There were blue curtains at the windows, and blue cushions on the big rocker where Essie sat to do the mending. In the center of the room was a large marble-topped table, and James Clement got out eggs and chose one of the copper frying pans, took a blue bowl and cream and butter and some herbs and arranged everything on the table. Then he said, "Cotty, where were you tonight?"

"At Ursula's, doing homework."

Her father broke four eggs into the blue bowl. "Cotty, I didn't know you were in the habit of lying to me."

"I'm not," she said. "Not in the habit, that is."

"But you were lying when you said you were at Ursula's."

"Yes. How did you know?"

James Clement took a fork and began to beat the eggs. "That is beside the point, Charlotte. I happened to have occasion to call you during the evening and discovered that you were not where you said you were going to be. Why?"

She felt uncomfortable. Her father had a fierce temper, but since her mother's death it had been leashed; in any case he seldom loosed it on her. She looked at his stern face as he beat the eggs, his head a little lowered, so that she could see the way his fair hair lay scantily on the delicate skull. "I didn't think you and Essie and Reuben would approve."

"You didn't think we'd approve of what?"

She looked at him rather desperately. He was wearing a misty grey Norfolk jacket that he was very fond of, a blue tie she'd given him for Christmas, and an immaculate white shirt; he never wore anything but white shirts. "Well," she said, "it was just that I went out with this boy."

"Which boy?"

"Well, you know I went to this party down at Jane and Pete's," she started, but her father cut in.

"Which party?"

"Just that party I was going to last week when they had friends in to help them with their apartment. You said it was all right for me to go."

"Jane is a relative. One of the few we have left. She always seemed to me like a perfectly pleasant young woman. I try not to forbid you to do things unless it is absolutely necessary. How did a party at Jane's have anything to do with tonight?"

"Well, I met this—I mean, I met *a* young man there. A medical student. That's how he knows Jane and Pete. He's in Pete's class in medical school. And he asked me to have dinner with him tonight."

"And you thought if you told me that you were going out to dinner with this young man I'd have forbidden it?"

"Well—yes. And I didn't think Essie and Reuben would like it, either."

Her father was silent. He put the frying pan on the stove and began making the omelette. "I'm afraid you're right, Cotty. But if you must do things we wouldn't want you to do—Charlotte, please don't lie about anything again. Is that what the nuns taught you, along with your charming manners? I've always thought I could trust you. I'd rather have you defy me, tell me you're going to do something anyhow, permission or no permission, than be underhanded about it."

"It was just—it seemed so much simpler this way."

"I've always told you that anything easy isn't worth a damn," James Clement said sharply as he dished out the omelette. She was no longer hungry, but she sat down at the table across from him.

"Cotty," he said slowly, "I haven't given you a proper life for a child. All those schools, and then the hotels all over the world during your holidays. But we were happier in the hotels, at least I thought we were, then when we were here with your Aunt Ada. But perhaps I should have brought you here more often; perhaps I should have let Ada take your mother's place more than I did."

"Oh, Father, you know Aunt Ada was never in the least interested in me. It was only you she cared about. She never gave a hoot what I did as long as I didn't bother you, you know that. I saw much more of you when we were at hotels than I ever did here as long as Aunt Ada was alive. I used to have to sneak into the library if ever I wanted to see you, she was so afraid I'd interrupt the muse."

"Don't scorn the muse, Charlotte, even in reference to me."

"I'm not!" she shouted. "I was just explaining about Aunt Ada! It was Reuben and Essie who loved me. They've been like my mother and—" she stopped.

"Finish your sentence," he said bitterly. "Like your mother and father, neither of whom were ever proper parents to you."

"You are, Father!" she cried.

"Oh, Cotty." His voice was heavy. "Oh, Cotty," and he pushed his untouched plate away from him.

She poked a bit of omelette into her mouth. She realized that everything she had said had been wrong. Everything she had said instead of making anything better was just making everything worse. Her father looked cold and pinched about the nose. He was no longer the gay young father the small Charlotte had adored. His blue eyes looked bleak the way they did when things were going wrong with his writing. She got up and went around the table and put her arms around him.

"Oh, Father, I'm sorry I lied to you about going to Ursula's. I won't do it again."

"Fight me if you have to, Cotty, but don't lie to me."

"I promise," she said. "And, Father, Patrick did a paper on your books in college!"

"Patrick's the young man you went out with?"

"Yes, and he thinks you're wonderful, and his mother, who's some kind of musician, thinks you're wonderful. What was it he said she called your books? Oh, yes, the brilliant apocalyptical novels of James Clement."

Her father pulled his plate back to him and began to eat. "Where did he take you to dinner?"

"He cooked for me himself."

James Clement shook his head, but he went on eating. Then he said, "I don't know what to do about you, Cotty. Suddenly I realize the fact that you are still in school doesn't make you still a child. And I realize even more strongly than ever that I haven't provided you with any kind of normal childhood."

"Oh, Father, I told you. There hasn't been anything in the world wrong with my childhood."

"You haven't had the love you should have had," he said somberly.

"But I have! You've loved me, and Essie and Reuben have loved me."

"You don't mention your mother. Don't you remember her?"

"Yes. I remember her. But she didn't want me. I interfered with things. She liked parties and important people and showing you off. She was much happier when she was in Nassau or on the Riviera or in London or Scotland or somewhere and could pretend I didn't exist at all."

"You're not being fair, Cotty, but you're too young to understand your mother."

"I'm sorry," she said, although she knew that she didn't sound sorry and of course she wasn't. But she should have been able to sound sorry. "I know people thought I was awful because I didn't cry and carry on when she died. But it was as though some glamorous movie star had died, not anybody who really had anything to do with me, Cotty. I was impressed, and I guess I was shocked, but it didn't— it didn't really touch me any."

Now why was it that she could talk to her father openly this way about her mother, and yet she had lied to him about going out with Patrick, and she knew she'd do anything possible to avoid telling him now about having had two martinis and too much wine and then that bath in Patrick's apartment with the man whistling at her: why?

"Shall I make some coffee?" he asked.

She shook her head. She'd had enough coffee. "No, thanks. But go ahead if you want some."

"No," he said slowly. "No. I think I'll just have a nightcap if you'll be kind enough to fix it for me. Let's go up to the library. And then we must both go to bed. It's late and you have school tomorrow. I don't watch your bed hours properly. All your life I've passed that kind of buck to nuns and other hired help."

"Essie watches my hours," she said. "She's always coming down and telling me to put out my light."

She picked up the plates and put everything in the sink for Essie and Reuben to wash up in the morning, and they went back up to the library. She mixed her father his nightcap, then sat on the couch while he sprawled out in his desk chair. He sat silently, glass in hand, not talking, and she did not feel like talking any more, either. She felt only very tired. She looked at her books across from her, and at the shelf where her father's books were, his published books. She had not read all of James Clement's books, and she was not sure why, because she liked them. She did not wholly understand them, but they fascinated her.

Perhaps one reason she hadn't read them all was Sister Thomas More; no, it wasn't Sister Thomas More, but Sister Mary Michael at the school in New York, who was for Charlotte in New York what Sister Thomas More had been for her in England. Sister Mary Michael told her class that there were two of Shakespeare's plays she still hadn't read, because she couldn't bear to have read all of Shakespeare. Charlotte couldn't bear to have read all of James Clement because there was something too final about it; it would somehow have been relegating him to the past, to an unused, undusted library.

"I'm tired," her father said. "Oh, Cotty, I'm so tired." He finished his drink and stood up. "Come along." They started upstairs.

When they got to his floor she said, "I'll come down and kiss you good night when I'm ready for bed." He just nodded, and she went upstairs and took a long, hot bath.

She knew that her father would not be turning out his light for a long time, because he read until daylight, until dark had turned into light, wearing a cashmere cardigan and a silk handkerchief at his throat. So she luxuriated in her bath, so different from the lukewarm inch of water in Patrick's tub, then sat on a stool wrapped up in her big towel to dry. She would have to ask her father about having dinner with Patrick on Friday. She couldn't just go without telling him. And Essie and Reuben wouldn't think it proper. They'd be much worse about it than James Clement.

She put on her nightgown and bathrobe and went down to say good night to him and to ask him about Patrick at the same time. When she got to his room and knocked on the door and he said, "Come in," he wasn't in bed reading as she had thought he would be. He hadn't even started to undress. He was sitting on the side of his bed. Just sitting. Not gone off to wherever it was he went. Just sitting.

But he smiled when he saw her. "Ready so soon, Cotty?"

"It's been an hour, Father."

"Oh. Time can be deceptive. And I'm tired. I'm so tired, Cotty. There is nothing more physically exhausting than a sense of failure."

"But you're not a failure, Father," she said.

"Oh, Cotty, let's not fool each other any longer. Why do I go on groping in the dark? Why can't I accept the absurdity of existence and laugh, as the absurd ought to be laughed at? Why can't I face the fact that it's all an accident, that man is an unattractive skin eruption on an improbable planet, that what came gurgling up from the void will die down again into darkness." He stood up. "Why does all of me reject this, Cotty? Why must there be beauty and meaning when everything that has happened to me teaches me that there is none?"

Her throat was tight and it was difficult to say, "But there is."

He clasped her tightly in his arms. "Why do I drag you into the pit with me?"

"You don't," she said. "You don't, Father. And there isn't anybody for you to talk with, and I'm glad I'm the one, truly I am."

"Cotty, sweet, sweet, go on up to bed and don't worry."

"I don't want to leave you when you're feeling this way."

"I'm all right."

"You're not feeling all right about your writing."

"That will pass, too. Do you know how applejack is made?"

For a moment she thought that he must have made himself another drink. "No."

"You put apple juice in a keg and leave it outdoors all winter and let it freeze. Almost all of it will turn to ice, but there's a tiny core of liquid inside, of pure flame. I have that core of faith in myself. There's always that small searing drop that doesn't freeze. Don't worry about me, darling. I'm all right. And you must get some sleep."

"And you, too, Father. I won't wake you when I come down for breakfast. I'll try to miss the squeaky stairs." She kissed him and hurried back upstairs, quickly, because she knew that she was going to cry.

The salt of tears.
The cleansing, the purifying.
The reducing to the core.

Why are tears salty?
When the oceans weren't?

"Did you know, Cotty, that in the beginning there was no salt in the oceans? They were pure, crystalline water from those first torrential, primordial rains. It took billions of years of sedimentation, of mineral deposits being washed down from the rocks, from the hills, before the seas became salt . . ."

"If there is too much salt in the sea, Cotty, it becomes dead. Its life is killed . . ."

Were tears once clear and crystal and without the taste of salt?

There is too much salt, now. My tears are dead.

. . . But because she was afraid Antonio would think she had been crying she pulled up out of her slumped posture as she heard his footsteps; she managed a courteous smile.

"I had to make the coffee," Antonio said. "Sorry to have been so long."

Charlotte sipped it gratefully. It was steaming hot, and he had been generous with the brandy.

"Mrs. Napier, forgive me. But it isn't just that you are ill. You are troubled."

She looked at him over the cup. "Isn't everybody, one way or another?"

"I know I have no right to ask." He held out his hands, the long fingers curving in a supplicating gesture. "But I feel a concern for you. I would like to help."

"Thank you. It's very kind of you."

"That you are unhappy distresses me."

She put the coffee cup down on the bedstand. "My unhappiness is unimportant."

"No unhappiness is unimportant."

"Mine is," she said. "I love my husband and I don't think he loves me. It's as simple as that. And as common."

Antonio immediately jumped to the obvious conclusion. "But with you—he could not love somebody else."

"He could, very easily. But it's not that. It's not *that* simple. Or that common. I suppose everybody's unhappiness is particular in some way. Let's talk about yours."

She had hurt him; he flinched. But he said, *"I* would love you."

She reached for her coffee cup. "That's nonsense. And furthermore, quite beside the point." Her voice was as chilly as the room. "We met only yesterday."

"It took Mariana and Noël only the meeting of their eyes."

"But I am not a dead nun and I take my marriage vows seriously."

"So, I think, did she," he said. "There would have been no problem otherwise."

She took a long drink of the rapidly cooling coffee. At least the brandy held its own heat. "Oh, Tonio—"

"Yes?" He pulled the chintz chair away from the window, dragged it close to the bed, and put his hand on her cold and trembling fingers.

She said, "Don't—please don't ask me things or I might talk about myself and we'd both regret it."

"I cannot imagine myself regretting anything you could tell me. Haven't you heard all the things I've been trying to tell you today? I have talked about battles and a long-dead nun but I have been trying to tell you something else. Haven't you heard?"

She withdrew her hand. "Tonio, go away. I came to Portugal to talk to Violet." She finished the coffee and automatically handed him the empty cup. She moved deliberately in her imagination from the dank room in the pensão to Violet, Violet seen in her feverish mind sitting in the blue-tiled room in the convent in Beja, the room that had known not Violet but the long-dead abbess: what was her name? Brites. Yes. Two syllables, Bree-tesh, with the *s* slurred the Portuguese way.

Why did the quondam abbess, like all the reverend mothers of Charlotte's past, wear Violet's face? How would Violet like *that*, Violet who was so passionately Violet and who spent so much time fending off any relationship that might become clinging or demanding? How would Violet like it that Charlotte could see no longer the faces of the nuns who had ruled the schools of her childhood, but only Violet wearing their habits?

Violet would not like it at all.

So Charlotte must not seem to cling or depend on her now.

To depend. To hang from.

No.

Violet, always troubled with hangers-on, detested them.

"Mrs. Napier—"

She looked at Antonio. He was too beautiful. The dark hair was too thick, too soft, the eyes too burning, the features too finely chiseled

it is not his fault

any more than it's Patrick's

the two so dark

so different

"Mrs. Napier, he'll be right here, Dr. Ferreira. He's probably been held up by a patient. They lie in wait for him. Why don't you rest until he gets here?"

"I'm all right," Charlotte said. "I'm all right just sitting here

. . . at

the abbess's feet on a low stool, bending slightly forward, her veil falling so that it half hid her face, her hands loosely clasped at her knees. She spoke softly, earnestly, ". . . most of the Rule is so easy for me that I hardly notice it. I think the part that troubles me most is the Examination of the Conscience."

The abbess regarded her calmly through serene, light eyes. "How so, my child? Are your sins, then, so grave?"

Mariana raised her face to the older woman. In the young nun's features the strength of the bone structure was not so pronounced, though the close blood relationship was revealed in the delicate line of cheekbone, the curve of lips, the wide spacing of the eyes. Mariana's eyes were more variable; they were the same extraordinarily light blue, but flecked with gold. She said, softly, "I think my gravest sin is that I do not feel sinful."

The abbess regarded the trusting face, utterly devoid of guile. The girl was more innocent that most of the children; she would have to grow up, face evil, to recognize the sinfulness of man. An abbess must know and not be shocked by the ways of the world, so Mariana must now learn more than charming French, more than the delicate copying of old manuscripts, the illuminating in red and blue and gold. "Continue, Sister Mariana," the abbess said.

"It's so easy, living here, in this beautiful place, surrounded only by the gentleness of your Rule—"

"Gentle?"

There was a certain irony to the question, but Mariana answered, "For me it is, so that as I follow through day and night I feel in—in a state of grace. Forgive me, but that's the way I feel, you see. It's not something I'm looking for, it's what happens. When I teach the little ones, when we walk through the gardens together, I don't feel grown up and beyond them; I forget my veil. I talk to them only of the joy of life instead of preparing them for the harshness they'll find when they leave here and return to the world. How can I prepare them for it when I have no experience of it?" She paused, but the older nun gave no sign of either approbation or disapproval, simply indicating that the girl should continue.

The young voice became hesitant. "It's so difficult . . . how can I say it . . . well, perhaps this is a sin, your Reverence, I don't know . . . I sometimes confuse God with his creation . . ."

The abbess looked at her sharply. "Explain yourself."

"God speaks to me not only through his son, but through the children I teach, through the moon sparkling against the fountain at night, a child's soft skin against my fingers, the sweet odor of growing things. . . . Mother, I lose myself in delight, and whether or not in this way I am worshipping God I do not know. But when I try to find him in dogmas and sermons, as Sister Joaquina does, I confess that these seem to me dead things, and I feel impatience and irritation."

"But that is Sister Joaquina's way, not yours, isn't it?"

"Yes, your Reverence."

The abbess was not angry, nevertheless she looked formidable. "It is arrogance in you to feel that you must praise him in Sister Joaquina's way, in Sister Beatriz's way, that no way should be closed to you. Do you understand that, child?"

"Yes, your Reverence. I never realized—but—yes, I think I see."

The abbess surprised her by laughing. "You want to try all ways, Sister Joaquina only one. I wonder what would turn out if I could shake the two of you together in a sack so that you'd be all mixed up?"

Mariana laughed. The abbess put her hand gently on the young nun's shoulder in a tangible gesture of affection she seldom allowed herself. "At least you bring laughter to this place, child. A strict rule should not discourage merry faces. But speak to Father Duarte about this in your next confession. He will help you to straighten it out. It does need straightening. You may go now. You have duties to attend to. And so do I."

The duties were part of the structure of the Rule, the framework that held her joy. She left the abbess and almost ran along the cloister to the chapel to steal a few moments in its golden peace. She dropped to her knees, her head bowed submissively, but slowly her face raised itself, for it was always easiest for her to pray outwards, upwards, towards the heavens.

"Oh, my dearest Lord, is it all right? It it all right? to be this happy? to love the children? Is there no grace in loving them because they are so beautiful and simple to love? And the soldiers riding by this morning, how beautiful they were! It was very easy for me, as I watched them, to understand that man is made in your image."

An unexpected shudder rippled over her body, like a cold wind moving across water.

. . . At the shudder that shook her, Antonio said, "You're still cold. Perhaps some more brandy?"

"No—" Charlotte started, but there was a knock at the door and it was Dr. Ferreira, battered black bag in hand, apologizing for the delay. He took a thermometer and put it under Charlotte's arm, European fashion, then looked around the room.

"This will never do," he said, beard and mustache quivering with the ferocity of his frown. "It is much too cold. You should have asked for a heater last night. No wonder you are ill. Of course we are unprepared here for this kind of weather. It gets cold in Beja, but not like this. A cold wave like this is almost unprecedented. Tonio, can you get a heater?"

"Of course, I'll go out and buy one—"

"But that's nonsense, for a few hours." He took the thermometer from Charlotte and looked at it. "Influenza. You will have to go to bed."

Charlotte said, in blind panic, "I can't—"

"At your mother-in-law's, where you will be taken care of. Not here."

Charlotte stood up. "I can't. I can't go to Violet."

"Why not?"

"She's not expecting me—she doesn't even know I'm here—nobody knows I'm here—"

"Your husband—"

"Patrick doesn't know. I left him. I came to tell Violet. So I can't go to her. Don't you see? I just came to—"

Dr. Ferreira put his hand against her forehead. "Mrs. Napier. Be quiet."

Antonio started to the door. "I'll buy a heater and we can put her to bed here and I'll take care of her."

The doctor brushed this aside with one of his big, clumsy gestures. "We will take her to my house and put her on the sofa in the library until we can get in touch with Dame Violet. At least I have a fire going in the grate; the room is moderately warm; I cannot even think of examining her here in this icebox. It was raining so abominably when I left that I took the car, so there is no problem in transportation . . ."

She was perfectly contented, now, to let them go on talking, pack her up, tuck her under a moth-eaten fur rug in the back of the car for the short drive. She moved through a haze of fever and discomfort until she was lying on a long and rather lumpy divan covered with a threadbare oriental rug. The doctor's library was warm and smelled of his fire and tobacco and undusted books: there was a feeling of comfort in the dark volumes filling the shelves, in the papers cluttering his desk. She submitted passively to his slow and thorough examination. As she felt the stethoscope cold against her skin she turned her head, half expecting to see Antonio looking at her, and almost screamed as she saw, instead, a skeleton standing in the corner. The flickering of the fire made the shadows move against the bare bones so that for a mad, feverish moment she thought it was Antonio, divested of flesh, three hundred years old, moving towards her. Then her brain cleared: there was nothing macabre about a skeleton in a doctor's study.

"Open your mouth and breathe, please," he said.

She did as he bade her, closing her eyes and relaxing under the absolute authority of his hands.

"You are not allergic to penicillin?"

"No."

She felt a swift, sure prick of hypodermic needle. Everything, at last, was under control; she was as much under his jurisdiction as though she were again a child

as though she were back in school

as though she were in a dormitory and the safety of rules was so absolute that they could be broken without fear because rules were so firm that breaking them could not really touch them.

. . . The ground near the frog pond at the foot of the convent grounds was hard and damp and Charlotte lay flat on it, pressing her nose against it until the patterns of grass and twigs were printed across her face and her tears were mixed with the wetness left from the morning's rain. Hard bits of stubble pricked through her uniform and jabbed into her, but she pressed against the ground even more closely, welcoming the pain, digging her toes into little tufts of grass and pushing, trying to concentrate her misery into simple physical discomfort.

"Oh, God," she whispered. "Oh, God." And then quickly she sat up, staring furiously at the sky, and said, "Damn you." And then, "Damn you to hell." She held her face up and waited, looking at one small white cloud (but surely any cloud was large enough for a thunderbolt). It floated past her and nothing happened. She had known that nothing would happen, but it was worth a try.

If he struck her down at least he would be there.

She became conscious of someone near her, and she stiffened, holding her breath, checking her sobs by pressing her face even harder into the ground. Someone was standing beside her, committing the unpardonable breach of privacy in watching her misery. She lay perfectly still, desperately trying to become invisible in the short, stubbly grass. But the dark shadow remained beside her. Why were nuns spying on her? "Go away," she whispered. "Go away."

"Charlotte."

"Go away," she said savagely into the ground. "Go away, damn you."

The voice, when it spoke again, held just a tinge of bitter amusement. "I'm not one of the nuns. Nor likely to become one now. Go on and swear if it will make you feel better."

Charlotte wriggled a few inches nearer the pond and stretched her arm out so that she could dabble her fingertips carelessly in the water. "I'm watching a tadpole turn into a frog," she said.

"That's very interesting, isn't it?" The voice was light. "I'd rather they stayed tadpoles, though."

"Would you? I like frogs." As conversation seemed inevitable she rolled over and sat up and saw that the voice belonged to one of the secular teachers, a teacher nobody liked.

"Hello, Miss Benson," she said courteously, trying to pretend that her face was not covered with tears, covered with bits of grass, marked with lines where the twigs had pressed into it. She pulled her lips into a smile. "A long face is a breach of manners," her father had told her.

"You may call me Sunset if you like," the teacher said. "I'm not ashamed of having red hair." She was a young woman in an ill-fitting tweed skirt and a baggy hand-knitted sweater and her face was hard and unhappy.

"I don't call you Sunset," Charlotte said.

"I wouldn't mind if you did. Except for the incongruity of it. A sunset is one of the loveliest things in the world. It's an oddly flattering nickname for me. Do you know that I came down to the frog pond just now for the same reason you did? Because I wanted to cry?"

Charlotte looked at her, at the red hair and the too-white skin covered with freckles. Then she remembered her manners. "I'm sorry."

"Don't be," Sunset said. "It's good to have something to cry about sometimes. That's how you grow." She dropped beside Charlotte at the edge of the pond and put her hand in the water, swishing it back and forth. Charlotte watched the long, knobby white hand, the back covered with fine red hairs, the nails cut off short and a little dirty. Sunset followed Charlotte's glance. "I know my nails are dirty." (But a teacher, even a secular teacher, shouldn't apologize to a student. Should she?) "I've been digging. Up on the hill above the Roman ruins. I've been digging gentians and planting them in a shoebox. I suppose they'll die, though."

"Maybe they won't." Charlotte kept on watching the thin, unshapely hand. "Why doesn't anything happen when you swear?"

"What did you want to have happen?" Charlotte did not answer and Sunset said, "Sometimes it makes me feel better if I yell at God. But not often. Not unless I can really shout."

"He doesn't strike you down . . ." It was barely a question.

"No," the teacher said sadly. "It doesn't work that way. Too bad, isn't it? At least we'd know he was listening. And we do want to be listened to. Far more than we're willing to listen. See here. I'd rather you didn't tell the Reverend Mother or any of the sisters, if you don't mind."

"All right."

"Even if I am leaving tomorrow I—I'd just rather you didn't."

"All right. But why are you leaving tomorrow?" Charlotte stared into the teacher's defiant face, suddenly aware of a pain not her own.

"I handed in my resignation half an hour ago," Sunset answered, "because if I hadn't I'd have been asked to leave in very short order anyhow. I admire the Reverend Mother and I thought I'd spare her that. When I came here I thought I was a teacher, and I thought perhaps I had a vocation. But it seems that I have no vocation, not as a teacher, not as a Religious. So where does that leave me? I can't discipline myself, and I certainly can't discipline you children. As a teacher I am worth exactly nothing to the Reverend Mother. Not one of you pays the slightest attention to anything I say."

"I pay attention," Charlotte said politely.

"You're different."

"I don't want to be different!" Charlotte cried furiously, digging her fingers into the ground.

Sunset looked at her sharply. "It was meant to be a compliment. I shouldn't have been talking to you like this if you weren't."

"Sorry."

"You won't tell the others about this?"

"Of course not."

Sunset looked at the child again, then began pulling out the short blades of grass, saying lightly, "Now I've told you why I came down to howl, you ought to tell me about you."

"Ought I?" Charlotte began pulling up grass too, laying the separate short strands across the sensible toe of her uniform shoe.

"It's only fair, isn't it?"

Charlotte had been well taught that fair play is all-important. She felt trapped but she said, obediently, "It was only that Perry Alfreds and I were the only new girls in our dormitory this term and she was my best friend, but none of the other girls in the dorm like me, so she doesn't any more, either."

"And that was why you were crying?"

"That. And because I lost the netball game for our form."

"You lost singlehanded?"

Charlotte gave a wry grin. "From the way they were yelling at me you'd think so. I'm terrible at sports."

"Yes. Well. There does seem to be rather an overemphasis on physical prowess. You still like Perry?"

"Yes."

"Under the circumstances, why?"

"You don't just turn friends on and off," Charlotte said with some dignity.

"Even if they do?"

"What they do," Charlotte said, "has nothing to do with what *I* do."

"Then why don't you get her aside sometime and have a talk with her? Or write her a note? If she's worth having as a friend she'll snap out of it."

Teachers were supposed to know everything, even secular teachers. "Well. Maybe I will."

"Good girl. You do that. You'd better run along now. It's almost suppertime and someone will be out looking for you if you don't get on back to the dorm."

"Yes," Charlotte said. "Thank you very much. Are you coming?"

"No. I think I'll stay and have my howl. You run along."

"All right." Charlotte started off, then turned back politely. "I'm sorry you're going."

Sunset looked at her, then at the frog pond. "Thank you."

Charlotte went back to the dormitory, pausing in the lavatory to splash cold water on her flushed face. The others—or at any rate a group of them, including Perry—were sitting in the middle of the dormitory floor, between the long rows of beds, playing jacks, the latest school fad. They had changed to dinner uniforms and were snatching this moment while waiting for the bell. They didn't look up or speak to her, so she changed quickly, then sat on her bed, rubbing the palm of her hand over the rough grey of the school blanket, watching Perry.

She knew then that she couldn't speak to Perry. She couldn't go up to her while the others were around—and the others of course were always around. Solitude was not encouraged. Didn't Sunset know that? Everything that was wrong was because of the others. When Charlotte and Perry had been moved up a form and put in the big middle-school dormitory Perry was accepted and Charlotte was not, and why? If she wrote Perry, would she find out? Sunset (who after all was a teacher and an adult even if she had no vocation) had told her to write. Charlotte pulled down her pad and a pencil from the shelf over her bed, sat down on the edge of the bed again, and started writing.

"Who are you writing to?" Perry asked suddenly.

"Father."

"You wrote your father yesterday."

"I can write him again, can't I?"

"If you want to. What are you writing him for?"

"Because I want to. He's my father, isn't he?"

"I suppose so. I never heard otherwise."

There was high laughter. One of the girls said, "Come on, Perry, it's your turn. Leave baby alone."

Charlotte watched Perry turn back to the game, bit her lip tightly, and went on writing. The bell for dinner rang and the others rushed off to get into line, not waiting for her. She folded the letter, wrote *Perry Alfreds, Private,* on it, put it under Perry's pillow, and ran off to get into place in the dinner line.

As she brushed her teeth in the lavatory that night she felt light and gay. She was happy as she had not been since the day the Reverend Mother had called Perry and Charlotte into her office and told them that their work merited their being moved up a form, although she usually didn't approve of doing this in the middle of the year. But Charlotte and Perry were such good friends that they would be able to make the adjustment together; each would help the other in areas that might be difficult for them singly . . .

Charlotte spread a second long white squirl of toothpaste on her brush, thinking that Perry was probably reading her letter at this very moment, and everything would be cleared up and she wouldn't be odd one out any more.

She hung her toothbrush on its hook and left the lavatory; she must give Perry plenty of time to read the letter. Because she wanted to run she made herself walk unusually slowly, placing her feet carefully in the center of each of the diamond-shaped patterns in the green carpet, holding off the joy she longed for so desperately, tasting every moment of anticipation as she had anticipated Christmas—no, not Christmas, her father had not been with her; it was the Christmas he had left her in the convent . . .

It was cold in the passage and she shivered in her flannel bathrobe.

At the end she couldn't hold off but ran the last few yards to the dormitory. She jumped into bed without a word and then looked over at Perry in the next bed. Perry was sitting up in bed, wearing bright-red pajamas and reading the letter. She was smiling a very little smile, and Charlotte's heart bounded with hope. She stared over at Perry, mouth a little open, breathing quickly. Perry turned to her and said, "Why did you lie to me this afternoon?"

Charlotte felt everyone in the dormitory looking at her. "What do you mean?"

"You said you were writing your father this afternoon, didn't you?"

"I guess so." Charlotte's hands reached out and held the edges of her thin mattress.

"You did. But you weren't, were you?"

"No."

"You were writing to me, weren't you?"

"Yes."

"Listen, everybody," Perry's voice was clear in the expectant silence. "I got a letter from Charlotte. Charlotte wrote me a letter."

"Please, Perry," Charlotte tried to whisper, but Perry didn't hear.

"Read it to us, Perry, read it to us!"

"It begins, *Darling Perry*—"

Charlotte scrabbled out of bed and flung herself on Perry. "Give me my letter."

Perry pulled away. *"Darling Perry, why don't you like me any more?"*

"Give me my letter!" Charlotte screamed. "Give it to me, give it to me—"

Perry jumped out of bed, choking with laughter, and ran up and down between the rows of beds. *"We were such good friends—you were the only one who called me Cotty—"*

Charlotte pursued her. "Stop it, Perry! Give it to me! Give it to me!"

"Cotty!" Perry cried. "It's a silly name. Cotty! Cotty! Cotty!"

Two of the girls held the screaming Charlotte, trying to clamp their hands over her mouth. "Stop it, Perry! Stop it! Stop it!"

"What's all this noise?"

Perry stopped reading and the others let Charlotte go and turned around. Sister Mary of the Ascension stood in the doorway.

"I want my letter," Charlotte whispered as the others climbed quickly into bed.

"Here, baby," Perry shoved the letter into Charlotte's hand.

Charlotte took the letter and got into bed.

"Give me the letter," Sister Mary of the Ascension said. "I shall burn it. I do not wish to see whatever is in it. In the future if you have anything to say to Perry, say it openly, Charlotte. I don't want to hear another sound out of any of you tonight. The last bell has rung. No wonder you didn't hear it. You will all take tardy marks. Stop crying, Charlotte. Control yourself."

Charlotte pressed her knuckles tightly against her mouth to keep her lips from trembling and shut her eyes.

"Now good night," Sister Mary of the Ascension said. "If there's any more disturbance from this dormitory for the rest of the week not one of you will be allowed to go to the concert on Saturday night. Remember that."

"As if we cared," Perry muttered, but said loudly, "Oh, we'll be good, Sister, we promise."

"We'll be good, Sister." The too-sweet voices echoed up and down the lines of beds. "Honestly we will, Sister. Good night, Sister."

"Good night." Sister Mary of the Ascension turned out their lights.

❖

The next afternoon during games period Charlotte's group had archery on the lawn near the driveway. Sunset was just finishing packing her little car and was ready to leave ("And please be gone *before* the children come out for games, Miss Benson") when the children came out, carrying their tall bows, their quivers of arrows. Now that Sunset was going they all crowded around her, curious, shameless.

"Are you going, Miss Benson?"

"Oh, we'll miss you, Miss Benson."

"Oh, Miss Benson, why are you going?"

They took a malicious pleasure in accentuating the *Miss Benson*. Sunset turned from stowing her gentians in a safe place in the back of the car and looked at them with a half smile.

"Goodbye," she said, holding her hand out to the girl nearest her, one of the girls in Charlotte's dormitory.

"Goodbye," the girl said and put her hand behind her back.

Sunset's smile disappeared for a moment. Then she turned to Charlotte. "Goodbye, Charlotte."

Charlotte looked with hostility at the outstretched hand, white and bony and covered with fine red hairs on the back. "Goodbye," she muttered, and turned away. She walked over to an oak tree and leaned against the heavy trunk, watching Sunset climb quickly into the car, not saying another word, not waving. The others waved for a moment, then ran back to the archery target, while Charlotte stood, leaning against the tree, and watched the car disappear down the road.

Thank you, God, for rules. Thank you for bells that ring for meals and for classes and for games and for bed and for— Thank you for the wall around the school, the silence in the corridors. Thank you for everything that holds the day together and keeps it from falling to pieces.

Sister Thomas More sought her out. Charlotte was alone in the dormitory, where she had no business to be, sitting on the side of her bed, looking down at the floor, not thinking, simply feeling all over as though she had a toothache. —But it is not my tooth, she thought vaguely. —You can't have a toothache in your heart. And you can't pull out somebody you love the way you can a tooth . . .

When she heard the *swish* of habit, saw out of the corner of her eye the white of skirt and scapular, the black of girdle and cross, she scrambled guiltily to her feet.

Sister Thomas More did not mention the fact that the children were not allowed in the dormitory at that time of day. Instead she said, "If you will stop wallowing for a few minutes, Charlotte, I would like to talk to you about your last Religious Knowledge paper, the one on love, particularly *agapé*, Christian love. I am thinking of entering it in the regional contest for church schools."

"I know nothing about love," Charlotte said.

"I never thought for a moment that you did. Now, Charlotte, if you will spare me a few minutes of your full concentration, we will go over your paper. Your writing is abominable and your spelling even worse. I understand you write honor with an *o-r* instead of an *o-u-r,* since you are an American; why, then, do you spell forty *f-o-u-r-t-y?*"

"I am never going to love anybody again," Charlotte said. "Not my father, or Reuben or Essie, or anybody here, not even you."

Sister Thomas More smiled. "You just said you knew nothing about love, didn't you?"

"Well, then," Charlotte demanded, "how *do* you love anybody? I mean properly?"

"We're taught that we mustn't become involved with people because this keeps them from loving God," the nun answered slowly. "To me this is blasphemy. I can only love God through loving people. I think that is what God meant us to do, because that's exactly what he did. That's exactly what the Incarnation means. But we must learn detachment, because far too often our love isn't sharing, it's demanding. We don't think nearly as much about giving love as we do about getting. We have to be involved in the people we love, but we have to be detached from our own selfishness. And this hurts, Cotty," Sister Thomas More said, for the first time using the name that Charlotte had shyly proffered her. "But where did anybody get the idea that it wasn't supposed to hurt? Think of the Incarnation again, and that the person who walked the earth who was most fully a self was also the only one who completely gave himself. And he never pretended for a moment that it didn't hurt. And he never lost sight of the joy that it leads to." She laughed. "Poor Cotty. I've been talking to you as though you were— But I've been talking to myself, you see. To myself. Thank you." From laughter her voice slipped into infinite sadness.

Charlotte looked across the row of white and empty beds, then back to the brooding face of the nun. "I'll try to do that paper if you really want me to, Sister."

. . . There were ten narrow beds down each side of the long, spotless white room. The windows were open to catch any breath of air coming across the Alentejo plains, but the white curtains hung limply, not moving. A wick burned low in a bowl of olive oil. Three of the girls were crouched together on one of the beds: Sofia, fat and intense; Urraca, skinny, with red hair and white skin like Sister Joaquina, and equally apt to feel wronged; and Ampara, sleek and feline and the newest girl in school . . .

". . . well," Urraca said, looking across the room to an empty, unturned-down bed, "you remember Peregrina's father knows Sister Joaquina's father—"

Ampara giggled. "I didn't know Sister Joaquina *had* a father."

Urraca put her hand to her mouth and gave a fishlike smile. "Even Sister Joaquina was produced in the normal way."

The three of them went into spasms of laughter, stuffing their long white nightclothes into their mouths to stifle the sound, looking up and down the room to see that no one else was awake.

"Sister Joaquina's father's a major in the army," Sofia said, proud of her contribution.

But Urraca always knew, had to know, more than anybody else, and Ampara must be shown that Urraca knew. "Yes, but he's a nobleman, too, Dom Alipio de Vasconcelos, though my father says he doesn't act like one. Mostly because he's never learned to act his age. My father says he still thinks he's an eligible young bachelor, and he doesn't want a grown-up daughter around—"

"Well, certainly not if she's Sister Joaquina." Ampara looked around the bare dormitory in distaste. "I hate it here. It's dull and unfashionable."

"Oh, come, Ampara, don't you know it's fashionable to be austere now?"

"I don't care. Even if Dona Brites Alcoforado is abbess, it's *not* fashionable and I *hate* it and I *won't* be a nun no matter what."

Urraca widened her too-innocent eyes. "Who said anything about being nuns? I don't want to be a nun, either."

"*Sst!*" Ampara jerked upright. "Someone's coming."

The girls scrambled into their beds, feigning sleep, as Mariana came to the doorway, carrying a small bowl of burning oil, which she raised so that she could see down the length of the room and check each bed. Three of the twenty beds were empty, three of the children having been given permission to go home and share in the festivities over the victory. The counterpane to Peregrina's bed was smooth and white and untouched; Mariana's gaze lingered on it; was the child asleep in the Alcoforado villa in one of the huge, carved beds? More likely, Mariana thought, she was still up, running wild with excitement, and with sips from too many people's wineglasses.

Mariana turned from the empty bed, sighing deeply, unconsciously, so that Ampara pricked up her little cat's ears and opened her eyes.

But Mariana had turned and was leaving the dormitory. She had already checked the younger children, so that when she left the dark corridor her evening duties were done, and she went swiftly down the marble stairs and hurried along the cloistered walk. Under the stone arches there was darkness, though a residual light lingered in the garden. Her lamp faintly illumined the pattern on the tiles that decorated the inner wall. At the end of the cloister she set the bowl down and stepped into the rectangular garden.

She moved slowly, with a controlled joy, among the flowers, holding out her arms to the moonlight. The hood of her loose night robe slipped down as she raised her face to the tingling silver light, and her fair cropped hair was suddenly haloed with radiance. In the garden insects called and the frogs clunked from the lily pond. In the streets there was more noise than usual. Celebrations were going on in many of the houses; laughter rose and fell; from a hidden street came the sound of running feet, shouts, more laughter, a shriek, silence.

Beneath the arches slid the shadow of another nun and a soft, childish voice called, "Mariana," as Michaela stepped out of the darkness.

Mariana looked up, startled.

Michaela's voice was tentative. "Mother Escolastica said I might—she said since we had been given permission to talk this evening I might—but only for a moment—and not to bother you if you wished to return to silence—"

Mariana turned to Michaela as though waking from a dream. "You wanted to talk to me—"

"Yes. Please."

Mariana smiled, then, as though Michaela were one of the children she taught in the early morning. "What is it, little Sister?"

"I wanted to ask—"

"Is it important? I'm not sure Mother meant— No, I can see it's important. Let's sit down." She led the way to a wooden bench that circled an ancient eucalyptus tree. Michaela picked up a long shard of the silver bark and pulled it nervously through her fingers, her face seeming to quiver as the light breeze moving the branches patterned the two nuns with a constant shifting of shadow and light. Finally she burst out, "I'm like Sister Joaquina."

At this incongruity Mariana laughed, and Michaela looked at her pleadingly. "I mean, I'm not like her, but I wasn't brought up in the convent the way you and Beatriz were. Joaquina and I came together to start our postulancy. For you and Beatriz it was home. That's how I'm like Joaquina. Do you see?"

Mariana leaned back, her head against the soaring trunk of the tree, and let her eyes rest on the water of the fountain spraying up into the moonlight. "Not yet. Go on."

Michaela cried out, as though it were a great tragedy, "I have three sisters!" and stopped again.

Mariana prodded patiently. "Yes?"

"And of the four of us I'm the only one who isn't talented . . . and gifted . . . and full of graces . . . and my father thought . . ."

"Thought what?"

Michaela began to cry. "That probably no man . . . no man worthy of our name . . . would have me . . . but that probably our Lord would . . . because . . . and he thought . . . my father, I mean . . . that I might be happy in the convent . . . and I thought so too . . ."

"And I thought so, too. I thought you were one of the happiest people here. Was I wrong?"

Michaela rubbed the back of her hand against her eyes to wipe away the easy tears. "No, no, I *am* happy. I've been happier here than I've ever been in my life. But—"

"But what?"

"This morning, when the soldiers came by . . . and then hearing them on the streets all day, and tonight . . . and seeing them from the balcony . . . and then . . ."

"Then?"

"Have you ever . . . have you ever wanted to leave the convent and go back into the world?"

"No," Mariana said. "No, little Michaela. No. I've been back. I've visited my father's house. I don't want to go back again."

"Never?"

"No. Though of course I will go if her Grace sends me. But how could anything in the world give me half what I have here?"

Michaela's voice was low. "I thought that, too. That's why I've been so happy. People haven't . . . haven't made me feel that I'm a fool . . . and silly . . ."

"You aren't."

"Oh, yes, I am. I'm the foolish one. I've heard the others talking about me often enough. First at home. And then here. In the Chapter of Faults. Even the older sisters. I'm the foolish virgin who'll always forget to have enough oil for her lamp. I'm stuck into a pigeonhole. And so are you."

"I am?"

"Yes. Of course. You're the abbess's niece. Everybody knows you're being prepared to be the next abbess. You're in that pigeon-hole. Even I forget who you are sometimes. I have to remind myself that you're Mariana and I love you, and when I remember that, I'm not afraid of you."

Mariana looked at her in quick surprise. "Nobody could be afraid of me!"

"Nobody is. We're afraid of the abbess's niece."

"Is this what you came to talk to me about?"

Michaela, sensing reproof, became immediately apologetic. "No. No. It was the soldiers. This morning when I saw the soldiers go by . . . and then I thought how everybody here likes me . . . and then I thought . . . I thought maybe if I went back into the world I wouldn't be so bad at things any more, and it wouldn't be impossible for my parents to arrange a good marriage for me."

"Is that what you want?"

"I don't know! I never thought I'd feel like this! I don't even know if I *do* feel like this! I thought I had a vocation, a true vocation, not like . . . and I still don't know if I do or not . . . because surely I shouldn't have been excited when the soldiers came by."

"But we were all excited," Mariana explained.

Michaela glanced at the other girl slantwise, looking darkly through her long lashes, and whispering, "Sister Joaquina wasn't."

"Of course she was," Mariana said impatiently. "And so was I."

"It doesn't worry you?"

"We're happy here. Isn't that enough?"

"You're going to be the next abbess. You know where you're go-ing. But for me . . . I don't know." Michaela's voice rose to a thin, childish wail. "I just don't know."

Mariana put her fingers for a moment lightly on the other girl's knee. "Sister, dear, don't fret so. After all, we're human beings. We can't retreat entirely. I don't think we're supposed to."

"But the soldiers—," Michaela said.

"Remind us that we're women! That we're still young. It seems to me we'd be half dead if we could watch the men who fought for us march by our convent and be unmoved."

"It didn't make you want to leave?"

"Why should it? How could any man hope to compete with our Lord?"

Michaela looked at Mariana and said in a small voice, "You make me feel foolish."

"I don't mean to. I don't think you're foolish. Just natural."

"I know that if I stay here I'll never be rejected again . . . and then sometimes I think that this is cowardice . . . and I ought to go back instead of taking the easy way . . ."

"The way of a sister is not the easy way!"

"For me it is. Far easier than the world."

"Then you have a lot to learn," Mariana said brusquely, but broke off into laughter. "Oh, dear, that's what Mother Escolastica and her Grace keep telling me. I expect we both have a lot to learn."

"You, Mariana? All of us feel that you are the wisest and closest to sainthood of us all."

Mariana's voice was suddenly ice-cold, sounding startlingly like the abbess. "Please stop, Michaela, or you'll make me angry."

"Don't be angry. Please just let me thank you. I came to you for help—"

"And I haven't been much help."

"But you have! I don't feel guilty about the soldiers any more. I'm surer about my vocation. I can go back to my cell and pray."

"I'm glad," Mariana said, but her eyes were troubled.

"I shouldn't have kept you so long. Mother thought I meant only a word. But I couldn't talk to her about it—"

"It's all right," Mariana said, the warmth returning to her voice. "Sometimes we need to talk." She stood up and walked with Michaela back to the shadow of the column where she had placed her lamp. She held the shallow dish of smoking oil until Michaela had walked the length of the arcade and into the convent.

Mariana put the lamp down by the column again and went out into the open gardens. At the far end of the convent grounds she walked past the frog pond and stood on tiptoe to see over the wall. She gazed out into the dark street that led to the great, open-air market; during the daylight wagons constantly creaked by, and patient, panniered donkeys. Now, in the dark hours, the shadows lengthening as the moon dipped, a horseman approached. Was he on a black horse? Straining on her tiptoes, the nun watched. Yes, the horse was black, it was— No. It was a Portuguese uniform, the horse was dark brown, the soldier was Alipio de Vasconcelos, Sister Joaquina's father. Mariana ducked, but he had seen her. She heard his coarse laugh as he called, "Looking for someone, Sister? Shall I send him a message?"

She turned and ran back to the protection of the cloister. The fountain splashed, pure and clean. Her lamp—yes, there was enough oil—burned low in the shadow of the column. As she bent to pick it up a gust of wind blew out the wavering light of the wick and she was lost in darkness.

. . . She opened her eyes and met Violet's cool, blue stare, heard Violet's cross voice. "Idiot. What is this all about?"

She closed her eyes again, refusing consciousness, giving a small, rejecting movement of her body. The roughness of the rug scratched her into wakefulness, and Violet's voice came again, probing, demanding. "Cotty."

She sat up and there was Violet standing by the couch wrapped in a long coachman's cloak of soft, grey fur, a fur cap pulled down on her head so that her sharp eyes and beaked nose made her look more like a wise and predatory grey owl.

"How do you feel?"

The question was peremptory. If Charlotte did not say, "Fine, thanks," Violet would be annoyed. Therefore Charlotte simply looked at her mother-in-law warily.

"Well?"

Goaded, Charlotte responded with all the dignity she could muster. "I feel abominable, thank you."

"Idiot."

Charlotte untangled herself from the moth-eaten fur rug the doctor had wrapped about her, and put her stockinged feet on the drafty floor. Where were her hideous new shoes? "It was a great mistake for me to have come," she said. "Go away, Violet, please. I'm not going to bother you. Don't worry."

Violet took an angry step forward as though she intended to strike the girl. But the doctor moved out of the shadows and put his arm around Violet in a rough hug. "Leave the child alone, Violet. She's not well."

To Charlotte's surprise, Violet did not turn on the doctor but permitted his arm to rest about her shoulders. "She's not a child, João."

"But she is not well." He left Violet and put the back of his hand against Charlotte's cheek. "She has high fever."

Violet glowered, as though it were Charlotte's fault. "Now I understand why Patrick called me in Paris last night."

"Patrick?" Charlotte looked up, startled.

"Yes. Patrick, being Patrick, of course did not say what was on his mind. But it is not Patrick's wont to make transatlantic calls to me about a successfully performed minor operation on an equally minor Manhattan politician. Now I understand. At least a little."

"I'm sorry," Charlotte said faintly.

"It is not a matter of being sorry or not sorry. Please do not attempt to use me as a confessor."

The doctor's voice boomed. "Violet, you are impossible. If you are going to continue to behave badly I shall keep Charlotte here."

"You called me to come get her."

"I am changing my mind. Antonio and I will care for her."

"Antonio?" Violet's scorn was sharp.

"A young man. Attractive. Ambitious. A poet."

"Be quiet, João. Do not pretend I don't know Tonio far better than you do. Blackmail will get you nowhere. Attractive, ambitious young men are always, for some obscure reason, drawn to Charlotte. All right, Cotty. The car is waiting."

"Both of you leave me alone." Charlotte's voice trembled. "I'm going back to the pensão for the night. Tomorrow I'll go back to Lisbon and return the car. I should never have come."

The doctor came over to her, speaking gently, calling her softly by her first name. "Charlotte."

She turned her head away. "What?"

"You are here. You have fever. You must accept both these facts. You can't eradicate them by running away again. Do you want to get pneumonia? And you know Violet. She is being completely in character. She is angry only at the people she loves. She is concerned and upset about you and therefore, because these are painful emotions, she tries to rid herself of them by a display of temper. It won't last. She'll calm down and face things. As you must."

Charlotte bowed her head submissively. "All right."

He looked at Violet and smiled. "Am I still invited to dinner?"

The sharp face softened. "João, you're an old fool."

"I take it that means yes. Go ahead, then. I'll bring Charlotte. If she goes with you, you'll be at her, and I don't want her bothered tonight."

In the doctor's car, wrapped again in the moth-eaten rug, Charlotte leaned back, letting her aching limbs relax. "Will I see you again?"

"Of course. I'm not going to abandon you now."

She looked at him. Although his lips were partly hidden by the unkempt mustache and beard, she could see that he was smiling; but he was not laughing at her.

"I see now how stupid it was of me to come," she said.

"Since I don't know why you've come I can make no judgment."

"But I told you, didn't I?"

"Some wild talk about leaving Patrick. This tells me nothing."

"I love him."

"Evidently."

"But I do."

"You don't need to repeat it."

"To want someone to love you, and to want him to be *in* love with you are quite different things. I haven't ever wanted anybody to be in love with me except Patrick, but it seems to have happened the other way around, so I'm confused, you see . . . about Antonio's nun—"

"What about her?"

"She really loved this French soldier?"

"Read the letters."

"I have."

"And?"

"I don't know anything about love. I'm asking you." She was suddenly conscious of the black mourning band on his sleeve. In the dining room at the pensão it had simply presented itself as a curious surprise to her, a reminder that in Europe customs that she had thought lost in the past persisted in the present. Now she felt suddenly the presence of a person, a loss, a grief.

He did not answer. He drove out the gates of the town, turned and headed uphill. After about five minutes of driving in silence, during which the coldness swept over her again, he turned the car through tall whitewashed gateposts and down a long dirt driveway lined on either side with poplars which were being lashed by wind and rain. At the end of the drive was a large, low house, with light spilling out of long windows.

"If I were a nun perhaps I could pray," Charlotte said.

"Is the qualification necessary?"

"It might help. I assume a nun would believe in God."

"And you don't?"

"Not any more. So I can't pray. So I wish I were a nun."

"But you are not. And I do not imagine that Mariana always found prayer easy. Or God available. Or comprehensible."

. . . "My nuns do not know how to pray," the abbess said. "Portuguese convents are either completely given over to the things of this world, or are filled with religious hysterics."

"I do not think this is hysteria," Father Duarte said.

Father Pessanha looked down his long nose. "It is very suspicious."

Mariana had been alone in the chapel when the first unusual happening occurred. She was twelve years old, no longer a child, certainly not yet a woman. She had been kneeling quite quietly, not praying, her mind not even wandering, but resting on the golden cross that soared heavenwards. Suddenly she was, as it were, taken, translated from the gold and light and warmth of the chapel into coldness and darkness. It was as though she were being taken through death, and it was her terror that brought her back to consciousness. Her body was ice-cold and she was shaken by shivering. It was not what one would imagine a vision, a beatific experience, to be at all. And yet she was left with a profound conviction of having been almost unbearably close to God. She had dutifully reported the experience to Father Pessanha, her confessor until her profession. He had accused her of letting her imagination run wild, and had, with her dazed permission, since she had spoken in the confessional, reported it to the abbess and Father Duarte.

"No, I do not think this is hysteria," Father Duarte said again. He was Father General of his own order and in priestly charge of the convent. "It has the ring of authenticity. But we must watch it—and the child."

Fortunately she was unaware of their watching. At first she had been afraid to go to the chapel alone in case the shattering experience should come again. Then she overcame her reluctance, and when the cold and dark came again she was not as frightened; she did not fight against it; she went in, in, into the dark which was at the same time a blast of light. The experience never came when she was looking for it; it could not be asked for; when it happened it was always totally unexpected and she was wracked by the wildness of it. When she returned to herself she was ice-cold and trembling. She did not need to be told not to speak of it to the other children or, later, to the other nuns, though Father Pessanha enjoined her to silence so often that she could not help realizing that what happened to her did not happen to everybody, that it was not ordinary. Nevertheless she simply accepted it without overmuch thought. It was, in its strange, wild way, as beautiful as the bursting of the pear tree into bloom. But one did not question the blossoming of the pear tree. One simply accepted and rejoiced.

"We must neither encourage nor discourage," Father Pessanha said nervously.

"Leave her alone," Father Duarte warned. "Do not interfere with God."

"O God," the abbess alone on her knees on her prie-dieu petitioned heaven, "can not the superior of a convent in this day and age expect moderation in anything? I am not looking for saints with their ecstasies—and what an odd ecstasy this is—but only temperate and disciplined nuns who wish to dedicate well-ordered lives to you. And certainly in my niece I looked not for a mystic but for the next abbess. But it was you who sent me this child, and if you have sent this, too, then you will have to help me. Meanwhile I shall keep her busy."

So Mariana moved happily through the years and it was her very happiness that was most baffling to the abbess. She was as happy as a professed sister, and in very much the same unthinking way, as she had been when she was a child. Everything seemed to be a source of joy. She seldom noticed the weather, the dank cold in winter or the stifling heat in summer, except to delight in it. Therefore the day after the victorious parade, the day after she had seen the two young men on the black and white chargers ride by, it was completely puzzling to her that in chapel her habit seemed for the first time to be unbearably heavy. The stiffness of coif and wimple for the first time choked her. She opened her mouth and gasped unexpectedly like a beached fish, so that both Joaquina and Beatriz turned to look at her in surprise. This wandering of attention was not unusual for Joaquina, who was more aware of what went on outside her than within her, but Beatriz's beautiful and rather stern concentration was seldom broken.

Mariana closed her mouth and started to pray silently, but her mind would not rest on any of the familiar words. —It's the battle, she told herself,—and the excitement of seeing the soldiers. It's seeing Baltazar so close and not being able to speak to him. It's— *"Hail, Mary, full of grace, the Lord is with thee, blessed art thou among women and blessed is the fruit of thy womb, Jesus . . ."*

Slowly the old peace began to settle about her, as tangible as the long golden rays of the early morning filtering dustily through the chapel windows, and she slipped, almost without realizing it, from formal prayers into her practice, unbroken since childhood, of talking to God in much the same unthinking way that she had prattled as a child to the sisters, for God was less strange to her than they.

—Dearest my Lord, they were so beautiful. They kept riding through my dreams, the horses pranced, and the black horse neighed, and sometimes his nostrils breathed flames. It is all right, isn't it, to have dreamed about it? For isn't it you who send me my dreams? Does it have to be all difficult, the way it is for Joaquina, for it to be worth anything? The soldiers riding by—I loved them in my dreams—I love them now—

From her stall the abbess rang her tiny silver bell in signal that the Divine Office was to begin, and Sister Isabella, old as Mother Escolastica, and almost blind with cataracts, rang the brilliant brass bell for the Office.

"O Lord, make speed to save us," the abbess sang.

"O God, make haste to help us," the sisters returned, making the sign of the cross. The Divine Office began.

Mariana sang. Peace was over her again like a mantle. Beatriz participated with the usual cool concentration that bordered on detachment from God as much as from man. Joaquina's eyes flickered to Mariana on her right, to little Michaela on her left. The abbess's eyes never left her diurnal, but nevertheless every sister in the chapel felt naked under her pale blue scrutiny.

"Mine eyes long sore for thy word, saying, O when wilt thou comfort me?" sang the nuns across the choir from Mariana.

"For I am become like a bottle in the smoke . . . ," came the response.

She was, indeed, not seeing or thinking clearly. In the middle of teaching French to the older girls she broke off halfway through a phrase and raised her head, listening, as a clatter of horses' hooves was heard out in the street. She stood up, at least remembering to bow to the children, to say, "Excuse me for a moment, girls, I will be right back. Sofia, go on with the translation—" She left the room and hurried down the vaulted corridor, her swift stride accelerating. She ran, ran, up the stairs, out onto the balcony. It was an hour when everybody was, or ought to have been, busy, and the balcony was empty.

She hurried over to the balustrade and looked down into the street as the horse clopped over the cobblestones, a black horse ridden by a French soldier.

The French soldier who had ridden beside Baltazar.

As the rider reached the convent he slowed the horse down and looked up to the balcony. When he saw that a nun was standing there he reined in so abruptly that the beast reared and seemed, for a moment, to go out of control. Then the soldier mastered him. The horse stood there, panting, pawing, while the Frenchman looked towards the balcony. He did not stand in his stirrups or wave, but he looked at Mariana deliberately, steadily. The sun struck against a fresh scar that slashed across his cheek. Then he spurred his horse and galloped off.

Late that afternoon the abbess sent for Mariana.

"Would you like to go to your father's house and bring Peregrina back?"

Mariana looked startled. "Of course. If you wish me to."

"It will be your first visit in some time, and you can thank your father for it. I asked to have Peregrina returned this morning, and he has as usual disregarded my instructions. How long has it been since you've seen him?"

"A long time, your Reverence. At least six months."

"I cannot presume to be judgmental about him, particularly since I understand him with my blood as well as my mind. Do you know why your visits to his house have been so few and far between?"

"Yes, your Grace. I think so."

"How do you feel about going home now? Secure enough?"

Mariana did not answer directly. Instead she said, "I want to see Baltazar."

"You love him very much?"

"You know I do. He's never hurt me or upset me. Neither Baltazar nor you."

The abbess started to dismiss her, then stopped. "I should have spoken to you about this before, and I'm sorry to bring it up now, but it has come to my attention that you and Sister Joaquina are sometimes irritable with each other. What is it all about? You know that I cannot allow anything like this."

"I know, your Reverence. It's my fault. I seem to Sister Joaquina to—not to take things seriously enough."

"Is she justified?"

"I don't think so. Not really. It's because I take things so very seriously that perhaps I appear to be too lighthearted about them."

"Yes. I understand that." The abbess leaned back in her carved chair. She looked tired. The bruised lids dropped heavily over the pale blue of the eyes. The lines between the beak nose and the warm mouth were drawn tight. "You must try to help her, child."

"I'm the last one to help her, your Reverence."

"And should be the first."

Mariana said, with some hesitancy, "She feels that because I'm your niece, and therefore almost your daughter in blood as well as in spirit, that—"

The abbess cut her off, eyes sparking, voice sharp. "That is not true! I have never let this influence me."

"I know you haven't, your Reverence, and the other sisters know it, too, especially the ones who've known me since I first came here."

The young nun looked slowly around the quiet room. Nothing had changed since the days when she had run toddling in, unmindful of position and authority, to scramble with unhesitating assurance into her aunt's lap.

"But Sister Joaquina is so—so unsure of herself that it helps her to think that when you are gentle with me and a little harsh with her it is because I am of your blood and she is not."

"Yes. Poor Sister Joaquina." The abbess sighed and smiled, her head still leaning back against the dark wood of the chair. It was unusual for her to reveal weariness. "I have been aware of this for some time now. It's a strange thing: Sister Joaquina feels that because of the generosity of her father's dowry, which, I'm afraid, was to get her off his hands, she is entitled to special privilege. She is entitled to no more than any other choir sister."

Mariana was seated on her usual low stool near her aunt. Without looking up she asked, "Shouldn't our dowry be the gift of ourselves, rather than money?"

The abbess answered briskly, "It should, and I'm sure that to our Lord it is. Nevertheless we have to eat. The tuition of the students doesn't begin to meet our needs. We are dependent on the dowries of the choir sisters and the gifts of their families. Dom Alipio is generous in his gifts. Conscience money? Perhaps. In any case, I cannot afford to refuse him. I see that this shocks you. Good."

"I hadn't realized—"

"No. You have been overprotected. It is time for your real training to begin, now. I hope I haven't put it off for too long. In many ways it is a pity that because you are an Alcoforado it is taken for granted that you will be abbess after me. I do not think, fortunately, that Dom Alipio has any ambitions for poor Sister Joaquina here. Certainly the thought is an impossible one. No. It is Sister Beatriz, with her man's way of thinking and making decisions, her lack of illusion, who would probably make a better politician than you. But there is no money or blood, no family backing behind her. This is the world we live in, and you must face this. You know, child, an abbess must be a politician as well as a Bride of Christ."

"But this is wrong!" Mariana cried.

"Oh, no, and you'll come to realize this as you grow older."

"How?"

The abbess drummed her fingers lightly on the arm of her chair. "You're very young for your age, child. You're quite right when you compare yourself to the children you love so dearly. Without a strong abbess a religious community will fall apart. You know that, don't you?"

Mariana looked at the abbess imploringly, but said, "Yes, your Reverence."

The abbess's hooded lids almost covered the icy blue and she did not see her niece's gaze. "There is nothing easy in a life dedicated to Christ, and doing many things that seem to take me far from the business of the spirit and into the business of the world is part of my way of serving him. Do you see?"

Now she looked directly at Mariana, who flinched. "I'm trying."

"It is particularly difficult at this moment in time, when it would seem that to serve Christ one must deal with more than one master. Our bishop is not recognized by Rome, nor should he be. It is a trying position."

"You haven't told me this before," Mariana said wonderingly. "Why?"

"I've been waiting for the right moment. Now that the Spaniards are finally being pushed out of the Alentejo the time has come. I need not say that you are not to talk of this."

"Of course not, your Reverence."

"Are you disturbed by what I have said?" As the girl did not answer, the abbess continued, "If I must confuse and upset you, I must. But there is no need for any other of the young sisters to be worried by the problems you will have to handle singly one day. I *must* begin to teach you. I can see that it is going to be even more difficult than I thought. You know, my child, it is sometimes easier for me to understand Sister Joaquina's struggles than your simple acceptance of your vocation."

Catching her breath, Mariana said, "You have only yourself to blame for that."

"I?"

"I've been with you since I was a small child. All my real life has been under your influence. Whereas Sister Joaquina left her father's world only a short time ago."

"No, child, it's not that easy."

Mariana forced a smile. "No?"

"The world has always been at our doorstep, and it has been neither desirable nor possible to keep it out. We are a teaching order, and we have always maintained close contact with the world. It is our one hope of changing it."

Mariana murmured, "Sometimes I wish it weren't quite so close." The abbess looked at her sharply, but Mariana raised her head and continued, "I'll try to be more patient with Sister Joaquina."

"You must love her."

Mariana looked across the room at the crucifix. "I know that I should have learned more about love. Sometimes I think that I don't understand it at all."

"Then learn with Sister Joaquina. There is no virtue in loving the lovable."

"I know . . ."

"Remember that in choosing his disciples, our Lord showed us that he could love even where it was most difficult. Remind yourself that one of the disciples was a tax collector for the Romans, and about as popular with his countrymen as a Spanish agent with us. Nevertheless our blessed Saviour gave him love. Remind yourself that he could love and give the keys of his kingdom to a man who was to deny him thrice in one night, and that he could love even the man he knew would be his betrayer." She paused, looking thoughtfully at Mariana, at the pattern surrounding the girl on the tesselated floor. Mariana's hand fell lightly to her side, her fingers touching the floor, her index finger moving gently in the small hole in the pattern where one of the tesserae was missing.

The girl stirred under the probing gaze, but did not speak until the abbess asked, "Sister Mariana, is something troubling you?"

Mariana looked away, raising her fingers from the floor and locking her hands about her knees. "Why, your Reverence?"

"You seem not quite yourself."

"I'm sorry."

"Is it anything you would like to talk about?"

"No. I don't think so. Not yet, at any rate."

"You are seeing Father Duarte tomorrow?"

"Yes, your Reverence."

"You will discuss whatever it is with him?"

"Yes."

"Then I need not worry." But a questioning ran through the statement.

Perhaps the unanswered questions were what caused the abbess herself to see Mariana off that evening, to stand, keeping the young nun at the gates, while the carriage waited.

"You do not question my sending you home tonight?"

"No, your Reverence. Of course not."

"*Of course.* You say it so easily. I put your obedience to the test more often than that of any other of the younger sisters, and yet it has never really been tested, has it?"

"I don't understand."

"Nor do I," the abbess said. "What I mean is that it has never been difficult, has it, for you to obey?"

"No, your Reverence, but—"

"Yes?"

"It is no virtue in me."

The abbess's voice was as cold as her eyes. "I never said it was." She took Mariana's arm and herself helped the girl up the high step and into the carriage, then stood by the open door as calmly and unhurriedly as though they were in the quiet of her study. The coachman stood aside, respectfully, though undoubtedly his ears were cocked. The abbess spoke almost as though to herself. "It will not become a virtue until it is put to the test. It is too simple for you. Sister Michaela obeys because it is safe for her to obey and she longs for safety. Sister Beatriz obeys her own will to obey. She will have to watch for spiritual pride. But she is aware of this. For Sister Joaquina all obedience, even over the most trivial things, is a hurdle."

She looked once again at Mariana in the shadows of the carriage, leaning forward so that she could listen. "All right, child. Go. And God be with you. I will see you in the morning."

She shut the carriage door and gave an imperious gesture to the coachman, who mounted his box and cracked his whip. The carriage jolted out of the convent gates and through the streets of Beja.

The gates to the Alcoforado villa were, like the gates of the convent, elaborately wrought iron swung between two heavy white pillars, one pillar attached to a small gatehouse. The convent coachman climbed down from the carriage and rang the bell, and Serafino, the old gatekeeper, shuffled out to let them in. He had known Mariana all her life and had to come to the carriage window to greet her, to be blessed by her, to exclaim over her, his old voice cracking with age and pleasurable emotion.

Mariana, nervous, impatient, tried to be gentle with him. At last he let her go and the carriage moved on up the long, straight drive, sandy, rutty, and bordered on either side by tall poplars. Almost all the windows of the villa spilled out light, and Mariana could hear music and voices. Evidently a party was in progress; a solitary evening, she knew, was anathema to her father, and Ana Maria, Mariana's sister, and Ana's husband, Rui de Melo Lobo Freire, entertained for the old man constantly.

Rui was at the door to meet Mariana. He was always courteous with her, overformal. To Mariana's knowledge he had never been to visit Nossa Senhora da Conceição or any other convent, and she had a feeling that he was not sure how he ought to treat a nun. Now he kissed her hand as though he were courting her and drew her into the large front hall. The double doors to the ballroom on the right were open, and a couple, the man in Portuguese officer's uniform, whirled by in a dance, broke apart, and the officer ran to Mariana, flung his arms around her and kissed her, first on one cheek, then the other.

"Baltazar!" Mariana cried joyfully.

"My darling girl," Baltazar said, gently disengaging her and gesturing to Rui to take care of his partner. "I'd made plans to come see you tomorrow."

"Oh, come anyhow, please do come," Mariana cried. "I'm here only for tonight. I have to take Peregrina home."

"Take her home? Isn't this home?"

"Oh, Baltazar, it doesn't matter, they both are. Do let's go somewhere where I can see you and talk to you!"

"We'll go to the library," Baltazar said, "and I'll bring you some wine." His arm around her, he led her up the rosy marble staircase to a large room over the ballroom; music and laughter rose to them undiminished. He led her to a chair upholstered in gold damask and seated her, saying, "There. If I can't get you out of that dark habit I can at least put you against a less somber background. Now wait right here, my sweetest sister, don't move, and I'll be right back."

He bounded out, pulling the door to behind him. Mariana, feeling suddenly weak, leaned back in the chair. As the door was pushed open she jumped, but it was only Pinto, Francisco Alcoforado's pet monkey. He came gibbering across the carpet, leaped up into Mariana's lap, and flung his skinny, hairy arms about her neck in a stranglehold. Mariana laughed, scolding him and loosening his grip. He plunged his pink leathery fingers into the pocket of her habit, looking for tidbits.

"I don't know why you're so skinny," she told him. "You're the greediest little thing I've ever seen in my life. Even greedier than the children."

"Even greedier than I am?"

Mariana looked up as Peregrina came into the library and stood in the center of the rug, twirling around slowly.

"Maria Peregrina Alcoforado!" Mariana exclaimed.

"Yes, it is I." Peregrina curtsied solemnly. "Do you like it? Of course it's Ana's, and we had to take it in in one or two places, but it's a proper dress for a dance, not the convent uniform or the baby clothes papa's been keeping me in when I come home. Do you like it?"

"I don't know," Mariana said helplessly. "I wasn't prepared. I wasn't ready to have you be grown up. No, I don't think I *do* like it. I'll be glad to see you back in your convent clothes and looking your own age again."

"I'm fourteen years old," Peregrina said, "almost fifteen. I'm a woman and I'm tired of being treated like a child." She sat down and complacently stroked her own bare shoulders. "Rui de Melo said he ought to have waited for me, and Ana was furious. She's got a jealous streak as wide as the Tagus, that girl. And she looks older than you do, for all she's two years younger. Dom Alipio said I have beautiful shoulders and Sister Joaquina's are scrawny. It's really unfair to poor Sister for me to know her father. Your shoulders aren't scrawny, are they, Mariana?"

"Stop it, Peregrina," Mariana said, moving restlessly on the gold damask of her chair.

Peregrina stopped stroking her shoulders, still rounded with baby fat. "Mariana, did you ever have a ball gown?"

"No," Mariana said quietly. "Why should I?"

Peregrina twirled again. "For the same reason that I should. And I *should*. My life would be blighted if I should have to become a nun and I'd never, ever had a ball gown."

Mariana smiled. "Do you think my life has been blighted?"

Peregrina stared at her, squinting, as though threading a needle. "If I *think* about it, then I'd have to say yes. But when I'm with you, and *feel* about it, then I'd say no. You certainly don't strike any of us as being blighted. You're the one who's always singing and laughing and being happy and getting scolded by Sister Maria da Assunção. That makes you popular, I can tell you. I suppose if one really has a vocation then not having a ball gown wouldn't be an utter blight—"

Mariana's laugh pealed out. "You're absolutely impossible. And you're still an infant, ball gown or no."

The door was pushed open and Baltazar came in, carrying two glasses of wine.

"Wine!" Peregrina cried.

"For Mariana and me, not for you. You've had enough. And don't shout at me like that. You made me spill."

"Mariana's a nun. She oughtn't to drink wine. It's sinful."

"Nonsense," Baltazar said. "It *is* nonsense, isn't it, Mariana? It's not a sin?"

Mariana took the wine and smiled at him over the rim of the glass. "Not when it's to welcome your brother home from the wars. Oh, Baltazar, I'm glad to see you, I'm glad to see you!" They raised their glasses, and drank.

"When did you have wine last?" Peregrina asked her curiously.

"Oh, Peregrina, I don't know, I don't remember, what does it matter?"

"You sound cross," Peregrina said, surprised. "All right, I'll propose a toast, even if I don't have anything to drink it with. To our brother, Baltazar, and all the Spaniards he killed."

Mariana raised her glass again, "To Baltazar."

Baltazar raised his. "To the Spaniards: better dead than alive. Now go, little one."

"I want to stay with you."

"You've been with me. Mariana's only here overnight."

Peregrina rose reluctantly. "All right. Though somehow I can never feel sorry for Mariana. She's just not someone you go around being sorry for, like Sister Joaquina. But it's true, she never gets home, and I come whenever papa gets bored and needs someone to amuse him. If he weren't always dashing off to court, I'd probably be here as much as I am at the convent."

Pinto left Mariana's lap, ran across the floor on all fours and bowed at the open door, as though inviting Peregrina to leave. They all laughed.

"Go find Rollo and Mathieu," Baltazar said to Peregrina, "there's a good girl."

"What about Noël?"

"He's not here tonight. Other fish to fry."

Peregrina explained. "He's the one on the black charger, who was with Baltazar. He's absolutely marvelous, Mariana, and he saved Bal's life. A horrible Spaniard jumped him from behind when he was already fighting someone else, and Noël came leaping in and killed the Spaniard, and the Spaniard cut him across the cheek, you can see the scar, and if it hadn't been for Noël, Baltazar wouldn't be here at all, and we'd be singing horrible requiem masses for his soul. Of course Noël says Bal saved *his* life. I wish I were a boy. Then I wouldn't have to worry about being a nun."

"You could be a monk," Baltazar said. "Stop talking and go."

—So his name is Noël, then. Noël.

As Peregrina left, Mariana asked, "You were nearly killed?"

"Darling girl, I'm a soldier. Who knows, really, how nearly nearly is? But yes, there was at least one time when Noël did save me from what would have been certain death. And I knew nothing about it until afterwards. As Peregrina said, the Spaniard was coming at me from behind—as death usually does, I suppose. Even if one is lying in bed waiting for it, I imagine at the last minute it takes one unaware. More wine?"

"No, thank you."

"Think it's wrong?"

"No, I don't. But one glass is quite enough. I'm glad he saved your life. Am I to meet him?"

"Yes. I've promised to bring him to the convent. God knows why he wants to come, but he asked me. Something about needing a change and peace and quiet. It will be a change for him, all right. Sure you don't want more wine?"

"Quite sure."

"Would you like to meet anybody? I have another French friend here tonight, Mathieu de Berenger, and a thoroughly mad Englishman—"

She shook her head. "No. Please. I only came to fetch Peregrina. And to see you."

"You think our esteemed aunt would be annoyed? That you would be corrupted by such company?"

"No. It's not that. I would just prefer not to. We have to be up early and I still have my night offices to say, so if you'll excuse me I'll go to bed." She twined her fingers nervously.

"Rules even on vacation?"

"This isn't a vacation. Good night, Baltazar. You will come?"

"I said I would."

"But—soon?"

"Very soon."

"Say good night to papa for me. And tell him I'll see him in the morning."

Her bedroom had the musty smell of a room seldom used. At least it was still considered her room, even if months or sometimes years passed without her crossing the threshold. Her bed had been turned down, the linen sheets sprinkled with herbs so that they smelled fresh and clean in contrast to the dark red velvet bed hangings which were seldom if ever aired and dusted.

The monkey followed Mariana in and clambered up one of the carved posts of the bed and sat grinning at her from the foot of the canopy. She reached up to take him down, and he twined his arms about her like one of the smaller children at the convent, but she put him out the door and shut it, then pulled the velvet drapes over the windows, cutting out the slight breeze that had been drifting in. She undressed quickly in the luxurious and unusual light of a candle, put on her nightdress and pulled the cowl up over her head before pulling back the drapes and opening the door. Between the windows hung a crucifix, and below this a prie-dieu, and she knelt to say her prayers.

She was deep in concentration when she felt the bottom of one foot being tickled and turned around in exasperation. Pinto sat back on his haunches and whickered wickedly. "I suppose I can call you a bodily mortification," she told him, and turned back to her prayers. Pinto continued to tickle her feet; she shuddered, but managed not to pull them away or to move, and slowly her concentration returned. Pinto, disappointed at the lack of response, gave up and clambered up onto the canopy again and sat looking down at her.

She was almost through when she felt the hood being pulled from her head, and then lips brushed the back of her neck. "Pinto!" she said without looking around.

Her neck was kissed again, moistly, and she turned. "Papa."

His breath was heavy with wine. "You went to bed without coming to tell me good night."

"I asked Baltazar—"

"You do not say good night to your father by proxy."

"I'm sorry, papa."

"And I hear that you are planning to leave tomorrow morning, and with Peregrina."

"Yes, papa. That is what the Most Reverend Mother Brites has asked me to do."

"She's not your mother. She's your aunt. My holy, horrible, hate-stinking sister."

"Please, papa." She pulled the cowl to her gown back up over her head, and he jerked it down.

"You don't need to hide yourself when you're around me. Pretty girl, my little Mariana. Damn shame. Hard choice to make, you or Ana. Brites was a pretty girl, once. What I could tell you about that holy, reverend, so-called-mother of yours."

Mariana did not say anything. If she spoke he would undoubtedly tell her whatever came into his head about his sister, whether it was true or not. But her submissive silence did not stop him.

"Lovers," he said. "Can't even count her lovers. Can you?"

"Yes," Mariana said clearly. "Because there haven't been any."

"How do you know, hah? All nuns have lovers. All decent nuns, at any rate. How do you suppose she got where she is? How do you suppose she's built the convent up? How do you suppose she winds the bishop around her little finger? Or gets boarding students from the best families in Portugal. By being pure and holy?"

"Precisely," Mariana said, her lips cold.

"Maybe now. Maybe she's pure and holy now. Getting old. Older than I am. Don't think I don't know about the bishop. Don't think I don't know about that priest, what's his name, Duarte."

"You're disgusting," Mariana said angrily. "The church isn't like court. It's a different world. It's a world you don't know anything about, and you can't take your world and put it over the church and make it fit."

"Pretty when you lose your temper. Give Francisco a kiss." He reached out to her and she pulled away.

"You're papa," she said, "not Francisco. Not to me. Remember that."

"Very pretty with anger flushing those cool white cheeks." He grabbed at her, pressing his lips against her chin. She twisted around, away from his tender pink mouth, his mouth shockingly like the abbess's, and shoved at him. He was so drunk that he staggered away.

"Papa. Go to bed."

"A pleasure, my angel, a pleasure." He leaned against one of the bedposts and the monkey dropped down and sat on his head so that Dom Francisco let out a yelp of surprise.

"Papa, go to bed," Mariana repeated. "Do you want me to help you?"

"Papa's little girl will help him to bed." Dom Francisco's knees began to sag and Mariana was afraid that he would slide to the floor. She took him under the arms and pulled him upright.

"Come on, papa, I'll help you to your room." He let her lead him down the hall, down the stairs to his bedroom. His manservant, waiting outside, gave Mariana an odd look that was close to insolence, and took his master.

"Good night, papa," Mariana said. "Perhaps I'll see you in the morning before Peregrina and I leave."

Once back in her room, which held the reek of his wine and tobacco, she flung open the windows, then moved blindly to the prie-dieu. She dropped to her knees and the familiar posture itself gave her a small sense of reassurance, although she could not find any words of prayer. Her mind groped wildly, but she could hear only her father's drunken voice. Then the cowl was pulled from her head again. She whirled around in fury and anguish, but it was only Pinto, shut out from his master's room. He looked up at Mariana, shook his head forlornly, and wrinkled his wizened little face as though he were about to burst into tears. She picked him up and held him against her breast, rocking him slowly, trying to pray.

There was no farewell to Dom Francisco in the morning, or to Baltazar. The great house was sleeping as Mariana and Peregrina climbed into the carriage.

As they drove off, Peregrina looked at Mariana and said, "Well?"

"Well, what?"

Peregrina sighed heavily, looking for a moment as ancient as Pinto. "Oh, I don't know. Well anything. So I'm back in my convent uniform. Like it better?"

"Yes."

"I look more like your sister now, and less like Ana's."

"Probably."

"Ana was mama's favorite, wasn't she?"

"I suppose so. In a way."

"Didn't you—resent it? I would have."

"No," Mariana said. "I don't think I did. I loved our aunt as though she were my mother. So calling her Mother has been very simple for me. And Ana was at home and I was at the convent. We never saw much of each other."

"I wonder what would have happened if mama hadn't died when I was born?" Peregrina asked. "I wonder where I'd be now?"

"Probably right here, on your way back to the convent," Mariana said firmly.

Peregrina swiveled around in the carriage to scowl at her. "It's a pity you have to wear that stupid old habit all the time. You'd look ravishing in one of Ana's ball gowns."

"That's enough about ball gowns."

"I don't think I shall ever have enough of ball gowns. Or wine. Rollo—he's one of the English soldiers—gave me some. I had three glasses."

"Very wicked," Mariana said absently.

"Aren't you going to scold me?"

"No."

"Why not?"

Mariana said slowly, "If I can't manage to understand two worlds at once, how can I possibly expect you to?"

Peregrina looked again at her sister as though seeing her for the first time. "You'll have to, if you're going to be the next abbess."

"I wish people would stop all this talk about my being abbess." Mariana tried to keep the trouble out of her voice. "And you, of all people."

"But it's obvious. That's why her Reverence—fancy calling *you* your Reverence, Mariana!—has her claws into you all the time, never letting you go home, calling you to her study, jumping on you. I gather you came home this time only to fetch me. She probably didn't dare expose anybody else to papa and Rui. She hardly ever let you come home, even before you professed, even when you were just a pupil at the school, but she doesn't care what I do."

"We're two different people, you and I."

"And where does all this leave *me*? Ana got the husband and you got the church and what's left for me?"

"Don't worry about it so much. Whatever's best for you is what will be."

"You believe that?"

"Yes."

"I wish I did."

The carriage stopped in front of the convent gates. The coachman stepped down and rang the bell, and old Sister Portress, half blind, half deaf, completely toothless, doddered out and gestured, with smiles and nods, for them to drive in.

"Back to embroidering dove's feet," Peregrina said. "And codfish for dinner."

"Is it so terrible?"

"Yes. It's part of being in oblivion. When we go through the convent gates we're lost from the world. It's as though we'd never been. We're forgotten."

As Patrick had forgotten Charlotte?

. . . He had called her, perfectly courteously, to cancel their date, the one that was to follow that strange first evening. He had a load of studying he couldn't get out from under, he said, and he'd call again soon.

And that, it seemed, was the end of Patrick. For a long time the telephone was a dark, malignant personality. At first she ran to it when it rang. Then she refused to answer, waiting for Essie or Reuben, because if she didn't run to pick up the receiver then it would be Patrick. But it never was. She learned from Jane that he had left New York, was in Boston, where he had some kind of grant from his father's old hospital.

So Charlotte tried to put him out of her mind, to forget that all that remained in her memory of their evening together was the humiliation of too many martinis, of being sick, of being whistled at in the bath . . .

She spent her time on schoolwork, in museums, going to concerts, at first deliberately anesthetizing herself with "culture," then getting caught up in painting, in music, for its own sake. What had started as a narcotic became a catalyst. She saw more of Sister Mary Michael and less of Ursula. She graduated, to her own rather startled pleasure, at the top of her class and went to college, not a convent college, but a female institution: her own choice: was it because she was afraid?

She knew what to expect from females, even those who did not wear long habits or navy-blue uniforms, and in a sense she did well in college, was on the dean's list, was a class officer, was active in clubs, was busy, busy, busy, laughed a great deal, was popular . . .

Several times her friends arranged blind dates for her for the proms. Each time she swore never again, and each time they talked her into it. "But you *must,* Lottie, how are you ever going to get any experience with men?" The nuns had supposedly taught her to dance *(nuns?)* and her friends gave added instruction, but invariably she trod on her partners' toes or fell over their—or her own—feet. She learned every legitimate excuse to go to the ladies' room and to stay there. She could spend half an hour taking off and putting on makeup; she could rip a garter or a hem or a shoulder strap and have to sew it back on; she knew exactly how long it was permissible to stay in the water closet. It was a moot question as to where she was most unhappy, on the dance floor or in the ladies' room. The morning after a prom she would hurry to her classes or to her stall in the library with the gasping relief of a swimmer grasping a spar. She stopped listening when her friends told her that she was beautiful, that all she needed was self-confidence. On weekends and prom nights she managed to have a meeting to attend or to find another dateless girl willing to go to the movies.

On a Friday afternoon during the Christmas holidays of her junior year in college the telephone rang. She went to answer it; the phone was no longer a demon; neither did she expect anything from it. She didn't even recognize Patrick's voice. He had to tell her who he was, that he was back in New York, had done his internship in Boston, was now resident at Columbia Presbyterian, was going to be a surgeon. Did she happen by any chance to be free? He knew it was the last moment but he had an unexpected evening off . . .

Why did she go with him?

Her heart was jolting so that her ears rang. But Patrick, thank God, did not know this. He took her to a small French restaurant where he offered her champagne. She refused, going back to her childhood drink of lemonade sweetened with grenadine. Patrick had an extra-dry vodka martini, "with a twist of lemon, please." He offered her a cigarette.

She sat upright and rigid next to him on the banquette of the restaurant; perhaps it was because her nervousness was so intense, so different from the prom kind of nervousness, that she didn't care what she said.

"No, thanks. But it's no virtue in me. I choke. I guess I'll survive without smoking."

"And drinking?" he asked.

"Oh, I drink," she said. "Just not tonight."

"Why not tonight?"

She lied quickly. "Too much last night."

He laughed and turned on the banquette so that he could look directly at her. "I don't believe you. And you're still incredibly young. What would you like to eat?"

"Oh—you order for me, please. I've never been allowed to have a mind of my own when it comes to food."

He studied the menu, asking, "Can you cook?"

"I've never cooked anything," she said. "I've never even boiled water."

"Are you proud of this?"

"It isn't something to feel either proud or guilty about. It's just a fact."

"It could be remedied."

"You think cooking's a remedy? Okay, doc, when I'm out of college I'll try it and see."

There was no trouble talking; her posture became less tense; she went with him happily to his apartment for more coffee. She felt slightly drunk, as though she had not refused the champagne. Patrick was living uptown now, in a pleasant studio apartment on Riverside Drive. It had somewhat the flavor of the room on Bleeker Street; it was definitely Patrick's apartment, but the bookshelves were better built, the coffee cups matched. As she sat curled up in a black leather chair, quite different from the canvas slings, he curved down on his knees before her, leaning towards her until his lips touched gently against hers. Then he sat back on his heels. "Cotty—"

She was not called Cotty at college.

"You're really staggering. You're marvelous. I don't know what I expected from you tonight. But not that you would be this way. Is it that you've grown up?"

"I'm afraid I haven't, very much."

"I'm glad I got you tonight," he said. "I didn't know whether you'd even be in town. Violet—my mother—is about to do her first American performances in ten years, and I think she'd like to meet your father. All right?"

So it was for James Clement and Violet Napier that Patrick had called, and not for Charlotte at all. She sat rigid again, her fingers closed tightly about her empty cup.

"She doesn't know," he said, "what a favor she's done me. More coffee?"

She rose. "No. I think I'd better go home now."

Without question he took her. On the bus. He announced that he would pick her up at the same time the following week. When she did not respond he said nothing, merely smiled. He did not, as she had half expected him to, attempt to kiss her good night, but simply waved as she ran up the brownstone steps and let herself in.

She went to the library but her father had already gone upstairs. She turned on the light and stood there a moment before going up, looking at the skull that sat grinning like a monkey from the top of the bookcase. The skull shone whitely in the darkness.

❖

. . . then, dangling below the thrust of lower jaw, the rest of the skeleton gleamed out

"Love," Antonio said from the cleanness of his bones, "must be enfleshed—"

But the doctor had been alone with her in his strange and stuffy library. Antonio had not been allowed in the room during the examination, so who was it who had once enfleshed those bones? The doctor had stood over her as she lay there, looking quietly down at her, and he was not angry with her.

"Oh, Father," she said. "Father."

. . . "It is not so extraordinary," Father Duarte said, "that we seek to understand divine love in terms of human love. It is our only means of understanding it because we *are* human. It is never God but only we who make a travesty of human love."

"I wasn't looking for it," Mariana whispered. "I didn't expect it. I didn't understand it. I don't understand anything any more." The walls of the confessional seemed to close in on her.

He said, "You are asked to renounce human love not because it is wrong but because it is so marvelous a thing that it is a fitting gift. And possibly—though of this I am not sure—that you may feel the thrust of God more deeply."

He had not understood, then, what she had started to tell him. Perhaps she could put it off.

. . . "I am cold," she said. "My bones hurt."

They put her to bed.

Where was she? She did not know.

The doctor sat by her, his fingers lightly against her wrist, and for a moment her mind stopped reeling. She turned towards him, her words slightly blurred from fever. "I suppose it's arrogance or self-ishness or something to care so much about being loved that I could feel that no one loved me. It was only with Andrew in all the world that I knew I was loved, that I was worth loving. Not because of me, Charlotte, but because I was his mother. Not because I was a good mother, but because simply, biologically, I was his. No matter what I was like, no matter how much I was lacking, I was still his mother; there was this basic, primary fact that was there and that nothing could ever change, not anything I did or didn't do. So I believed that he loved me. And so I was—I was freed. With every-body else in the world I haven't believed it, and so I haven't been free." She had never put this into words before; it hurt to hear it, but it was true; it was Charlotte. "And if anybody is for a moment gentle with me, then I am—I can't explain, I dissolve, I'm completely undone."

"What about Patrick?"

"I love him. But I can't—," she gasped.

"Never mind, Charlotte. You've said it. But if the fact that you are Andrew's mother is unalterable, what about the fact that you are Patrick's wife?"

"Patrick only came back to me because he wanted to introduce Violet to my father. It wasn't for me at all."

"But you love Patrick?"

"Yes."

"Then does it matter why he came back to you? Isn't the important thing that he came?"

"But did he?" she asked. "Did he really?"

If he answered she did not hear. His hand was placed briefly, gently, on her burning forehead. She lay still, obedient to his touch, to his command to sleep.

An English setter with a soft, sad face put his moist nose against her cheek and breathed anxiously. In the strangeness of her waking she thought it was the doctor, that she was still wrapped in the rug in his library. Then the concerned face became unblurred as her eyes focused; she broke into an actual peal of laughter as she realized that it was not the doctor but a dog, standing on his hind legs, his feathery elbows on the coverlet, gazing at her inquiringly.

She was not in the doctor's library but she had no idea where she was. Her eyes had cleared but her mind still whirred. She moved one hand gropingly across the bed, then one leg, but encountered nothing.

Patrick, then, was already up, eating breakfast, or at the hospital— No.

This was not their low bed in New York, extra-length to accommodate Patrick's long legs. Carved posts at each corner of this bed loomed up to the ceiling. This bed was high, and the dog (where did the dog come from?) continued to stand there leaning against the bed.

Violet's villa.

She was in bed in Violet's enormous place in Beja.

Nothing had gone as planned. Charlotte let out a shuddering sigh, and the dog matched it, then began to pant, his breath warm on her face, and waved his plumed tail in eager demand for love. She caressed one of his ears, murmuring thoughtlessly, "Yes, you're beautiful, you're sweet, yes, you're a gorgeous beast, absolutely, I quite agree . . ."

At this lack of proper attention the dog removed his forepaws from the bed, thudded to the floor, and left the room with great dignity. After all, she had not even asked his name.

Charlotte sat up. At the long windows heavy ivory damask curtains were drawn. In the fireplace were the ashes of the fire she now remembered the doctor ordering the night before. She put her hand to her cheeks; they were hot, but not burning as they had been; the penicillin was working. Her limbs still ached, but no longer intolerably; her mind was clearing; if she was still inadequate to the situation it was because of the situation itself and not because of fever.

She got out of bed and her feet met the comforting warmth of a rug. Her legs were surprisingly unsteady. She crossed to one of the windows and pulled back the drapery so that she could look out. Rain was pelting in cold and angry gusts against the glass; the comfort of the room had nothing to do with a change in the weather. She looked at the poplars on either side of the long drive writhing in the wind.

Yes. She had come up that drive the night before with the doctor, and an elderly maid had undressed her and put her to bed, a maid named Julia with a cross mouth and infinitely kind hands. An old man in a brown leather apron had come in with piles of firewood and built the fire. Violet had kept stalking in and out, making suggestions which the doctor vetoed. He had sent everybody from the room and put his hand on her forehead and then she had gone to sleep . . .

She was waking now as though to a new world, as though she had been swimming all night and come at last to land, to a strange shore, exhausted but cleansed.

She climbed back into bed and turned on the lights on either side. They were soft, but powerful, not isolating the bed in a small pool, but spreading their rays across the room. She sat in the center of the bed like a small child, her hands locked across her knees, unwilling to leave, even in her mind, the safety of this bed, this room. She looked warily about. It was an intensely feminine room, white and gold, but there was nothing precious about it, or cluttered. The furnishings, though beautiful, were sparse, so that there was a feeling of strength. Like Violet.

—I hope I behaved well last night, Charlotte thought. —It would be incongruous to play any kind of an ugly scene in here.

But life was full of incongruities. Patrick himself was one; only his surgeon's knife was congruous in his long, strong hands.

There was a light knock on the door and Julia, her mouth still fierce and disapproving, entered. Enter the maid. As she saw that Charlotte was awake she spoke very rapidly and in full voice in Portuguese, as though by sheer volume she could make Charlotte understand. Then, still speaking loudly, she disappeared, shutting the door firmly on her words.

Why did Charlotte feel rejected and angry because Julia had looked cross and had shut the door against her?

On the right-hand bed table were three books; always, in Beja, things seemed to be in threes. An English murder mystery: good. An ancient Tauchnitz edition of Milton's *Paradise Lost* with an occasional marginal comment in Violet's angular, distinctive handwriting. *Paradise Lost* always reminded Charlotte of a small but shattering experience from her schooldays. There had been a nun, little and pretty and gay, always friendly and open, a favorite of students and parents: Sister Felicity. Charlotte, searching after school for a forgotten book, had come across her in the deserted classroom, weeping wildly. She had looked up at Charlotte, controlling her sobs, and said, "Which way shall I fly wrath and infinite despair? Which way I fly is hell; myself am hell."

Charlotte had not recognized those dark words as being from *Paradise Lost* then, but she had never forgotten them. The next day Sister Felicity had not been in school, nor the day after, nor ever again. There was the usual gossip and speculation among the students, the usual silence from the sisters. And a priest, giving the girls a meditation of the uses of silence and the necessity for silence in the life of a Religious, had mentioned that a popular nun may be a very poor Religious.

So no *Paradise Lost* this morning, thank you.

In any event Charlotte did not need to be reminded that she had been expelled forever from the Garden of Eden.

—What is forever? It cannot be in time, because time can be measured, and forever cannot. Time is inextricably tangled up with place, and can be measured only against place (dark of night in New York; grey of morning in Beja). Time has meaning only in relation to its position in space, the movement of a planet about a sun, of a night through stars.

Time for Charlotte had been measured against Patrick and Andrew.

Patrick was still in time, in night that would turn to day, to sunlight, and she, despite the clock, in night and darkness. Andrew was, presumably, in forever, whatever and wherever forever is.

The third book, the bottom book on the table by Violet's bed, was the French edition of *The Letters of a Portuguese Nun*. Was this Violet's? Did people in Beja read nothing else? More likely Charlotte had brought it with her from the pensão. She had a vague memory of asking Antonio for it.

Another knock, this time peremptory, and Violet came in, followed by Julia bringing a breakfast tray.

"You are to eat," Violet said without preamble, "and then I am to take your temperature and report to João. You seem to have had your usual effect on him."

"That then," Charlotte said, putting her head down on her knees and moving her fingers across the blanket as though trailing them through water, "would be no effect at all."

Violet sat on the white brocade of the chaise longue. "It is not clever to underestimate yourself."

"I'm not clever." Julia brought the tray to her. "And I don't mean to underestimate myself. I know I have acquired a certain flair with men. But it's on the surface. It doesn't count."

Julia poured hot milk and coffee from silver jugs, lifted a china dome to reveal two delicately poached eggs, removed hot rolls from the folded linen napkins.

"Are you hungry?" Violet asked.

Charlotte looked directly at her. "Unto starvation. Unto death."

Violet returned the look. "What did you expect?"

The maid left.

Violet drummed her fingers on the foot of the chaise longue, not aimlessly, but with definite pattern. She was, as always, practicing, perhaps one of the finger exercises she had worked out for herself, perhaps a phrase she considered was giving her difficulty.

Charlotte, sipping coffee, looked with relief at the strength of the disciplined hand. Violet's hands were shorter, squarer than Patrick's, their power and reach extraordinary for a woman.

Strength: it was this that had driven Charlotte to Beja in the dead of winter to see violent Violet, whose violence was turned to gentleness by the structure of her music, who could play chaos into order. Who could perhaps even now take all the senselessness with which Charlotte was darkened, and play it into meaning.

As she had the night of James Clement's burial. Because of Reuben and Essie they had come back to the house on Seventy-fourth Street. "But they need us there," Violet said when Patrick started to protest. "Go on to the hospital, Patrick. Charlotte and I will be all right." She went into the drawing room and sat at the piano and played Bach until Reuben called them to dinner. They sat at the long table in the dark dining room and Violet managed to keep some kind of conversation going. After dinner they went up to the library for coffee. They were silent while Essie puttered around with the coffee cups, the silver pot. When they heard her heavy footsteps going downstairs Violet leaned back on the black leather couch. The small coffee cup was held in one strong hand.

"If I have a reputation for arrogance now," Violet said, "God help me if I had been a failure. Humility is possible only if one is a success. It takes tremendous arrogance to sustain one's faith in one-self, as an artist or as a human being, if one must do it alone. The feeling of failure is more destructive to the creative artist, like Clement, than to the interpreter, like me. I have Buxtehude and Scarlatti and Vivaldi; but Clement had only himself."

She put her coffee cup on James Clement's desk, picked up his paper knife for a moment as though weighing it, turned the hour glass. "To be driven by a vision that is ignored or misunderstood, and to be faithful to it, as he was—dear God, no wonder he—" She turned from Charlotte with an angry cry, leaned her forehead against James Clement's bookshelves, and wept.

Violet's fingers stopped. Her square hands lay on the ivory brocade, holding power suspended in their stillness.

"I am not very objective about Patrick, Charlotte. I am not even very objective about you. If you want to talk to me, to tell me what all this is about, why you have come unannounced to Beja, I will try to listen with dispassion and compassion. But I can't promise you any help except bed and board until you're well enough to be on your own feet again. Meanwhile please eat your eggs while they're still warm."

("She's rude," James Clement had said. "She has no manners. She has an abominable disposition. She is utterly glorious.")

Obediently Charlotte took her fork and broke open one of the eggs so that the golden yolk spilled out of it. "I came wanting all kinds of things from you I shouldn't have wanted," she said.

"And that I couldn't give you."

Charlotte nodded. "But I thought you could. I went to a priest for absolution and he gave it to me, but even though I tried to tell him everything as honestly as I could, I felt unabsolved."

"Why?"

"Because he didn't blame me enough."

"Do you want to be blamed?"

"Not in any masochistic sense. Not for the pleasure of wallowing in guilt. But he seemed to think that I am not at fault. He kept letting me off the hook. So I knew that I must have slanted the picture. Blame is never that unequal. Or maybe it was just that I was having what you call my usual effect."

"You are as vague as Patrick was," Violet said. "He pretends that the subject, whatever it is, does not exist. And you are walking in enormous circles around it. One of you is going to have to center on it."

"Yes," Charlotte agreed. "I thought it would be possible to talk to you about it, but it was easier to tell the priest."

. . . "It seems to me, my child," Father Duarte said, "that you have spent a great deal of time today recounting peccadilloes to which you usually give very little thought."

Mariana bowed her head. A small trickle of perspiration ran down her back. The midafternoon sun poured hotly through the stained-glass windows of the chapel. A shaft of golden light drifted down through the open ceiling of the confession box and seemed to leave a film of dust on her veil. There was always a feeling of dust in the air of Beja in the dry season, borne on the hot wind from the Alentejo plains.

"Sister Mariana," Father Duarte passed his hand over his rough head in a tired gesture, "is something troubling you?" Mariana gave an almost imperceptible nod. "You are not yourself."

"No, Father."

He said in a quiet but definite voice, "You want to confess something but you are afraid." He looked at her, and this direct confrontation, counter to regulations, unnerved her. She bowed her head but did not speak. Father Duarte said dispassionately, "Remember that you are confessing not to me, but through me, and that there is nothing you need be afraid or ashamed to tell your Lord."

Mariana spoke with great effort. "I have lied."

"To whom?"

"To her Reverence. To my Sisters." She stopped, was lost in silence. She did not hear the voices of the children outside, the birds in the garden, the fountain, a sudden burst of quarreling among soldiers and civilians out on the street.

"What was your lie?"

Mariana raised her head, looking above the grille and at the dark wall of the confessional with eyes that were focused far beyond it. "I tried to pretend to them, to myself, that nothing was changed." Again she stopped.

"What is changed?"

She licked her dry lips, pushing her words out painfully. "I can't tell you." She turned from the wall and looked at Father Duarte, the old brown priest waiting with controlled strength. "Next time—"

His voice was deceptively gentle. "Now."

"I lied," she said again, and swallowed.

"You have already told me that."

Focusing her eyes carefully on the bars of the grille, she said, "About the soldiers. The French soldiers who ride by the convent almost every day."

"How could you lie about the soldiers?"

"That they don't matter to me."

"They matter to us all," he said quietly.

"That's what I said, too. That's how I explained it to the others. But that's not it."

Again he had to break through the heavy silence. "What is it, then?"

Mariana's voice was suddenly bitter. "Sister Joaquina saw. She always sees." Father Duarte raised his eyebrows slightly but did not speak. Her voice came angrily. "One soldier . . . just one soldier . . . is all that matters."

Duarte did not want to hear what he was going to hear. He tried not to know that it was coming. "It is forgivable to feel a special pride in your brother."

"Not Baltazar."

Duarte gave a deep sigh of acceptance and sorrow. "Who, then?"

"I don't know."

He looked at her in quick hope. "You don't know?"

"One of the French soldiers."

"Which one?"

"I don't know. I don't know his name. But I see him. And he sees me. No. Now I'm lying to you. I do know his name now. Part of it. I learned it last night. Noël. He is called Noël."

"You learned that when you went home?"

"You knew I went?"

"Yes."

"He's Baltazar's friend. I don't know any more of his name than that. Only Noël."

"Did you see him?"

"No. He wasn't there. I wanted him to be there. I prayed for him to be there."

"My child, do you know what you are saying?"

"No. Yes. Father, I don't know!"

Now it was Father Duarte's turn to be silent as he struggled for words. Mariana looked at him, saw his struggle, and closed her eyes against it. If she could have closed her ears she would have, but his words came so quietly that she listened in spite of herself. "My child, we have all been overwrought and overexcited by the victory and the presence of the soldiers. For us here in the Alentejo to be free from Spain at last is enough to raise our emotions to an unstable pitch. I think that you are letting something perfectly normal loom too large, that you are giving an importance to a guilt in yourself that does not really exist."

Mariana replied wearily. "That is the kind of thing I tried to say to Michaela. I've tried even harder to say it to myself. It doesn't work. Because I see him. I see him. Whenever they ride by. And he sees me. He sees me far more than if we waved at each other the way the others do. We . . . and when my eyes are closed I still see him. His face is all that I see."

"At least you are aware. Thus there is something you can do about it."

"What?"

"Do I really need to tell you?"

"Never to go to the balcony when they ride by. Never to look over the garden wall. Yes. I know."

"And when this face of an unknown man comes unbidden to your eyes you must replace it with the known face of your Lord and Spouse."

"Yes."

"I've known you all your life, Mariana. You have great strength. Now you must call on God to give you even more."

She did not hear the words of the absolution, though she knew he had given them. She crossed herself and stumbled out of the dark heat of the confessional into the gaudy gold of the chapel.

There she knelt: had Father given her a penance, given her prayers to say? He must have. But what?

O God, I can keep myself from going to the balcony, from looking over the wall for him. It is not going to be difficult never to see him in reality. But not to see him in my heart—I see him now. It is you who will have to stop that for me, dear my Lord, because I can't do it myself. But I don't want you to stop it, Jesu, I don't want you to stop it. If you have once seen a heavenly vision, you long for it over and over again, don't you? If you have seen the archangel Michael— but why should he make me think of the archangel Michael who has no buttons at all to count?

You made me, God.
You made me this way.
This is the way I am.

If you want me to change you'll have to help me. I can't do it by myself.

. . . "I've tried to change, but I can't seem to do it. Sometimes I can manage it on the outside, and this seems to satisfy Patrick, but on the inside I'm still—Charlotte."

"But why should you need to change?"

"One of us has to."

"Why?"

"But don't you see why, Violet?"

"No. I don't."

"You mean you accept the myth: Charlotte and Patrick Napier are the ideal couple?"

"No, Charlotte. I'm old enough to know that there's no such thing. But I thought you were both mature enough to have worked out reasonable compromises."

"Is that your definition of a marriage? Compromise?"

Violet lay back against the chaise longue, closing her kohl-rimmed eyes. "I don't believe in definitions of abstractions."

"You think marriage is an abstraction?"

"As you seem to be using the word, yes."

Charlotte pushed her tray aside, one egg untouched, rolls unbroken. "All right. No more abstractions. Let's be specific. Let's talk about compromise. Did you?"

Violet's fingers began to move again with controlled, calculated precision. "No."

"Well, then?"

"I am not an admirable person, Charlotte. I wish you would get that clear. I am driven by a passion that has overridden honor, decency, love. I destroyed my husband, which is one reason I have never married again. I have picked up love, if you want to call it that, as the need has arisen—and it does arise—and dropped it as it has become an interference with my work. Your father and I: I have sometimes wondered if Clement and I would have married if he had lived, but I think not. My success would have been intolerable for him. And then it would have become so for me, so *he* in turn would have become intolerable. But he is the only human being in the world who has ever—"

She stopped, turned her hawk's face away for a moment, then continued, "Patrick is my son. I have been an abominable mother to him, though on occasion a good companion. I gather he is an excellent surgeon. But I know him very little as my son—or your husband."

"He *is* your son, though."

Violet's fingers continued to move on an invisible keyboard. "And your husband. Who loves you."

"Does he? He picks up a scalpel with more real love than when he comes to me. The hospital, the operating room, the problem of the patient, this is what puts everything in its place in the universe for him. I don't. I'm part of the chaos. And there's nothing that orders the universe for me. Nothing."

. . . There was disorder everywhere, in the town, and even, it seemed, in the convent, though the rules were reinstated; the life of the nuns was again centered in the chapel, structured by the Divine Office . . .

But they could not help being aware of the disorder outside their walls. Schomberg's soldiers, although officially stationed in the neighboring town of Mertola, were often in the streets of Beja, and children and sisters found excuses to go to the balcony and look down into the street.

The children were quick mimics of the French and English soldiers as they struggled to speak Portuguese. "English is even funnier than French," small round Dolores told Mariana. "How hard it must be for them to learn to talk when they have such a peculiar language."

At night the town never seemed to quiet down; only in the heat of the day was there any diminution of the merrymaking. The streets were constantly filled with brawls, with soldiers and girls, with dancing. Only the oldest of the lay sisters were allowed to leave the convent to attend to the laundry in the river that was still full and clear from the winter rains, or to go with Sister Cellaress to the market that sprawled down the hill beside the convent. The bell at the convent gate was rung continually by visitors for sisters and children, and, each time it rang, even if she was in the chapel, Mariana would raise her head and listen. It was impossible not to.

Where was Baltazar, who had not kept his promise to come?

Joaquina's father, Dom Alipio de Vasconcelos, had not been to visit his daughter, either, but then, he never did. . . . As she realized this, Mariana looked with pity on Joaquina. Baltazar always *did* come. Eventually.

—Oh, dearest Lord, why doesn't he come? Are you keeping him

away to make things easier for me? But it isn't easier. We don't always have to like your will, do we?

—Help me to want what you want for me. Only I don't know what it is that you want . . .

My soul thirsteth for thee, my flesh also longeth after thee: in a barren and dry land where no water is

no

help me O Lord
you have to help me
it is so dark

She walked in the safe rectangle of the cloister garden. Her fingers moved against her beads, but the words were only a habit and could not command her attention. The fountain splashed up towards the sun, caught gold, and the breeze, coming in a brief gust of coolness, blew spray in her direction. She held her face up to it.

From behind her came the old, cracked voice of Sister Portress. "There you are, dear child. Sorry to interrupt, but you and Peregrina have visitors in the locutario, and Peregrina is already there."

Mariana turned to meet the ancient, smiling face. "Visitors?"

"Your brother and a friend."

"A friend?"

"Did I interrupt a prayer or a dream? Wake up, child. It's just your brother and one of his friends. Run along and see them."

"Yes, Sister. Thank you."

It might be anybody, the friend.

It might be the Englishman who had given Peregrina wine.

It might even be Rui de Melo. Sister Portress wouldn't remember him because he never came

So it wouldn't be Rui de Melo because Rui de Melo never came

So

Baltazar had said he would bring him

Baltazar had said he would bring the Frenchman

To see him. To see him face to face.

To have the stars stop, shuddering, in their courses.
To have her heart wrenched in her body.

The locutario was a divided room. The large anteroom was for guests and contained some statues the abbess had banished from other parts of the convent, was brightened and cluttered by palms and plants in colored pots and jars, by massive chairs of carved wood and dusty velvet. Waste not, want not, and the lay sisters enjoyed puttering about, cleaning, polishing. Guests could see and speak to the choir nuns through a grille. On the nuns' side of the partition the room was bare except for a crucifix and a number of plain chairs. It was to this room that Mariana hurried now.

An Alcoforado—no, a nun trained by the abbess who was also an Alcoforado—could smile, could laugh, could be gay, could hide what was going on in her heart . . .

Could thank the Frenchman for saving her brother's life, for coming to the Alentejo, for taking up the cause of the small, enslaved country . . .

Could offer her prayers on learning that Schomberg was taking his soldiers into the field again, that despite the victory the war was not ended, that there might be more fighting . . .

"But I thought the danger was all over," Peregrina cried. "I'm tired of praying for you."

"But I count on your prayers," Baltazar said. "And yours, Mariana."

"You will both have my prayers."

The Frenchman: Noël; Noël Bouton Saint-Leger, Count of Saint-Leger; now she knew all of his name. He met her eyes, smiled. "Then we are invulnerable."

"My own prayers mean very little," Mariana's eyes were properly downcast, as a sister's should be when talking with a secular. "But all of us will pray for you. For all of you."

Again his eyes tried to meet hers. "And perhaps when you stand out on your balcony you will think of us riding by?"

She did not look up. "I will think of you."

"When we come back we'll be riding by again. Will you be watching?"

She turned away so that he could not see even the curve of cheek within her coif and pretended to smooth Peregrina's curls. "It may not be possible."

"But you've watched before—"

Her voice was light, impersonal, hardly her own voice at all. "Father Duarte thinks, and quite rightly, that we've spent too much time on the balcony in the past days."

And Baltazar's voice, somehow pompous, as unlike Baltazar as she was for the moment unlike Mariana, "Sometimes it is hard for us to remember that the sisters have spiritual duties, just as we have military ones." And then, down to earth, back to Baltazar again, he was wanting to show Noël the convent, "To show that not all Portuguese convents are the same."

The Frenchman said lightly, "But you're too sensitive."

Baltazar shrugged. "Perhaps. But it's no secret that Rome sides with Spain because of the Inquisition, and that there's only one bonafide bishop in Portugal at the moment. And you've made it quite clear to me that our convents don't have the most delicate of reputations."

"Royal whorehouses." Peregrina's voice came clear.

Mariana turned swiftly. "Peregrina!"

Peregrina had the grace to redden.

Mariana, trying to erase the words, turned back to her brother. "Only one bishop?"

"I forget how isolated you are. Doesn't Aunt Brites tell you anything?"

Mariana's face still showed shock. "Yes, of course. But not about—"

Peregrina, trying to make amends, chanted as though reciting a lesson: "When John of Braganza claimed the throne it put Rome in an awkward position, so they appointed a lot of Spanish bishops to the Portuguese sees, and of course we weren't going to be very happy about that, so John of Braganza has been appointing his own bishops who aren't recognized by Rome, and ecclesiastically speaking, the situation is confused. I quote."

"Accurately, I hope," Mariana said. "In any case I accept it as my history lesson for today."

They had turned the distasteful and embarrassing subject so that it could be dropped, but Baltazar clung to it. "Accurately enough. I want Noël to know that there are places in Portugal where religion is neither a matter of politics nor of lewd laughter."

"My dear fellow," Noël assured him, "I don't believe all I hear." There was more than a hint of amusement in his voice.

Baltazar's frown deepened. "I haven't liked some of the talk. Particularly when it includes my sister."

Peregrina, recovered, made a face, directed at Noël. "Bal talks like a priest. I want to hear more about the war."

Baltazar, still scowling, said, "Noël and I came here this afternoon to forget war for a few hours." Then he relaxed and smiled. "Come on, imp. You're supposed to take us to Aunt. And we all know better than to flout an order from on high."

Noël turned to Baltazar in mock terror. "Must I go? She doesn't want to see me; I'm not her nephew. I'll talk with Sister Mariana here. I'm frightened enough of *her*. Don't make me go beard an abbess in her den. I'm no Daniel."

Both Baltazar and Peregrina burst out laughing, and Baltazar said, "All right, all right. We won't be long. Aunt has little time for visitors, even those just returned from the wars."

"I'll stay here, too," Peregrina said.

"You will not. You know no man is allowed to go unaccompanied to the lion's lair," Baltazar said.

"Let Mariana go, then. She's a proper nun."

Noël Saint-Leger said lightly, "You're a naughty child. It will do you good to see the lion. I hope she eats you up. Run now. Military orders."

"All this obedience," Peregrina muttered. "It's as bad as a convent." But she said to Baltazar, "All right. I'll meet you in the hall."

Mariana watched after them, holding her breath as though waiting, as though poised for flight. Noël reached up and held with both hands on to the bars of the grille, looking at her intently. He did not speak, and the silence seemed to grow louder and louder, until Mariana turned slowly from the empty doorway to the grille, asking in a low voice, "Why did you say you were afraid of me?"

For a moment Noël seemed surprised. He looked at her, a half smile on his lips, his brown eyes lit with curiosity. She waited, and he said, his smile fading, "You know, Sister, I've thought each day as I've ridden by the convent and seen you on the balcony that our lives must be alike, yours and mine."

"Alike?" Mariana indicated her dark robes, his bright garments. "It's night and day."

"But night and day both obey the rule of the sun. And you and I both live our lives in obedience to a rule. We're both responsible to a law higher than ourselves. You submit to the orders of your abbess, your convent, and I to my commanding officer and my king."

"I never thought about it that way. You seem to be from—from a different world. One that my world can see only from a distance and never know. Your world is so large and mine is so very small. . . . I didn't even know about—about the bishops."

"Perhaps you were better off not knowing. I don't know anything about bishops either, and I don't want to. What I want is to know something more about you."

At last Mariana raised her eyes to him. "About me? But why?"

The lightness drained from his voice, the smile from his lips. There was a tenderness in the velvet brown of his eyes. He stretched both hands through the grille, bending towards her. "I don't know. Dear God, I don't know. I say casually that our lives are alike because we must both submit to authority. And yet, as I come by and look at you and your Sisters, standing on your balcony, moving about the garden, perhaps even calling to each other, your voices so light and peaceful in contrast to the rough voices of the men surrounding me or the shrillness of the women we see—this is what attracts me, makes me go out of my way to take the convent road. It reminds me—"

"Of what?"

"I think of something I've lost. Or maybe it's something I've never had."

. . . "Stop looking for something you've never had," Violet said crossly. "Settle for what you have. You've been married for six years. You are twenty-seven. God knows that's young; nevertheless you're a woman now and it's time you stopped this schoolgirl sentimentalizing."

"I don't—," Charlotte protested.

Violet picked up the book of letters. "Stop reading this junk. It's not going to get you anywhere."

It was difficult to try to look dignified lying down in that enormous bed; nevertheless Charlotte tried. "I find the letters interesting."

"Of course they're interesting," Violet slapped the book down on the bed table. "They wouldn't be still in print if they weren't. Or if they weren't controversial. But they aren't going to tell *you* anything."

"How do you know?"

"Because it's time you stopped looking for answers outside yourself. You are really the most superstitious human being I've ever known."

"I fail to see where superstition—"

"This nun is not going to tell you anything. She was a dull, self-pitying creature. The Frenchman thought it would be amusing to seduce a nun and she evidently found it amusing to be seduced by him. That is all. Half the nuns in Portugal in the seventeenth century never even thought about God. They simply transferred their worldliness with them when they took the veil. They had luxurious bedrooms, not austere cells, and it is well known that they entertained men. As for the French soldier, Mariana was probably the first and most available nun he could find."

"You're being vile."

"You might also be interested," Violet continued, unperturbed, "that in the army manual for the time there was a rather mild penalty for having an affair with a nun."

"I wish you wouldn't."

"All I want you to do is see things as they are, not as you would like them to be."

"Do you know how things are?" Charlotte demanded.

"I am *not* going to get into one of your abstract theological discussions. I am trying to get down to some kind of facts."

"So am I," Charlotte said. She would have liked to have asked Violet, "What is a fact?" but she kept her mouth closed.

"You are silly and young," Violet said. "It is not entirely your fault. But it is time you grew up."

"I know!" Charlotte cried. "I'm trying!" She lay weakly back on the pillows. Her throat hurt again. She wanted to see Dr. Ferreira. She wanted to get out of Violet's bed and run out into

the rain so that it would cool her cheeks so that she would be
cleansed . . .

. . . She ran. To the chapel. To Father Duarte. To help.

But he was, as she should have known he would be, hearing confessions. She saw Sister Michaela enter the confessional. She could
not burst in . . .

She stumbled down the aisle to the altar and fell on her knees.
Tears rushed to her eyes and she looked blindly through them at the
crucifix. She whispered, "I have seen him. Oh, God, God. I have
seen him. Help me. Help me."

During recreation it was Beatriz, not Joaquina, who asked, "Are
you all right?"

"Yes. Of course. Why?"

"You didn't eat."

Mariana shrugged in apology. "It's the heat. I wasn't hungry."

Beatriz looked at her with grave concern. "You don't usually let
the heat bother you. You let it roll off you, like water off a duck."

Mariana forced a smile. "An odd duck."

Mother Escolastica hobbled rheumatically across the room and
touched Mariana lightly on the shoulder. "Her Reverence wishes to
see you in her office after recreation."

Mariana nodded and Mother Escolastica, waiting a moment for a
further response that did not come, hobbled out.

Beatriz again directed her level gaze at Mariana. "You look as
nervous as when her Grace used to send for us when we were students and we'd done something wrong—as usual."

Again Mariana forced a smile. "That doesn't seem to change as
far as I'm concerned."

"Doing something wrong? Or being nervous?"

"Both."

"What have you done now?"

"Dear Sister Beatriz," Mariana said. "I made my confession to
Father Duarte—" and stopped short.

So did Beatriz. She gave Mariana a sharp look as Joaquina said,
"Why worry? We all know *you* can do or say anything."

Mariana's voice betrayed her by climbing a notch, though it remained steady. "I have no special privileges. There are none in this convent. You know that."

Beatriz came between them, saying to Joaquina, "I do admire your sewing. You can make the tiniest stitches of anybody in the convent, barring not even Sister Isabella before her eyes went back on her. Is that a new habit?"

"Yes." Joaquina refused to look pleased. "For Mother Escolastica."

"Her poor hands," Beatriz said. "She used to do such beautiful lettering. And she needs a new habit."

"She doesn't think so," Joaquina said. "Nor do I. But her Grace says it is time and we must obey."

Beatriz smiled at Mariana and frowned when the smile was not returned. She spoke quietly to Joaquina, "Can't we have a happy medium between wearing habits that are in shreds and dressing as though we were going to be presented at court? Her Grace is trying to teach us moderation in this convent."

"That's true, isn't it, Mariana?" Michaela asked eagerly. But Mariana, not having heard, did not reply. She left the chapter room and went to the abbess's study.

But the abbess was concerned only with a general loosening of discipline. "It's time we got back to normal. I don't like this continual buzzing in the convent. And there has been too much breaking of Silence. Among the sisters as well as the children. I look to you to be an example."

"Yes, your Reverence. I'll try."

There were two days of chill wind and driving rain during which the soldiers were away. Then the skies cleared and the sun burned high and hot again. The nuns knew when the troops returned to Mertola by the noise in the streets of Beja, by the shouting and singing that continued again through the small hours, although the presence of the soldiers was beginning to be taken for granted and neither children nor sisters ran to the balcony at the sound of bugle or hoofbeat.

Mariana held closely to her work, playing with the little children, teaching French to the older ones, copying manuscripts in the library, spending her fragments of free time praying in her cell or remaining on her knees in chapel after singing an office. As the temperature rose, chapel and cell held and contained the stifling heat of the noon-day sun, barbaric in its intensity, and she was driven out to the lily pond at the bottom of the convent grounds where a heavy, humid breeze stirred the leaves of the eucalyptus trees. She lay down on the browning grass, her fingers touching tepid water, and looked at the bullfrog on his lily pad. "I'm trying. Why don't you help me? Saint Michael, can't you hear me? I can't do it alone. I try not to think about him. I try not to see him. I try not to see him when I pray to you. But your face is his. I cannot tell any more who he is or who you are—"

She broke off as a shadow, deeper than those cast by the euca-lyptus branches, moved across her. She turned onto her side and looked up.

He was there.

He was standing above her. The buttons on his coat flashed in the sun. He took off his hat with the waving plume. He smiled, his smile that flashed even more brightly than the sun on the buttons . . .

She sprang to her feet, feeling the blood drain from her face. "Excuse me, monsieur le—excuse me—it is not allowed—" She fled down the path, through the arch to the cloister, past the brilliance of the fountain, into the stifling heat of the chapel.

There was no meaning to time while she was in the chapel. There was only a darkness that was outside time, and a light seeming to strike against her so that she kept shaking her head against it. She did not know whether she stayed on her knees for a minute or an hour, except that when she rose and stumbled out her knees were stiff, her habit damp with perspiration. Sofia was waiting outside for her.

"Sister—"

She was still in darkness, though she had to close her eyes against the sun, and her voice groped towards the child. "Sofia—"

"Sister Isabella asked me to wait until you got out of chapel to tell you that you have visitors."

"Visitors. Yes. Thank you."

"Sister said to tell you that she would have waited herself, but—oh, you know how blind she is and she'd already mistaken Sister Joaquina for you and told her that she had visitors and then of course when poor Sister got to the locutario there was nobody there for her. So Sister Isabella didn't want to make a mistake again so she sent me to find you."

"I see," Mariana said. "Thank you, Sofia." She left the covered cloister walk and went into the tiled main hall, moving rapidly down the corridor, robes and girdle swinging. She entered the nuns' section of the locutario. Peregrina was there already, and in the visitors' parlor were Baltazar and—who were they? So many people . . .

Yes, he was there. Noël. She was being introduced to the Englishman, Rollo Boundys, and to another Frenchman, Mathieu de Berenger.

She joined in the laughter, the gaiety, but she did not know what was being said, and after the men had left, with Peregrina running after them to see them out, she remained in the parlor, holding on to the bars of the grille as though she could not stand in any other way. The door on the visitors' side reopened. Noël Saint-Leger looked in, a half smile on his face.

"I believe I left my hat," he said formally. Then, as he approached Mariana and could see that there was no one else on the nuns' side of the locutario, he said, softly, "Sister—"

"No—," Mariana protested.

"No, what?" Again he gave her the brilliance of his smile. She only shook her head. His smile disappeared and he looked at her soberly, his whole face seeming to darken. "Sister. I have been in the army long enough to know that sometimes the best way to keep a rule in the long run is to break it in the short."

"Please," Mariana said. "I must not."

"In a few days we leave again. We will be going down into the Algarve, and this time there will be danger. I want to see you, to have your prayers before I go."

Mariana's lips were so cold and stiff that she could scarcely form the words, although the heat of the afternoon pressed heavily on the parlor. "You know that you have them."

"But I want to see you. Is that asking more than you can give?"

"It is not allowed."

"If I come to the locutario tomorrow—but without the others—would that be allowed?"

"I—don't know."

"I have a splendid idea." His smiled flashed again. "Baltazar tells me that you teach French to the older students—"

"Yes."

"So I could help you with your French—" again the smile, "—so that your accent will be better for your students."

"Is this—is this what you want?"

"It will have to do, won't it?" He turned on his heel abruptly, and left. Brusquely, not looking back, he left.

. . . As Violet had left, having crossly told Charlotte to "stay in bed until João comes."

Charlotte slept, roused briefly, slept again. For the moment it was all she had to do. No responsibilities. No decisions to make (Had not all decisions already been made? Were they revocable?). She put her arms around one of Violet's soft, square feather pillows, as though in this way she could hold the safety of sleep; as long as she clutched the pillow she needn't wake up. Then, perhaps because she was holding it too tightly, sleep left her. She was wide awake, her eyes dry, the lids like sand, her mouth like the Sahara. She poured herself a glass of water from the carafe on the bed table, pressing the rim of the glass against her teeth as though to keep from crying, although in this strange desert through which she was wandering she was still far from tears.

She had not cried for a long time.

She had not cried since—

Blindly she reached for the books beside her, for the letters of the Portuguese nun.

I gave my life to you the first moment I saw you, and it is my pleasure to sacrifice it to you.

No.

Things aren't the same. No two things are ever the same. So even after I take away the obvious differences, I mustn't put too much weight on the similarities.

She wanted to leave God for man.

But I don't want to do that. Or the reverse, either. I don't want to leave man for God. That would be very tidy, wouldn't it? And much too easy. Get thee to a nunnery, Cotty. It could be done.

There are convents that take widows.

I'm not a widow.

I'm not—

So it couldn't be done. They wouldn't have me, even if I wanted to. And I don't. I'm not that much of an idiot. I do at least know that this kind of thinking isn't only stupid and self-deluding, it's downright sacrilegious.

And there's not much point to that at this point.

I gave my life to you the first moment I saw you, and it is my pleasure to sacrifice it to you.

No—

why should I not try to remember all the wonderful ways in which you showed me your love? They made me so happy that it would be ungrateful of me now if I didn't still adore you with the same ecstasy my passion gave me when I was secure in your love—

No—

She turned from the first letter to the last.

—you have finally persuaded me that you don't love me any more, and that therefore I must no longer love you—

—I've asked the Most Reverend Mother to take care of everything for me. I have always confided in her, not only about this, but about everything

But Violet doesn't want to know, and I don't suppose the abbess did, if it came to that . . .

The doctor knocked and came into the bedroom. He put the back of his hand against her cheek, then took her wrist in his fingers. "You still have fever, though not like last night. How are you?"

"All right."

"That is no answer. Open your mouth. There is still some inflammation in your throat. Headache?"

"Yes. But nothing like yesterday."

"No. You are mending. Let me listen to your chest . . . Yes. That, too, is better. I think we need not worry any longer about pneumonia. You are bouncing back like a ball. Now." Methodically, deliberately, he put his stethoscope away. As he snapped his bag shut he said, "You have upset Violet. You and your Patrick."

"Her Patrick, too."

"But *you* came to her. Why?"

"I needed help."

"From Violet?"

She turned her face away. "It's not as illogical as it might seem."

He took her hands in his, turning her towards him. "Child, I am protecting Violet and hurting you, am I not?"

She moved her head numbly, but whether in affirmation or negation she could not have said.

"But you shouldn't be such a child," he said. "You are a woman. Why is it that American women are so immature?"

Here it came again, the generalities about Americans. She had affirmed her Americanism to Antonio; now she said, "I am not 'an American woman.' I am not a—a platitude. I am not a cliché. I am Charlotte Clement Napier, and if I am—backwards—it is because I am myself, and not a category."

To her surprise he smiled. "Bravo! Now you are being you. Do you think while you are being thus delightful, you could tell me why you came running so wildly and willfully to Beja?"

"For a point of reference," she said.

"I have heard Violet called many things, but never this. Would you care to explain?"

She looked at him warily, but his deep-set brown eyes were kind, concerned; it was simply his way of speaking. As she pondered, he pulled a small gilt chair over to the bed and lowered his bulk onto it.

"Supposing," she said, slowly, "you were sitting in a train standing still in a great railroad station. And supposing the train on the track next to yours began to move. It would seem to you that it was your train that was moving, and in the opposite direction. The only way you could tell about yourself, which way you were going, or even if you were going anywhere at all, would be to find a point of reference, something standing still, perhaps a person on the next platform; and in relation to this person you could judge your own direction and motion. The person standing still on the platform wouldn't be telling you where you were going or what was happening, but without him you wouldn't know. You don't need to yell out the train window and ask directions. All you need to do is see your point of reference. So I wasn't—I wasn't going to bother Violet. No yelling out the train window. I just wanted to see her. I wasn't going to dump everything in her lap. I didn't want her to tell me what to do. I just thought—if I could see her and talk to her, she could be my point of reference."

"But why Violet, child? Violet of all people?"

"There are reasons why she seemed the—only person."

. . . Violet had come to the United States for a series of concerts and Patrick had brought her to the house on Seventy-fourth Street.

And the house came alive again. James Clement came alive again. The small, vital, unfrozen core expanded, and he lay no longer on the black leather couch, gone off into some dark state of nonbeing.

And Patrick: long before he came back to Charlotte to take her out to dinner and ask to bring Violet to see James Clement, he had learned about martinis.

And Charlotte: if the cherry in the martini had saved her virtue it was Violet (not Patrick) who broke through the sheer glass wall of her innocence. There is more to the adult world than the correct making of martinis.

It was during her spring vacation from college and she was spending the evening with Sister Mary Michael; she always went to see Sister Mary Michael during vacations. Sister had been talking to her about the attitude of young people in schools and colleges towards morality, about their refusal to be responsible in love.

"I can't reach the students," Sister Mary Michael said despairingly. "The Reverend Mother wants me to talk to them and they put up great blocks of interference because—oh, I see all the reasons why. But I must go on trying and praying for grace and I must not forget that to think that chastity and sex are opposites is a blind mistake. A wife refusing her husband relations because she is angry or wants her own way about something is being just as unchaste as a prostitute, because she is equally prostituting the meaning of love. In the same way a prude rejecting sex as being vile is being unchaste. But this all must be seen in a Christian framework, Cotty. There are no new morals. There never have been. There never will be." And then, as Charlotte was saying goodbye, "Thanks for listening to me sounding off, Cotty. Thanks for understanding. God bless you."

Charlotte walked home, asking herself, "But did I—do I understand?"

She climbed the brownstone steps and let herself in. The library was dark; only the night light was on in the hall. She went upstairs and there was a light coming from under her father's door. She tapped and entered, and there was Violet, wearing enormous, horn-rimmed spectacles, sitting up in the bed reading the newspaper.

She knew only that where her father had been dead he was now alive.

She knew only that Reuben and Essie, paragons of rectitude, worshipped Violet.

. At first she had thought that of course they would get married, because wasn't that what one did? But the only marriage that was talked about was hers and Patrick's.

She came home from an evening at Patrick's apartment and, as she turned her key and pushed open the door, she heard a cry and Violet came running down the stairs, loose robe flying, eyes wild. "The doctor, quickly, call him, Cotty—"

There had been life in the house and now there was death. Charlotte and Violet had stood by James Clement's bed waiting for the doctor during those brief moments of unspeakable pain. It was over before the doctor rang the doorbell. It was Charlotte and Violet who had shared it.

. . . She could not tell Dr. Ferreira.

"It was just—there are reasons why she seemed the only person."

He pressed her hand. His voice was gentle. "It is a dangerous thing to have a living person as a point of reference."

She spoke over an edge of desperation. "Why?"

"A living person is usually found to be moving, too. You can't ever expect living people to be predictable, and if your point of reference starts moving, and in an unexpected direction, then where are you?"

She closed her eyes. "What about a dead person?"

"That sounds rather macabre. How dead?"

"Oh—about three hundred years."

He smiled. "Sister Mariana?"

"Yes."

"You have to have somebody?"

"Yes. At this point, yes. Yes. I do."

"Why?"

"I'm lonely. Abysmally, unutterably lonely."

He spread out his great, gentle hands (far too gentle for a key-board, a harpsichord) in a gesture of half-amused exasperation. "But my poor Charlotte, loneliness is the natural state of humankind. It is what distinguishes man from beast. An animal can be solitary and live, but in loneliness it dies. But we: we live in loneliness. There is nothing else."

Behind his beard, below his mop of bear-brown-grey hair, his mouth and eyes were bleak with pain. Charlotte, unwilling to add to his hurt but unable to contain herself, turned her eyes away from his and let her gaze rest on the black band circling his un-pressed sleeve, and asked, "Were you lonely when—your wife was alive?"

A feeling of tension came into the room, but his voice, as always, was courteous, controlled, "It was easier to bear. That's all."

"Then——," she said eagerly, "then maybe that's what I mean. It's— I can't bear the loneliness right now. I'm torn in two by it."

He covered her hand with his. The nails were ridged, a little horny, cut short, immaculately clean. The touch of skin felt warm and vital. "But nobody can bear it for you," he told her. "Even when you love, and are loved, you have to bear it yourself."

"But when you're loved it's easier. You said it yourself."

"Charlotte. Dear Charlotte. Yes. In a sense you're right. But easi-ness has never been a criterion of value."

Now she could not restrain herself. She sat upright. "So, because it makes things easier, you're devaluing love?"

He brought both hands down in a definite gesture on his knees. "Not in the least. Its value is so high that it cannot be estimated. And there is nothing easy about it."

"But you just said—"

162

"No, Charlotte. You said."

. . . "Then you think—you think I
don't really love the Frenchman?"

"My child, you will have to answer that question yourself."

"It would be so terribly wrong to love him?"

"Love, the kind of love I have been trying to show you, can never
be wrong because it is always an expression of God's will. And,
since God has led you to a vocation, how can this—infatuation with
a Frenchman you hardly know be anything but counter to his will?"

It was hot in the confessional. Father Duarte's beard was damp
with sweat. Mariana's hands were moist as she pressed them together.
"I'm so lonely, Father. All of a sudden I'm so terribly lonely—"

"Because you are turning away from God and that, Mariana, is
the ultimate loneliness."

"Father, help me—"

"My child, if only I knew how—"

She left the stifling confines of the confessional. There were others
waiting. They would be wondering why she had taken so long. She
knelt at the altar rail, stretching her arms out and up towards the
statue of the Virgin.

"Dear my Lady—sweet my queen—help me—"

She said the prayers of her penance not once, but three times,
then moved stiffly, blindly, out of the chapel, along the covered walk,
out the arch that led to the rose garden, past the kitchen gardens, to
a small herb garden at the back of the convent, and sank down onto
a marble bench, plucking at her rosary. In the center of the garden
was a little stone fountain, a purely secular fountain, a little grey
dolphin spraying out a cool shower. The garden smelled of thyme
and rosemary. Against the lichened stone of the fountain Sister Isabella, whose nose was as keen as her eyes were weak, had planted
mint and violas, hen-and-chickens and chervil. There was a homely
safety to the place. The young nun began to breathe more quietly,
her fingers moved less restlessly over the rosary. Then both breath
and fingers stopped as a shadow fell across her hands.

It was, as she had known it would be, the Frenchman.

"No."

"Sister—"

She rose, clutching her beads. "No."

He stood there above her, the sun flashing its brilliance against his buttons. His face was tanned and healthy, the scar hardly visible as the shadows of the playing water splashed across his face. His eyes were warmly brown, his full lips quirked up at the corners . . .

—St. Michael

He said, "I must speak to you."

St. Michael had a sword and flamed with passion, but there was no place for passion in the quietness of Sister Isabella's herb garden.

The rosary snapped under her tense fingers and the beads spilled onto the grass. "It is not allowed."

Rosary. Rosemary. The two together by the fountain. The rose of Mary. It stood, Sister Isabella said, for fidelity, for constancy.

He knelt on one knee to pick up the beads, to drop them into her lap. "Sister, I have noticed that the other nuns receive soldiers."

"If you will come to the locutario—"

"Damn the locutario."

But he came.

. . . Dr. Ferreira held the book of letters lightly, slapping it against the palm of his hand, looking thoughtfully down at Charlotte and chewing on his straggly mustache. "Be careful with these letters, child. They are hardly history. And even history as we know it is nothing but the opinion of a few people, the very few people among all the billions of people in the world who have bothered to write down a record of what they think happened. Even the most objective of historians is ultimately subjective, even if only in what, out of countless scraps of knowledge, he selects."

"So how can anybody ever know?" Charlotte asked. "How can anybody ever know what really did happen? If I don't know what is happening with me, how can I possibly hope to know what happened with Mariana and Noël?"

"Why do you want to know?"

"So that perhaps—just perhaps—I can know what is happening with myself."

"With yourself alone?"

She shook her head impatiently. "It's never anybody's self alone, is it?"

"No," he said. "I'm glad you remember that."

She looked down at the broad gold of the wedding band on her finger. "It would be rather difficult to forget."

So might Mariana have looked at her own hand; she might have stood there in the locutario, holding the grille, so that Noël could see the gold wedding band on her hand, the band of the bride of Christ.

It would have been impossible in the locutario
impossible

So, then, the end of the convent grounds, furthest from the complex of blazing white buildings, at the secluded corner by the lily pond, he would have come again.

And she, too.

She would have come there.

God. I did not come here of my own volition. Whose, then? You will have to help me. I do not understand. I do not understand anything.

. . . "I used to think about God all the time." Her voice was low, on one tone, as though the sunlight flashing against his buttons had hypnotized her. "Everywhere I turned he was in my thoughts. I was so close to him that it seemed to me that when I touched the bench where the sun had warmed it I could feel the touch of his hand."

It was the Frenchman's hand that moved against the bright surface of the bench, lightly touching the edge of her habit. "And now?"

She looked into the lily pond. There was no salt in the water, but it was not clear. A green summer scum was beginning to creep over the surface. "And now when I start to think about God I find that I'm thinking about you. When I look at the clean white marble of the bench I remember that you sat there, and the sun glinted against your hair, and the plume in your hat moved in the wind from the plains."

With one finger he stroked the dark material of her habit. "And this troubles you?"

She looked up at him with a painful honesty, then lowered her eyes, so that the brightness of the gold within them was shadowed. "Yes. I was always happy when I thought about God."

"You're not happy when you think about me?"

She looked at her hands that lay in her lap, hands that were seldom dropped in idleness against the dark fabric of her habit. The sun gave the tangle of her lashes a burnished glint. "I didn't know what happiness was until I thought about you."

He gave a deep, lingering sigh.

"The children have seen it," she said.

"Seen what?"

"How happy I am. Peregrina knows that there is—something. And the little ones, 'Sister, you're always so happy; you laugh so much,' they tell me. But I was always happy, I always laughed, but they know that now it is different. Noël, tell me. Is this wrong?"

For a moment a shadow moved across his assurance. "You are asking *me?*"

"Father Duarte says—"

"Father Duarte says what?"

She shook her head. Her voice came very low. "I cannot do what Father Duarte says."

His fingers reached again for the folds of her habit, held the dark material tightly so that his knuckles showed white under the curling hair. "Mariana, do you know what you mean to me?"

"How could I mean anything to you? I've been here in Beja all my life, and you've been all over the world . . ."

His fingers relaxed their grip on the material, moved slowly until they touched, through the habit, the long line of her thigh. "And never found what I was looking for until I came here."

Her body stiffened but she did not move away. "What are you looking for?"

"I'm not looking any more. I've found her."

Still not moving from the touch of his fingers through her habit, she looked directly at him. "What can you want of me?"

He answered only, trying to lighten the too heavily charged air, moving his fingers back to the resistance of marble. "The look in your eyes right now."

She started to turn away, then held her gaze. "That seems like a very small thing to give you."

"It is very much."

"I'm only a nun, and I've never—" She stopped, gasped, then went on, "while the women you've met in Paris and Lisbon must be full of elegance and wit."

"Yes, empty and shallow." He shrugged.

"I don't know how to talk to you—" She was almost panting. "If I don't say what's in my heart I get all confused. I don't know how to say the things I'm supposed to say."

His smile was gentle, as though for Peregrina. "I want you to say what's in your heart. Shall I tell you what's in mine?"

She nodded, breathing painfully.

"Oh, sweet Mariana, I'm not going to tell you what I came looking for, what I expected. You are nothing that I expected, or could even have believed existed in this filthy world. Dear girl, how difficult it is to talk to you here where at any moment some child may come running up, here where a bell may ring so that you will jump up and flee back to those white walls, here where one of the sisters may come walking, eternal beads clicking. How many times do I dare talk to you like this? or for how long? before Baltazar, before the other nuns will notice, will wonder? How can I tell you what's in my heart when I'm afraid that at any moment we may be interrupted?"

Mariana cast a half-fearful glance around her, but the path was empty, the browning lawn stretched to the hedges. "But if we're afraid of being interrupted—"

"Aren't we?"

Now she moved away from him on the bench. "Yes."

He challenged her. "And why?"

She moved still further, pulling her robes about her in a compulsive gesture of hiding. "The only time a nun should ask for privacy is to be alone with God."

He stretched his hands longingly toward her. "Mariana, I want to see your hair—"

Her hand flew up to the white wimple, the black veil. "Our robes are to—hide as much as possible anything that might be an earthly vanity. To make us as much like each other as possible."

He spoke softly, coaxingly, as though holding out a bowl of milk to a half-wild kitten. "Your eyes are so different from Baltazar's, from Ana's or Peregrina's. Is it the tiny golden flecks of light that seem to shine from within? And your hair—Peregrina's is chestnut and Ana has golden curls: and you?"

She did not move, but she seemed to draw further back. "Why do you want to know?"

He was pleading now. "Mariana, I am a soldier and you are a nun, but we are also two human beings who find pleasure in each other's company. And when two people like each other, when they find each other, they want to know everything they can about each other. I stand before you, right here, wholly revealed, for you to see. Is it fair that you should be hidden from me?"

She faltered. "But I'm not—an ordinary person—an ordinary woman—"

Again he stretched out his hands, bent his head towards hers so that the light fell on the scar across his cheek, the visible mark of his friendship with Baltazar. "And it's that in you that draws me to you. Mariana, is your head shaven?"

She shook her head in negation.

"But your hair is cut?"

She nodded.

"Very short?"

Again she shook her head.

"It can't be all artificial curls, like Ana's, nor a tangled mop, like Peregrina's. Is it curly?"

A faint shake.

"Chestnut, like Peregrina's and Baltazar's? Or gold, like Ana's?"

"Lighter—lighter than Ana's." She put her face in her hands.

His hands reached up to pull hers down. "Let me see your eyes. Golden eyes, lit by the Portuguese sun, brilliant, startling. Mariana, does your cell lead out onto the balcony?"

She nodded.

"Do you sometimes go out on it at night to watch the moonlight in the gardens?"

Again she bowed in acquiescence.

"Do you often see people on the road by the convent gates?" he asked.

Another nod.

"There have been a lot of soldiers lately, haven't there, and some of them drunk?"

"Sometimes."

"Do they never see you standing there?"

"If someone comes I step back into the shadows."

"And then you can't be seen?"

"No."

"Have any drunken soldiers tried to climb the convent wall?"

"Two of them did, once—"

"What happened?"

"Her Grace saw them and sent them away."

"How did she know about them?"

"They weren't very quiet."

"Suppose a soldier got drunk, but still climbed quietly. Do you think that's ever happened?"

She looked at him, not understanding. "Perhaps. But all he could do would be to wander about in the garden. The doors to the convent are all locked."

"And the doors to your cells?"

"They're locked, too. After we've retired. Sister Isabella goes down the passages and locks all the doors."

"So that you can't get out? Or so that no one can get in?"

The flecked eyes widened with surprise. "Nobody's thinking about getting out or getting in. It's simply a convent rule."

"But suppose you want to speak to someone?"

"We're in Great Silence from Compline till after breakfast."

"But if you should become ill during the night?"

"If we called, Mother Escolastica or Sister Isabella would come. Or Most Reverend Mother herself."

"Does she sleep lightly, like a true mother, one ear constantly listening for her children?"

She raised troubled, darkening eyes to his. "Why are you so interested in all this?"

"To know more of your life, your discipline, your Rule."

She relaxed. "It's light and easy for us all. When you serve someone with gladness then rules aren't hard to obey."

"Yes, we are alike, aren't we?" He pressed his advantage. "Orders that must be obeyed without question. For instance, there has been a small outbreak in the south again, and tomorrow I'm off once more for a few days."

"Again? So soon?"

"Orders."

"To go into battle?"

"Dear girl, I'm a soldier."

"Will there be danger?"

"No more than usual."

She breathed in, deeply. "I will pray for you constantly till you return. Will I—how will I know if you come back safely?" She clasped her hands in a childish gesture.

"I will come to you." He reached towards her again, but she drew away, hiding her fingers beneath her scapular. "Am I not allowed even to touch your fingers?"

She started to take her hands out but looked up and saw a man's figure hurrying down the path towards them, saw him over Noël's shoulder. She whispered, "Baltazar." Blood rushed to her cheeks.

Baltazar looked at the two of them. "I didn't mean to be so long. Aunt kept me talking politics. She knows more than most men, that old bird. Is it all right for you to be here, Mariana?"

"I'm free for a few minutes now. Monsieur le capitaine tells me," somehow she managed to make her voice sound casual, conversational, with only the proper edge of apprehension fitting for the subject, "that you're leaving tomorrow." Yes. She had been well trained.

Baltazar rested his hand lightly on Noël's shoulder. "Only for a short time."

"But there will be danger—"

Noël rose, and Baltazar took his place on the bench beside Mariana. "Where's your faith? You've never seemed this anxious about my welfare before."

"Haven't I? It seems to me you always scold me for worrying about you too much. And if I'm anxious it's because I know you have no fear of your own, and wherever there's danger you rush in."

"Danger's what makes life exciting. That's how Noël and I first became friends."

"Because you were the ones who volunteered for the dangerous missions?"

"There's safety in danger. It's the cowards who hang behind who lose out."

From behind Baltazar, Noël said lightly, "Bal and I are like cats. We have nine lives."

"And have no intention of losing them too soon. Come, Noël, it's time we got back." He rose, and Mariana stood beside him, her fingers plucking at her brother's sleeve.

"When will you be back?"

"We don't expect to be gone more than a few days. We should be back in Mertola by the end of the week."

"And then you'll come to Beja? And to Nossa Senhora da Conceição?"

"Don't I always? But it may not be possible for Noël."

Her eyes widened, but Noël stepped quickly back so that Baltazar could not see him, looked at Mariana, finger to lips, and shook his head.

Baltazar came forward, close to Mariana, speaking softly. "Everything is all right with you, Mariana?"

"Yes, Baltazar."

"You're not—disturbed about anything?"

"Why should I be?"

"I don't know. I just felt—"

"Everything's just the way it always is. Goodbye, Baltazar. God go with you."

He stood there, looking at her questioningly, but she simply returned his gaze, standing her ground. At last he turned on his heel, abruptly, and stalked down the path, calling to the Frenchman.

Noël turned to Mariana, saying clearly, rather loudly, "Goodbye, Sister Mariana."

"Goodbye, Monsieur le capitaine."

He whispered, "I will come to you," turned, and ran after Baltazar.

. . . "He was, after all, a soldier," Charlotte said. "He must have seen death over and over again. Does it ever become less terrible? Does it to you? Because you see it, too—"

"It is always terrible," Dr. Ferreira replied. The spindly chair creaked beneath his weight. "It is terrible even when one is grateful for it."

"One can learn to accept it," Charlotte said. "At least one can hope to. Isn't that all? When I was little I learned to accept going to bed alone in the dark, being alone in the dark during vacations, no matter where I was, in New York with Reuben and Essie or in hotels in strange cities all over the world. But accepting it didn't make me any less afraid. Was death terrible to Noël, do you suppose? If he was so used to the death of the body that it didn't matter, that he wasn't afraid to go into battle either to kill or to be killed, then the death of the spirit would have seemed unimportant to him, too."

(Andrew had stood near her in the kitchen as she was preparing dinner, and had startled her by announcing in his clear treble, "I don't want to die." Still stirring her sauce, paying more attention to the double boiler than to the small boy, she answered, "Nobody does, Andrew." He asked, "Do you?" "No," she said. He pushed up close against her, saying, "But people get old and then they get wore out because they're so old and so then they has to die." But not just when they're old . . .)

She shuddered as the doctor took his smelly pipe out of his pocket, and a roll of tobacco. With quiet concentration he began the ritual of preparation.

Charlotte watched him until his match flamed over the bowl. Then she said, "He was a soldier, and it was different then. I mustn't imagine it like war today, with tanks and molotov cocktails and gas and bombs and mushroom clouds. But is death from a hand grenade very different from death from a cannon burst or a rifle shot—they did have rifles then, didn't they?—or a sword thrust? He must have seen men lying on the ground and trying to hold their guts into their ripped bellies. Don't you think it must have been terrible to him? And he must have killed. So the way he killed Mariana was not the first death for him."

The doctor puffed on his pipe. "You're not thinking about Noël, are you?"

"Only partly."

"Patrick?"

"The death of the body," Charlotte said. "The death of the spirit. It seems to me that I have known them both ever since I can remember and they grow no less terrible to me. But Patrick: it isn't just that he sees death all the time. It's that he takes it for granted. He isn't shaken and shattered. It is so commonplace to him that even—" She stopped.

"Even what?"

She could not answer him. He looked at her intently but did not repeat his question. She shook her head. "Patrick has only an intellectual knowledge of death. He doesn't see its obscenity. But I'm not an intellectual—"

The pipe went out. Slowly, patiently, the doctor lit it again. The door of the room was pushed open and the English setter padded across the softness of rug, put his forepaws up on the bed again so that he could touch Charlotte's fingers with the moist coolness of his nose, then sat on his haunches by the doctor. Automatically, without thinking, the doctor pulled his handkerchief out of his pocket and put it across his knees. "There, Gibb," he said. "Dribble on that." So had Charlotte put a diaper over her shoulder whenever she picked the infant Andrew up to hold him there, to burp him, to walk with him when he was restless.

"If I could understand about Mariana," Charlotte said. "Why, when she loved so much, her Frenchman treated her so cruelly—"

"You still don't understand?"

"She was so happy and then: *what started with such happiness is tears, and deathly despair, and I see no help anywhere.*"

"And you still look to her for help?"

"I have to look somewhere. Because I know now I shouldn't have come to disturb Violet. And she seems to be everywhere here, Mariana, the nun. I keep blundering into her. There were her letters in my room at the pensão. And the convent itself is still full of her. I

Love Letters

173

could feel her there so strongly. . . . And this house of Violet's. It is the way I would imagine the Alcoforado villa. And Tonio—Violet says he rides a black horse. He sees himself as Noël but he can't quite make it. But he's in love with Mariana, probably more than Noël ever was. And even you. The way you and Tonio were fighting that battle on the tablecloth, and then yesterday afternoon in the convent—"

"Charlotte," he said gravely (When had he started calling her Charlotte, as though she were a child, instead of the more formal, adult Mrs. Napier? He did not seem like one who would easily drop the formalities and yet the gentle *Charlotte* fell completely naturally from his lips), "You must not become emotionally dependent on your point of reference, whether it's the living and unpredictable Violet or the dead, misunderstood nun. In order for you to see yourself in relation to a point of reference you must look at it with dispassion and objectivity."

"I don't feel very objective."

"That is quite apparent. But, as you yourself said, your point of reference does not tell you in which direction you are going. And I think you came wanting Violet to tell you."

She moved restlessly against the soft linen of Violet's sheets, but said nothing.

"Charlotte." The doctor stood up, the gilt chair creaking as it was relieved of his weight. "You have told me that your husband does not love you, or that you feel that he does not love you." He walked heavily to the window and looked out at the driving rain. "Was this a sudden and unexpected discovery?"

"No. I've known it for a long time."

"But this trip to Beja—to Violet—was sudden and unexpected?"

"Yes."

"Did something happen, something new, to precipitate so radical a move?"

"Yes." She looked at the bulk of his back in the brown tweed suit. It was a good tweed; it had once been an excellent suit. Now he wore it shabbily, carelessly, and his bearishness was somehow comforting. She wanted him to question her; she could not tell him unless he was willing to probe deeper, as though for a hidden splinter, and why should he? Why should he care enough to spend the emotional and physical energy when he was—even she could see this—already tired? Out of concern for Violet, perhaps, so that she would not upset Violet. But why shouldn't Violet be upset once in a while?

"I wanted to get things in perspective," she said. "I was—I was stuck in the moment. I couldn't see beyond it. And it wasn't just that I couldn't see myself. I couldn't see Patrick any more. I couldn't see him any more than I could see myself." She realized with horror that her voice was quavering, though her eyes were painfully dry. "I'm sorry. I'm really not very bright, you know."

He turned from the window and came back to the great four-poster bed, lowering himself carefully again onto the small gilt chair. "You're beautiful, Charlotte. And I think you're loving. You have a giving heart."

"But people don't want—don't always want to be given to. Mariana—"

"Charlotte," he said. "You're Charlotte."

She tried to laugh. "That's not much. To be Charlotte. Look at my father. At Violet. Patrick. All the people I've loved. They have so much. While I—"

He was looking directly at her. She wanted him to reassure her. She wanted him to hold her. She wanted to cry, after this long, dry time, against his great shaggy chest, to have him wipe her eyes with the handkerchief he had spread over his knees for the dog. But he said only, "I want you to sleep now, Charlotte. I have left medication for you, and I will phone Violet this evening to see how you are. I will be by to see you tomorrow."

Disappointment burned in her. She turned away from him and pressed her face into the pillow. She heard his footsteps as he left the room. She jumped slightly as the cold nose of the dog touched her hand again, the beautiful silky, arrogant beast. He sat on his haunches and looked at her with canine concern. If she could cry now it would be all right. If she could put her arms around the dog and sob and let him lick the salt tears away.

There would not need to be any pretense.

But she could not cry and the dog dropped to the floor and plumed from the room.

Dr. Ferreira had left

The dog had left

And Patrick?

You left Patrick, didn't you?

Be quiet, Charlotte, you're not the center of the universe. So what makes you think you have any right to be loved? What have you got to offer anybody anyhow? except love? Your own undisciplined human love.

Why does the joy of love contain so much sadness?

We're afraid of the sadness because it grows and spreads and becomes too terrible to be borne. And because it leads to tenderness.

Tenderness.

The moment of tenderness, the undoing, unbearable moment of tenderness.

❖

. . . From Violet, once, after James Clement's death:

Charlotte was sitting on the black sofa in the library and Violet came in, as usual unannounced. She had a key to the front door but she seldom (out of respect for Reuben and Essie) used it, only occasionally late at night when she did not want to drag the old couple downstairs. Violet had rung, then, and Charlotte, not caring to see who was at the door, had not moved from the black leather of the sofa. Reuben had climbed up the steep, dark stairs from the kitchen and opened the door to Violet, and Violet walked directly to the library, to Charlotte. She saw Charlotte sitting hunched there where James Clement had so often lain. She said nothing. She only crossed the room to Charlotte and put her hand on the girl's head, stroking it. Just for a moment. Then she left the house, letting herself out and hurrying down the brownstone steps.

And it was as though a world of love had exploded within Charlotte.

It was enough. It was more than enough.

It was Violet's music translated into a physical gesture.

And once from Gus. Gus was an obstetrician and gynecologist who had the office next to Patrick's, who was their friend, and Charlotte's doctor. A day had come when a mild discomfort had suddenly

Love Letters

176

become exquisite pain and Gus himself had taken her to the hospital, had placed his hand gently, tenderly, on her belly, saying, "The pain will soon be over, love."

And then afterwards (it had been an ectopic pregnancy, there wasn't anything imaginary about it after all) he had stood by her bed and adjusted the needle in her arm for the IV and said, "You're a good, brave kid," and placed his hand again over the appalling soreness of her abdomen.

It didn't mean anything. It didn't mean anything at all. It was simply doctor to patient. To any patient.

So why did it mean so much?

And if it really meant anything, if it really on occasion did mean something, if it came where there was love, could one survive the juxtaposition? Could the physical human body take the enormity of the cross of tenderness and love?

Make me nothing, Lord, so that my pride will not get in the way of love of thee. Strip me as my cell is stripped so that my worship may be only of thee.

If she had nothing to give Patrick
except love
then what did Mariana have to give Noël
except the glamour of being a nun?
an affair with a nun
Yes, it was, after all, exotic
There was that to offer, even in those wild and wicked times when the golden calf of court and position veiled the cross and the blinding demands of the God who moved in a cloud because his brilliance was unbearable to the human eye.

The Frenchman would have come back from his skirmish in the south, and would easily enough have found an excuse to ride by the convent, by the balcony.

And Mariana would not have been there.

She would have obeyed Father Duarte in this at least.

She would have prayed. On her knees on the prie-dieu in her cell. At the altar in the chapel. She would have heard the sound of horses' hooves, the sound of trumpets, and she would have trembled and buried her face in her hands.

And then night.

The convent and the garden at night, bathed in moonlight, with the shadows long and strange and disturbing, unlike the shadows cast by the living fire of the sun.

There would have been no statue of Queen Leonora on the plaza then, because Queen Leonora was outside that time, still unborn, unthought of. But the plaza itself would have been there, and the marble benches, white in the moon. And inside, in the shelter of the cloister, inside, in the walled protected gardens, moonlight would have fallen. There would have been a hot wind blowing, a dry wind from the plains, so that trees, flowers, shrubs, would move lightly in its embrace. The night would have been filled with the sounds of the tropical spring, insects, frogs, the rustle of leaves already beginning to sound dry.

Then a new sound. A different shadow.

❖

Noël.

Noël, climbing the wall, dropping lightly to the ground, standing, listening . . .

. . . The tower clock struck the quarter hour, starting a sudden crescendo of insect music. A bird called. The Frenchman walked softly towards the moon-drenched buildings and stood in front of the balcony.

As though responding to an act of his will a shadow moved from within the shadows, stepped out of the protection of the shadows, then drew back swiftly and was lost in darkness again.

He called: softly: "Mariana. Mariana. I saw you step back into the shadows. . . . Mariana, I've come to you as I said I would. I want your prayers of thanksgiving for my safe return."

It was more than an excuse. He wanted her prayers. The dice at the playing tables must be kissed to propitiate them so that luck will not turn sour. After a battle the young warriors in their war paint must leap around the fire in a ritual dance so that the gods of victory will have their desire for human gratitude sated. So if Mariana thanked her God for his safe return he would remain invulnerable in the next battle and the next . . .

The nun stepped out onto the balcony so that the moonlight clothed her. She was dressed for the night in a hooded robe of pearly white through which the lines of body and limb showed more clearly than in the darkly concealing daytime habit. She stood strung taut as a bow.

The Frenchman spoke quickly, persuasively. "You understand why I had to come this way? Baltazar would never have brought me here with him again. I had to come to you alone. Mariana, you are more beautiful than moonlight on water. Mariana. I keep saying your name because when my lips touch your name they seem to be touching you. Mariana, what I feel for you can't be wrong because it flows from me so freely, like a clear stream of water gushing out of the mountainside. Mariana . . . stretch out your hand to me that I may kiss it once."

Slowly she moved to the edge of the balcony and leaned over the ornateness of the wrought-iron railing, stretching her arms out to him. But the balcony was just too high; their outstretched fingers did not quite touch.

He asked, his voice as soft and strange as the moonlight, "Can't you come down to me? Dear love, can't you come?"

"The door of my cell is locked."

"Mariana, is your heart locked to me, too?"

Her voice was dark, as though a cloud had come over the moon. "My heart feels—so strange—it has never felt this way before."

"But it's not closed to me?"

"I think it's—opening—for the first time. I'm afraid—"

Gently, as to a child: "Of your heart? Or of me?"

"Both."

"Not of me. Never of me. Sweet love, I want to help you, and I don't know how. All I can do is give you myself. All of myself."

She breathed in, sharply, painfully, "My heart—hurts—"

"When a door has been locked for a long time, the first turning of the key is not an easy thing."

"But I never knew my heart was shut!"

Quickly he put his finger to his lips to silence her, poised himself for flight. She reached towards him again, and, as the quiet surrounding them was undisturbed by her cry, he said, whispering, "Let me come to you. Just to kiss your hand."

"How can you?"

"Easily. Let me come."

"But—"

"For just a moment. For your blessing. To kiss your hand."

It was, as he had said, easy for him, agile and young, to climb up to the balcony, to stand beside her. Through the white gown her long limbs trembled. He took her hand and bent over it in a long kiss. Then he pushed her hood back. "Let me touch your hair—" He raised his hand to the soft, fair locks, silvered by moonlight. As his hand brushed over her hair, lightly, barely touching it, a long quiver shook her body. With the tip of one finger he stroked her cheek. "You're trembling." She started to draw back, but he took her hand again, pressing it to his lips. "Dear God, I love you."

She did not speak or move away. She stood there, her lips slightly open.

Slowly, gently, he put his mouth to hers. Then they moved, as though in a dream, out of the moonlight and into the shadows.

Into Mariana's cell.

. . . When she woke up the rain had stopped beating against the windows, and the sun, the first time she had seen the sun in Beja, sent its warm rays through the room.

She yawned, stretched. The bed lamp was still on, weak against the sunlight, and she switched it off, and picked up the letters, the Portuguese nun's letters.

Again she opened the book at random: *I gave myself to you utterly. . . . I gave my life to you the first moment I saw you, and it is my pleasure to sacrifice it to you. . . . Shouldn't I have given you everything that was most precious to me? Shouldn't I be glad that I did? I feel that I haven't loved you enough, or suffered enough for you. Once I had begun loving you, my love became my honor and my religion. . . .*

She let the book fall onto the covers.

How can she help me? How can she possibly help me?

What does anybody really know about her?

That she was willingly seduced by a French soldier of fortune.

That's all anyone knows for certain, and even that's not certain, so why do I care? Is it that I think she must have learned something about love?

Or about God?

God

I would like to swear, every blasphemous word I've seen scrawled in subway stations, on walls, in public washrooms

God

(But I don't believe in you: remember?)

She picked up the book: *Stop, Mariana! Stop wasting yourself in vain. You are searching for a love you will never see again, a lover who crossed the ocean to flee from you—*

Only it was I who crossed the ocean to flee from Patrick.

What did she do to make him go back to France? What went wrong? Was it because the whole thing was wrong? Because she was a nun?

Yes. That.

It could not be more wrong.

But it wasn't only that.

As Antonio had been at pains to make clear, those were other times, and the climate of thought was different, too.

But the weather of love? Were not its storms and sunlights always the same?

Mariana became a nun and she broke and betrayed her vows.

And I, in my own peculiar and different way, am doing the same thing.

I married Patrick. I made promises. But he made promises, too. As God did to Mariana.

And as Noël must have done.

So why did he cross the ocean to flee her?

She cried afterwards. But did she pray? I cannot cry. I have never known how to pray. I know the words. All the words I have caught and held within my memory. They have been, somehow, like ladders made of angels. My hands have reached up and clung to the rungs so that I haven't fallen.

Prayers are dangerous: sometimes they get answered.

He came.

He came to her at night. He climbed up to the balcony. What he could do once, he must have done again. And then, before dawn, before the sound of the key, he would have to leave the cell and the balcony, to climb over the wrought-iron balcony rail; he would have to drop to the delicate pattern of mosaic.

And she would lean over the balcony and whisper:

"Noël—"

"My love!"

"When—"

"What?"

"When will you come to me again?"

"Soon."

"Tomorrow night?"

"If I can."

"No, no, you must promise, tomorrow night, when it is light again—"

"Light?"

"I'm all confused. . . . Days and nights are turned around for me. When you're gone, then it's dark and I can't see. But when you come, then it's light again, and my eyes are opened. . . . Come tomorrow night and bring me my light."

"My dearest heart, you must trust me."

"I trust you with my life."

"Then you must know, you must understand, I'll come as soon as possible."

And where would he have been, those other nights? the nights he didn't climb over the wall and into her cell?

He was, after all, a soldier, a soldier of fortune. Did he, when they were apart, think of her as constantly as she of him? Did the intensity of his obsession end once his desire was fulfilled?

One would think so, according to the letters.

It was easy to imagine him in one of the gaming houses in Mertola or Beja, perhaps playing rouge et noir and leaning back in his chair while one of the innumerable women of the half-world bent over him, brushing her lips against his ear, so that he laughed . . .

Did he laugh that way when he was with Mariana?

And while he was laughing there in the wine-reeking, smoke-filled cellar, Mariana perhaps was sitting in her dark robes in the refectory, soft white shoulders covered in darkness, eating in silence with ritual gestures to ask for bread and water; Sister Beatriz at the lectern reading, voice low, dispassionate; another sister kneeling throughout the meal in penance for some offense . . .

Or perhaps he was at the Alcoforado villa, drinking wine, laughing (how easily his laughter came), dancing with Ana, Mariana's sister of the beautiful, golden, artificially arranged curls . . . brushing his hand for a moment against the smoothness of her shoulder.

And Peregrina. Peregrina home again, standing at the refreshment table, babbling to a young officer and eating cake: "There's my sister Ana over there with the French soldier, Noël Saint-Leger. He comes to see us at the convent with my brother, Baltazar. That's Baltazar now, the handsome one, with that red-haired girl. She's a cousin of Alipio de Vasconcelos. He has a daughter who's a nun at Nossa Senhora, but she's cross and never lets us have any fun . . ."

And Baltazar, leading his green-eyed beauty out of the great ballroom and into an unused parlor, kissing her lightly, laughingly, beginning at the fingertips and working up her arm and into the soft warmth of her neck, and laughter suddenly gone . . .

And Mariana, sitting on the browning grass in the middle of a circle of little ones, teaching them a prayer, saying the words slowly, syllable by syllable, while they repeated in chorus after her, looking at her with love and trust . . .

And Noël and Baltazar in the forest hunting wild boar, Noël with a snarl of pleasure rushing after one of the spiny-backed snub-faced beasts, plunging through the underbrush . . .

Worlds within worlds within worlds

"Here's lunch, Cotty," Violet announced, preceding the poker-faced Julia into the room.

"I think I was asleep again," Charlotte said. "That's all I seem to do, sleep. Is Dr. Ferreira doping me? I could have got up for lunch, Violet."

"Nonsense. João would be most displeased with me. And he's not

Love Letters

doping you. You had a high fever, your temperature is not yet normal, and he said that in any case you were in an appalling state of over-exhaustion. No wonder you fell apart. But we'll eat lunch together at least."

"And I'll get up for dinner," Charlotte said. "I feel much better. I can't just stay here and sleep."

"Why not? Don't make any plans before you're ready to."

"I'm not making any plans. I just want to get up for dinner."

Julia wheeled a serving cart over to the bed, took a tray from the lower shelf, put it on Charlotte's lap, then wheeled the cart back to Violet, who sat again on the chaise longue.

Then they were left alone. Where was the dog? He answered Charlotte by barking out of doors.

"Just soup and bread and cheese and fruit," Violet said. "I cannot eat a seven-course meal in the middle of the day and do any practicing in the afternoon."

"I haven't heard you this morning."

"No, child, you wouldn't, from here. I put the guest room at the far end of the house so no one would be disturbed by my noises. Of course I can't control Orlando Gibbons. He's enough to waken the dead." So that's what Gibb is short for. She went to the window and called out to the dog, "Gibb! Gibb! Be quiet." He went on barking. "It's the man with the fish," Violet said. "Gibb can't stand him. So I myself am rather on guard. I have great faith in Gibb as a judge of character."

"He's lovely," Charlotte said. "He came to greet me this morning."

"He approves of you, then," Violet said. "Good. I thought he would. He's my Beja dog. I can't travel with him because of the English quarantine rules. Julia's very fond of him and he's an excellent watchdog. He also is very fond of music. He'll lie absolutely quietly underneath the harpsichord for hours, and he never howls no matter how intolerably monotonous my noises."

"I like your noises," Charlotte said, "even when you do two or three notes over and over again for an hour."

"Why? There's no beauty in the struggle to maintain and improve technique. It's just what makes for beauty later on, one hopes."

"That's why, then," Charlotte said. "It gives me a sense of foundation."

Violet did not reply. They ate their soup in silence, delectable soup; wherever Violet was, she would see to it that she had a good cook. She broke off a crust of bread, cut a morsel of cheese. "Cotty—"

Charlotte looked at her warily, broke bread in her turn, waited.

"If you want to talk to me about whatever this is all about—"

Charlotte shook her head. "No. I'm sorry, Violet. I was all wrong. I acted out of darkness and—and shock. It was thoughtless of me, and stupid. I'll get up for dinner tonight, and tomorrow I'll go back to Lisbon."

"And then? What then?"

"I'll have to trust that when then comes, I'll know what."

"That's not good enough, not for any of us. I'm back to myself now, but you shook me, child. I was completely unprepared for my own reaction. I was suddenly a lioness and Patrick my cub. It was unthinking and completely—animal—and it staggered me, I who have never in the proper sense of the word been a mother. Nor was this a proper reaction. Let's start over again. As we were."

"But we aren't as we were," Charlotte said. "I'm not. You see, Violet—you must have guessed—I came to tell you I was leaving Patrick. And I think that still holds—leaving him. I don't think—no matter how differently I feel about things now—that I can go back to Patrick."

"No. You can't go back to Patrick. It's possible that you can go forward to him, but only you can know that. If you tried to go back then you'd only have to leave all over again. Nothing can ever be repeated. Ever."

"What about when you play the same fugue over and over again?"

"It's never the same. It's never repeated. It's better. Or it's worse. I go forwards or backwards. You don't want to go backwards with Patrick."

"No. But I don't have any idea what direction either of us is going. That's why I had to get away."

"What did Patrick do to make it so sudden?"

Charlotte did not answer. She had thought that she could tell Violet, that she could dump it all in Violet's lap, but she couldn't, not until she had stood aside and looked at it objectively herself.

Violet peeled an orange with delicate precision. "You're stronger than you think you are, Cotty. With all your softness and vagueness you're stronger than Patrick or I with all our drive. And you have a tremendous sense of identity, with your feeling for names. Don't you know that's why you were such a strange little girl about being called Cotty?"

"Only you call me Cotty now," Charlotte said. "My father is dead."

"And Patrick?"

"That last time I saw Patrick he was calling me names other than my own."

Did she still think of herself to herself as Cotty? Not so much, not since she had, as it were, grown up. At school her interior monologues with herself had been to Cotty. (Cotty, my girl, there is nothing to be depressed about; you'll see Father during the spring holidays and he'll take you to the theater. Straighten the seams in your hideous black school stockings, Cotty, you idiot, pull up your bootstraps and go for a walk.)

It was her father who first had started calling her Cotty, during one spring vacation in Egypt when Shepherd's Hotel had still been in existence. He called her Cotty, and Reuben and Essie picked it up, and she only told the loving diminutive to the people she cared most about. At school it was usually Lottie. Ursula, during the period when they both expected, with no work or discipline, to become famous actresses, was allowed to call her Cotty in private. And there had been three nuns, Sister Thomas More in England, and Sister Felicity (who had betrayed the name and all names by disappearing), and Sister Mary Michael in New York. It was this that had made her reluctant to give "Cotty" to Patrick that first night. But she *had* given it to him, and this kind of gift can never be taken back.

Nor should it, once accepted, be rejected.

. . . "I've never rejected you," Patrick said. "It's you who have rejected yourself. Over and over."

They had just come home from a dinner party. She pulled her dress carefully over her head and hung it up. "If you try to make me into nothing, then I have nothing to reject."

"You're drunk," Patrick announced.

She sat down on the edge of the bed and started pulling off her stockings. "In vino veritas."

Patrick asked her (now why would he ask her such a question?), "Did you ever think of being a nun?"

Surprised, she answered him, rubbing her fingers over her toes where her new shoes had pressed. "Yes. Once, when Father couldn't be with me for a whole summer vacation and I had to stay at school, and there were only three of us there who didn't go home or at least somewhere. I tried to make myself think I had a vocation. But my reasons were all wrong. I was terribly pious for about a year and then I began to see through myself." She stopped. "Sorry." She stood up, stretched, and began to turn down the bed.

Patrick said, "But I have a vocation, Charlotte."

Folding the bedspread she asked, "You mean you want to be a priest?"

"Idiot. Medicine."

"Yes," Charlotte agreed, rather bitterly. "I've heard your white coats, your scalpels, referred to as instruments of your priesthood."

"One can be serious about something without being pompous," Patrick said. "And I'm serious about medicine, Charlotte. It's part of me. Part of what I am. It's my relationship to God and to man."

"And your relationship to your patients?" Charlotte asked. "Don't they ever resent being just bodies to you, to be opened up and re-arranged and put together again? I'm not a patient, and I resent not being more than a body."

"Then stop flaunting your body about as you did at dinner tonight."

She sat down on the side of the bed again, her hand rubbing against the soft nap of blanket, shivering a little in her slip. "I dressed for you, Patrick. Not for the others. And so that I would still feel alive."

Patrick turned towards her then. "Work is what keeps me still alive, Charlotte. It's my safety valve. I order my grief through work. Why don't you—"

"I keep busy," she said, shortly. "I'm going to bed. Good night, Patrick."

He did not say good night. Good night, Cotty. Or good night, Charlotte. Or good night, Mrs. Napier. That's who she was, after all. She had accepted Patrick's name and she could not reject it.

No matter
No matter what

. . . "Patrick was no help to you when the baby died, was he?" Violet asked her.

"Andrew wasn't a baby, Violet," Charlotte said, her voice carefully controlled. "He was five years old."

"But Patrick didn't give you the comfort you looked for, did he?" There was no sympathy or compassion in the question, only a cool probing, as Patrick, perhaps, might have used a steel probe on the wound of a patient.

"Patrick had his own grief. And he was perfectly kind."

"But you needed more than that, didn't you?" The probe dug deeper.

"If we had been able to share it," Charlotte said. "But he kept it to himself. He took it to the office with him, and the hospital, and bound his wounds with his care of other people's hurt. He kept his own pain away from me. He didn't bring it home with him. And there mine was, naked and raw. And he didn't want it. I'm not blaming him, Violet. If I'd had anything to contain my pain I'd have used it, too. But I have no vocation. I'm not an artist or a scientist and I couldn't find God. I still can't. When Andrew died God went away and anyhow it wasn't God I needed and wanted, it was Patrick. I wanted the tangible comfort of human arms. At night when Patrick stayed in the hospital I walked in the park where I used to take Andrew to play, and everywhere there seemed to be lovers, and all I felt about me was a cold wind. And Patrick was in the hospital when he didn't need to be there. And I understand, Violet. I had nothing to clothe my grief in and its nakedness repelled him. But I am—was—am—his wife."

There was a heavy silence. Violet put her perfectly peeled orange on her plate, sat holding her fruit knife like a scalpel. "Are you sure you don't want from him what your father—"

"I had everything from my father that I needed," Charlotte said. "The only thing Patrick and Father share in common is a passion for their work. I married Patrick, not a father image. But I wanted some of that, too, I suppose. A marriage isn't just an isolated emotion. It's—it's everything."

"When Clement died—" Violet started, and stopped.

"We shared it," Charlotte said softly. "You and I. We shared his death. We were with him. We bore his pain together. Patrick was in the hospital operating when Andrew—it was in the middle of the afternoon. He had an emergency operation and I couldn't even reach him. It was spring and Patrick knew I let Andrew play out on the sidewalk after kindergarten. Where else is there for a city child to play? Most days I took him to the park, but— And he was up on the sidewalk. He was very good about that. He never went near the street. He was up on the sidewalk trying to learn to bounce his ball against the building. He wasn't very good at catching. But it wasn't that the ball had gone out into the street and Andrew after it. The superintendent was there, he saw the whole thing, the truck went out of control. It wasn't anybody's fault. Everybody said it wasn't any-body's fault, not even the truck driver's, because his accelerator jammed. But I always felt that Patrick blamed me, somehow, because I was home, because Andrew was out on the sidewalk, because I wasn't in the park with him. But I know that's not fair. I don't mean to sound Freudian, I don't know enough about it, but I'm probably wanting Patrick to accuse me of the guilt I feel myself. But we're not supposed to have senses of guilt, are we? That's old-fashioned. We can be nasty, but we can't be sinful."

Violet sounded angry. "I should have flown to New York."

"No. We didn't expect you to."

"Of course you didn't expect me to. Violet never does that kind of thing, does she?"

"No, Violet. No. If you had been with us, if you had been there when it happened, maybe we could have shared it again, the grief. But for you to have come—it wouldn't have worked."

"No," Violet said. "It wouldn't. But it's rather amazing that you know it."

Charlotte smiled wryly. "It's odd. You found early that you couldn't—that marriage wasn't possible for you. You've always been strong and alone. Like Patrick. And yet this is what I'm turning away from in Patrick, and turning to in you. And why, under the circum-stances, I should expect you of all people to be objective about my marriage—I do see how funny this is."

Violet got up off the chaise longue and took Charlotte the peeled orange. "Eat it." She crossed to the fireplace and stood looking at herself in the huge mirror over the mantelpiece. Her body was thin and hard from the disciplines to which she submitted it, but the hardness was not bony nor angular, was instead the firm and supple curve of rhythm. The hair above the light blue eyes was a silvery ash blond so that it was difficult to tell where and how it was turning grey. She wore a suit of English tweed but it had been made by a French dressmaker. She looked at herself with displeasure and turned back to Charlotte.

"Don't look to me for any kind of model when it comes to marriage. I dishonored and blasphemed mine. I did what I had to do. But that doesn't make it right. Clement and I—we used to talk about you and Patrick sometimes, and how the simple fact of your parentage was always going to be a stumbling block for you. But Clement's lacks as a father were less than mine as a mother."

"You said that when you left Patrick's father you did what you had to do."

"Yes."

"But you don't think I ought to leave Patrick?"

"Do you?"

"I don't know. You're Patrick's mother. I'm asking you."

"Don't try to make us alike because Patrick and I have a passion for our work. We're not alike. On the most superficial level I'm a woman and he's a man, and that in itself makes a good deal of difference. It is generally accepted that a man ought to care about his work. He is the one to support his wife and in other ways be the head of the family. By the way, he called again last night."

"Does he know I'm here?"

"You didn't want him going to the police, did you?"

"Did he tell you—"

"He told me nothing. He didn't even ask me. I told him. He didn't even try to explain a second unlikely transatlantic call. This, for Patrick, is extremely irrational behavior. Patrick may be a successful surgeon but he still has a New England scrounginess about money. If you wanted to upset him, Charlotte, you have."

"What did you tell him?"

"Simply that you are here. That's all. Nothing else. Just so that he would know where your physical body is. I think you do owe him that."

"I hadn't expected to keep it a secret."

"How seriously do you take your marriage, Charlotte?"

"Seriously enough for this." She closed her eyes. "I'll get up for dinner, Violet," she said behind the darkness. She felt Violet pick up the tray from the bed, heard her leave the room.

God.

I thought the baby was the visible sign of the grace of love. I thought my love of the baby was my offering of love to you. But there was no ram caught by the horns in the thicket for me, God. And I do not understand.

. . . "I do not understand," Mariana said, kneeling at the altar, waiting her turn to go to Father Duarte for confession.

"I do not understand," Sister Joaquina said, kneeling in the small dark box. "Abel brought the Lord beasts from his flock as an offering, and the Lord accepted them. But Cain brought the fruit of the ground and the Lord wouldn't accept it, and he didn't even seem to understand why Cain was upset at having his offering refused. Why, Father? Why wasn't Cain's offering equally acceptable?"

The big priest in his soiled, browning cassock sighed, "One explanation we are given is that Cain did not bring his offering to the Lord with love, though I myself see little indication of this in the text. But I have never tried to hide from you, my daughter, that there are many things under heaven that we cannot understand with our minds. There are many things that may seem to us in the light of our limited knowledge unreasonable. But isn't this because it is our reasoning that is inadequate?"

"Father, I don't know! I'm asking you!"

"Perhaps we've allowed you to do too much studying."

"I'm only seeking to understand."

"You must try with your heart, not with your mind."

❖

Joaquina's voice was muffled. "The heart gets bruised with too much rejection."

"Who is rejecting your heart?" he asked. "I know your father's coldness and indifference is distressing to you—"

She cut in, "I'm not thinking of my *earthly* father."

During Joaquina's confessions Duarte sat turned away from her, his face hidden, but now his gaze flickered through the small barred opening, rested for a moment on her pinched features, distorted by tension. "My child, explain yourself."

"I feel like Cain. I bring the Lord my offerings, and they are not accepted. While Abel—"

"Who is Abel?"

"Don't you know?"

"Perhaps I can guess who Abel may be in your mind, but I think you had better tell me yourself."

"Everything she does," Joaquina said, "the sun seems to smile on. If she plants flowers they grow. Whereas my seeds, if they come out of the earth at all, are scorched by the sun or drowned by the rain and wither and die. The children love her. They'll do anything she wants them to do. Whereas they disobey me, they play tricks on me, they laugh at me— And she never reads, she never studies, she never uses her mind, and she seems to know everything. And I work and work and nothing, nothing—"

"My child," the great warm voice could be formidably stern, "your relationship with the Lord is between him and you. It is not in comparison with one of your Sisters."

Joaquina held out her hand with the gold wedding band on the third finger. "Sometimes I think he doesn't care about me, that he's never wanted me for his bride. While she—"

"Sister Joaquina, these are evil thoughts."

"That is why I confess them."

"Go into the chapel and feel God's love. At first do not attempt to pray. Kneel there and you will feel it as bright upon your shoulders as the rays of the sun coming through the colored glass of the windows. His love for *you*. His love for Sister Joaquina. You are infinitely precious to him."

She responded with obedience but with little conviction. "Yes, Father."

Father Duarte, with a look of pain, raised his hand and murmured the words of the absolution. Joaquina, crossing herself, rose from her knees, pushed aside the heavy drapery that closed the confessional, and went into the chapel. Mariana, next in turn, brushed by Joaquina without seeing her. Joaquina jerked rigidly, trying to control her anger and resentment, staring until Mariana had pushed through the curtain and into the box.

Mariana knelt, her head raised unseeingly. She did not make the sign of the cross. She did not speak. On his side of the division Father Duarte sat, waiting, his head bowed onto his big, gentle hands.

At last he broke the silence. "You still do not feel that you can make your confession?"

She shrugged. "What's the use, since you won't give me absolution?"

"You still persist in continuing your sin?"

She did not meet his eyes. "I cannot feel that it is a sin. I have tried, and no sense of sin touches me."

"This is blind pride, Mariana."

For a moment her look flickered towards his. "I didn't think one could be blind and honest at the same time."

He sighed, the sound gusty and unexpected after their hushed voices. "I don't think you are being honest, either with yourself or with me."

"If I'm being honest with Noël, that's enough."

"Are you?" She did not answer. "And what about her Reverence and your Sisters?"

Now she looked directly at him, challenging, "Would you want me to tell them?"

For a moment he put his head in his hands. "My child, I cannot reach you."

Mariana spoke with a flash of her old, spontaneous kindness. "Oh, Father, please don't be distressed on my account. If you could only understand how happy I am then you'd know that such joy has no room for sin. You'd have to know." She turned away from his loving, anguished face. "Father, do you think Heloïse's love for Abelard was a sin?"

"Heloïse and Abelard," he said softly. "Paolo and Francesca. Tristan and Isolde. Is that it?"

"You say it yourself."

"You really see no difference?"

"Only in my greater unworthiness."

His voice was harsh and grating, as though the words cost him a tremendous physical effort. "Forgive me if I hurt you. My poor child, how can it be the same when the love is only on your side?"

"Only on my—"

"For him it is purely carnal, the coition of two bodies with no communion of soul. It is a denial of all sacrament."

"No!" Her cry rang loudly through the chapel.

The heads of the waiting, praying nuns were raised in shock and curiosity. For a moment Joaquina actually turned her head and stared at the closed confessional box. Then, as no further sound came forth, beyond the usual low murmur in which individual words were inaudible, the dark heads bowed again.

Father Duarte pressed ruthlessly. "It couldn't have destroyed you so utterly otherwise."

She looked at her hands, at the gold wedding band that was not Noël's. "Oh, Father, I hoped you'd understand, you of all people . . . Father, can't you believe that it does have meaning?"

His voice was the barest whisper. "Love always has meaning. But sometimes only God knows what it is."

 . . . "God knows you've told me nothing," Violet said. "I know and love you enough to think that there is something to tell."

"Yes, I'm sorry to be so stupid about it."

"All I can say, then, until you see fit to tell me—and I am not a priest, Charlotte; I cannot absolve either you or Patrick, you are under no compulsion to tell me, and your coming to Portugal in this abrupt manner is really no more irrational than Patrick's transatlantic phone calls—all I can say is that if you truly love Patrick then it doesn't matter what he has or hasn't done."

Charlotte looked down at her hands lying loosely on the bedclothes. "But everything matters, Violet."

"But not your marriage."

"What do you mean?"

"Even if Patrick has been unfaithful to you, in no matter what sense of the word, if you took your marriage vows seriously it doesn't matter. You know the words you said at the altar when you married Patrick. I don't need to remind you of them. Or, to go to a more secular source, *love is not love which alters when it alteration finds.*"

"But *I* didn't—" Charlotte started.

"You married Patrick of your own free will, didn't you? You entered freely into this relationship. You were quite clear about that, weren't you? Without freedom you cannot have anything but a mockery of love."

Out of her hurt Charlotte turned on the older woman. "So you mean we're free to do anything we want? You'd say it was okay if I—or Patrick—did sleep around?"

Violet stood up, stiffly. "You think that wouldn't be a mockery of love? Are you misunderstanding me deliberately? Or is it just because you're unhappy? Your suggestion would hardly fit my definition of freedom. I have to go practice now, Charlotte. Get up for dinner if you want to. I really don't think it will hurt you." (Was there an implied "I don't care"?)

After Violet had left the room, erect, rather stiff, not violent at all, Charlotte dressed, putting on a skirt and sweater. Yes, the rain had stopped. Sunlight, thin as bouillon, was streaming into the room, and she stood by the window and let the warmth flood over her. In the garden the grass looked fresh and green, and in contrast the evergreens were almost black against the pale, clean sky. The bare branches of the fruit trees were softening. If the cold did not return they would soon be in bud. Lovers would walk the roads, the streets of Beja, the convent paths, now only a museum, where once

But all love is only once, is always and forever singular.

. . . "We are taught that we must avoid singularity. Our habits, both those of behavior and apparel, emphasize this." How well she had been taught. How poorly she was teaching Noël. "It is only when you look directly at us that you can tell us apart, and even this should be made difficult by our downcast eyes and carefully veiled expressions. If you see us from the side or the back you will not know which one of us it is, Mother Escolastica or Sister Joaquina or even her Grace or—me. Our habits are designed to minimize as much as possible all discrepancies of age or weight or even height."

He broke brutally into the careful recitation. "So you think that all nuns are alike in the dark? That I couldn't tell you from one of your Sisters in bed?"

"That's blasphemous."

"No. I am not being blasphemous, Mariana. I only want to convince you that you are unique."

"I've never denied that. It's I who keep telling you that I am—different. And that I must not be—singular."

"You mean you want me to take on the whole convent? I'm not in love with a religious order. I'm in love with one woman whose name is Mariana Alcoforado and who happens, through no fault of her own, to be a nun."

"Stop—oh, stop—"

. . . There were happier times (weren't there?).

When he would come at night and leave before dawn. When the glory of their love seemed to burst the bounds of the tiny cell, of the convent, of the world, of time.

I love you. Oh, God. I love you.

Oh, Patrick. Patrick.

And then the infinite sadness afterwards.

"There are tears on your cheeks," he said. And kissed them, tasting the salt upon his lips, his tongue.

They talked, as the young and in love have always talked, of love and life and death and eternity, of man and God, of passion and passions. They stood in the aseptic kitchen of Violet's suite at the Plaza after an evening at the theater when Charlotte had come to the city from college for the weekend.

Violet and James Clement were in the living room, Violet having ordered supper, "For you do not eat properly, Clement. What are Essie and Reuben thinking of, to allow you to abuse yourself this way?" In the kitchenette Patrick removed ice from ancient trays that had to be run under hot water ("I do not care about modern devices," Violet had announced carelessly; she wanted the results of them, nevertheless; she herself would not of course struggle with the archaic ice trays), fixed four scotches, took two into the living room, came back into the kitchenette and kissed Charlotte. Then he sighed, heavily.

"What is it?" she asked, panic coming into her voice.

But Patrick smiled. "Sadness always follows intercourse, little Cotty, even intellectual intercourse."

She put her cheek against his dark dinner jacket; even his dinner clothes smelled faintly of ether and disinfectant.

Rubbing her softly between the shoulder blades he said, "That's how I know our relationship has become real. By this sadness. Because it means there has been intercourse."

Where has the sadness gone?

Without sadness there is no joy

And the strange thing is that that is not a contradiction

While there was sadness there was laughter, there was singing, there was soaring

Where has it gone? Is it only the sadness that distinguishes us from the animals? We take our bodies so for granted that we're hardly aware of them, of what extraordinary means of life they are. We think about them most acutely three times: when we experience a birth; when we make love; when we watch a death. Perhaps a fourth time might be when we watch someone we love dearly in sleep. The face then is utterly vulnerable although we are shut away from the sleeping thoughts or dreams. We become suddenly aware of the intake and outlet of breath, of the faint rhythm in the chest where the heart beats. The creature ˅ strains our senses with its incomprehensibility. But that is ˄

kind of body Patrick sees now when he looks at me. He sees only a *thing*.

... "To love God is to honor his creation." Mother Escolastica said so. A long time ago. But I remember. And you created Noël, dear my Lord, and I am honoring you in loving him. We don't learn to love you more by loving people less, or by refusing to love them. "But," Mother Escolastica had said, "by loving them differently, by stripping love of selfishness."

At night the gardens were alive with sound and shadow. Did the birds never go to sleep? The fountain caught the distant silver of the moon and the silver was sound as it splashed into the marble bowl. A burst of laughter came from the street, a scream (no one paid any attention to screams now), a snatch of song. Frogs. Insects. From the convent the heavy creaking of a door. A nun: a nun coming out into the arched cloister, the hood of her night robe up and shadowing her face, her white garment a lighter shadow moving against the white stone of the vaulted arch. A nun hiding behind the deeper shadow of a column, listening to a new sound, a sound of—what was it?

So that she saw, she had to see, as the French soldier climbed over the wall. He was careless now. He did not stop to listen, to hear her sibilant intake of breath. He did not stop to look around him, to see the shadow of robe against shadow of stone.

She stepped out from the archway and watched him as he ran lightly across the garden and climbed up to the balcony. She stepped further out, out, in plain view if he had turned his head (but, single-minded, he did not), and watched as the French soldier moved, quiet and supple as a cat, across the balcony and into Sister Mariana's cell.

Her breath came in shallow gasps as she stood watching. But he did not come out. The open long window to the cell remained a dark scar in the white stone of convent. The moon moved across the sky and struck against the watching nun, cold as a whip. How long had she been there? She shuddered under the moon's lash and went back into the convent.

When the moonlight left the cell they knew their time was over. Raising himself on one elbow Noël looked out the long window and across the balcony. The eastern sky was beginning to pale with a light warmer than moonlight. He sighed.

Mariana echoed his sigh. "It's almost time for Sister Isabella to open our doors."

"Sister Isabella can—"

She laughed, putting her hand over his mouth. "Hush. It's her duty."

He stretched, slowly, fully. "I don't want to leave you."

"You must. It's time. If her Grace should find—" When she talked of the abbess to Noël she used the secular form of address. She could not, though she did not know why, say "your Reverence" when she was with him.

"What would happen?"

She shuddered. "I don't know. When she's angry she's terrible."

"You're afraid of her?"

"No. Not of her. But of her anger. Of what she would do to us."

"That priest won't—"

"How could he? I've spoken to him only in the confessional."

"God, how can time go this quickly? I don't want to leave you. I never want to leave you."

She pressed her face against him, breathing in the warm scent of his flesh, his sweat. "But you're leaving me today. You're leaving Mertola. You'll be far from Beja. Why do you have to go?"

He touched the short, springing vitality of her hair. "Because I, like you, have to obey orders."

She pressed closer. "How do I know you'll come back to me?"

"I said I'd come back before, and I came, didn't I?"

"Yes—"

"How can you doubt me now? After tonight?"

Her voice still was muffled. "Perhaps I don't doubt your desire—"

He raised her head and lightly kissed her. "But how can I keep from being afraid that you might be wounded?" She traced with her finger the line of scar that ran across his cheek, the scar that had faded to a thin line. "Or—even killed?"

"Dear love, have you so little faith in your prayers?" A tremor ran through her. "Mariana, I know that I shall dwell in safety."

"How can you know?"

"Because at all times I shall be clothed in the protective garment of the prayers of the most beautiful nun in the world."

"After what has happened I haven't any more right to be called a nun."

"Do you think you're the only nun who ever—"

"Noël!"

He put his hand quickly over her mouth. "Hush, my love. I know. I'm sorry."

Tears rushed to her eyes. "If I thought I were like—everything her Grace has tried to keep this convent from being . . . if I didn't believe that this is different . . ."

"Different from anything in the world. And I believe in your prayers."

"But perhaps now my prayers will be blasphemies in the ears of God."

"Never."

"I wouldn't dare pray for you now."

A tinge of impatience came into his voice. "It's that priest."

"No. No, Noël. He loves me."

"How dare he!"

"Not that way! Like a father!"

"Then why can't you pray for me?"

"Because I'm afraid my prayers might do you more harm than good."

"Nothing you could ever do or say could be anything but good for me. But I'm afraid of what I may do to you."

She raised her head to look at him, and the last rays of moonlight glinted against her tears. "You've shown me what glory means. Noël. My heart. I have prayed. I pray all the time. When I go to Father Duarte I try, oh, God, I try to confess sin. I have tried to use the word *sin*. And the word *fornication.*"

He stopped her words with his lips. When she tried to turn away he said, "Don't be afraid of words. That's all they are. Words used by dirty-minded priests. They have nothing whatever to do with what happens between us." Again he kissed her, caressing her to quiet her distress. "Dear girl, I'm only a soldier. I've never had time to think much about sin one way or another. It's my mother who says the prayers for the household."

She forced herself to look directly at him. "What would she think of this? An affair with a—nun?"

A veil seemed to clothe his eyes.

(Things are different in Portugal. It's a backward country. Women are a simple and necessary part of life like eating and sleeping. Everyone knows that Portuguese convents . . . even in France it is assumed that the cardinal accepts his right to a woman as long as he is discreet . . . one simply observes the rules and doesn't think about these things or all the fun goes . . .)

"Noël?"

"I don't know."

As she had given him her body, so now she must give him her fears, because it is only he who can do what Father Duarte cannot do, absolve her from guilt. "Noël, it says—it says in the psalms that we are shaped in iniquity, that our mothers conceived us in sin. That the night that made you was sinful—No! Not if it was like our nights. I try to understand, and I don't understand anything except that I love you and that it is right. When I touch you my heart is so full of love that there's no room for fear. But Noël, when you're away . . . then I lose my faith and in the corners of my cell there's a lurking terror . . ."

What is there to do to silence her except to kiss her, to let her cling to him?

"I'm afraid because you're leaving . . . I'm afraid you may be caught . . . I'm afraid we may be discovered . . ."

"Let's exchange tokens," he said, smiling at her as though at a small child. "I want you to remember only the joy of our love and forget your silly fears."

She apologized softly. "I'm sorry."

"What are you going to give me?"

"Noël, a nun . . . a nun in our convent has no personal belongings . . ."

He reached into the deep pocket of her night robe. "Here. I'll take your handkerchief to the wars with me as a good knight should."

"Yes . . ."

"And I'll give you this holy medal my mother gave me when I left France on my first campaign." He took it off his neck and started to put it around hers.

"But she gave you this medal for your safety! You mustn't part with it!"

He brushed away her hands and clasped the chain about her neck. "Love, travels and battles are the ordinary way of my life. My mother's prayers won't leave me with the medal. Whereas you are starting on the first journey of your life."

Mariana closed her hands about the medal, the medal that was warm from the beating of his heart. "Journey? But I can't go with you! God knows I wish I could."

"No, my sweet girl. You are starting on your journey into the seas of love, and it's a dangerous voyage for you. You need all the safety I can give you." He held her close, as close as the medal had lain on his chest. Then, with a final kiss, he left the cell, the balcony, the enclosure of the convent walls.

Within the enclosure of the confessional she stood. She did not kneel. She would not look at the grief in Father Duarte's face. She did not heed either his words or his silence. She said, "If you cannot absolve me, then you cannot allow me to receive the sacraments."

"And if you do not, if I forbid you—and this is what excommunication means, Mariana, you know this—then what will it mean to your Sisters?"

She was rigid as an iron bar. "They have nothing to do with it."

"They have everything to do with it. You are a member of a community and you cannot sin in isolation. If I withhold the sacrament from you it would be a matter of great concern and confusion to them. You assure me that they know nothing. I, too, am interested in protecting their innocence. I cannot have your blind willfulness causing them pain. Therefore I am not going to excommunicate you."

"But if I receive unabsolved then I am committing mortal sin."

"Child. Child, you have involved yourself in sin to such depths that anything you do now only compounds it. Whatever you do. Whether you receive or do not receive. And what you do now in regard to the sacrament affects your Sisters more than it does you."

"But I will not—"

He lashed out at her. "What you will or do not will does not affect the sacraments nor the presence of our Lord in them. For your Sisters' sake I order you to communicate. Perhaps the virtue in the sacrament itself will be able to do for you what neither I nor any other human being at this point can hope to do."

"You don't understand," Mariana said. "For me he is all the sacrament I need. He is—he is the archangel Michael, he is

. . . "But he's her lover," Antonio said in surprise.

Violet was walking the length of the long hall. The harpsichord was at the far end, as distant from the group of chairs around the great fireplace as though in a concert hall. Joaquim was curled up on a huge white fur rug in front of the fire, sound asleep, his guitar beside him.

"You're mad," Charlotte said. She was enraged. Why did Antonio see nothing but sex? Her cheeks burned with more than the fever that had returned with evening, though not as fiercely as the night before. Violet had not in the end allowed her to come down to dinner, but afterwards, when Antonio and Joaquim came with their guitars, she had come down to lie on the sofa, wrapped in a soft rug very different from the doctor's moth-eaten one.

"But why? Why should they not be lovers?"

"Violet and Dr. Ferreira!"

"Yes. Of course. Everybody knows this."

"The things that 'everybody knows' are frequently not so."

"But why should it not be so?"

"Because they're too old." —Because it would be wrong; it would be a sin, new sin compounding the old sin. Because she was my father's mistress. Yes, in Beja that would be the word. She belonged to my father. She left her own husband. But she didn't leave him for father— That was years and years— And she left Patrick when he was a baby. If she has to, she will leave anybody. So why should I expect her to stay with a memory? Even the memory of James Clement?

"This is the first American thing you have said. We do not consider people too old for love. We do not approve of—what I believe you call planned obsolescence. We are not refrigerators to be replaced in ten years. That is a cold concept. We are warm-blooded and our blood does not turn cold when we have acquired experience. We find knowledge not dull but desirable."

"That's not what I mean," she said.

"But you are shocked. Why are you shocked? Is it that we have a different feeling about these things here than in America? Is it that you consider this kind of an affair to be sinful?"

Sin was not what she wanted to think about. Why did it keep coming up? It was, in any case, impossible for her to think of sin in connection with Violet. Violet was a point of reference, and a point of reference cannot, of its essence, sin. Therefore Violet could not sin. Therefore what was not sin for Violet might perfectly well be mortal sin for Charlotte. No, sin was out of style.

—But I have always had my own style, she thought with unconscious arrogance.

She looked rather wildly round the room. On a table between two windows was a photograph in a silver frame.

It was Andrew.

No black and white photograph could really look like Andrew because it could not show his extraordinary coloring. He had Charlotte's lemon-colored hair and Patrick's Celtic blue eyes with the great dark lashes. The black of the lashes and the paleness of the hair were in beautiful apposition. Nor could any photograph catch the moving joy of the smile that lit the entire face so that there was no contradiction between the dark and light. Nor could it catch the vividness of Andrew's conversation that followed her about as she worked in the kitchen, as she ran the vacuum: holding the handle of the vacuum—he called it helping—he had said one day, "The wind was blowing hard this morning and I decided the wind was God blowing. God blows all over everywhere, all over the earth, and all over the whole world, and all over the earth planets. Mummie, why does gravelty keep us down? What *is* gravelty?"

Gravelty was not keeping Charlotte down or even keeping her in orbit. She was blown out with the cold wind.

Antonio's eyes followed hers to the picture. "It is a beautiful child," he said. "Is it perhaps an early picture of your husband?"

"No, my son. Be quiet. Violet—"

The first clear notes from the harpsichord rang through the room. Violet sat upright, her fingers moving in strong and simple structure of one of Bach's Two Part Inventions, her horn-rimmed spectacles making her look more than ever like an owl. Was it precisely Violet's discipline that allowed such a sense of passion to enflesh the bones of the music? Charlotte had struggled with this particular Two Part Invention as a schoolgirl: could it have been the same music?

("But you must listen, Charlotte," Sister Thomas More had told her, coming into the room where Charlotte was practicing. "In a Two Part Invention it is not just a monotonous repetition of a single theme. Bach is saying something, something important, and he is saying this one important thing in two clear and separate ways, and you must keep them clear and separate, at the same time that you must make us know that they are uttering the same cry. And with Bach, dear child, it is always a cry of affirmation, of passionate affirmation.")

—If Violet has a lover, if Violet truly has a lover, if any one of her affairs is completely monogamous, it is her affair with Johann Sebastian . . .

Antonio leaned closer to Charlotte, whispering through the form of the music, "I wish you would let me help you. I could, you know."

She whispered back, "You already have. Thank you."

"You know that's not what I mean. You do owe some things to yourself, you know. It hurts me that there is the strange, longing sense of unfulfillment in you . . ."

("All this emphasis on fulfilling ourselves," Sister Mary Michael had said to Charlotte, "is backwards. We do not fulfill ourselves. We open ourselves up so that we may be filled.")

". . . I could help you realize what you really are. You don't know how remarkable a person you are. I have never met anyone like you. Please—"

"Hush. Don't talk while Violet's playing." She leaned back and closed her eyes until the last clear notes died into silence.

Violet raised her hands from the keyboard. "Now Tonio and Joaquim will play it on their guitars."

The little boy picked up his guitar, shifting his unchildlike attention from listening to playing. "The Bach, Jacopo," Violet called from the end of the long room. "The one with the two voices calling back and forth to each other."

The music came sweet, a little shrill, from the two guitars, the round treble Portuguese guitar in Joaquim's grubby hands (Violet had made him wash, but the dirt was permanently ground in), the conventional, larger Spanish guitar in Antonio's slender fingers. The combination of the two instruments had a strange poignancy, and it was this, together with the look of concentration on Joaquim's child's face that almost undid Charlotte, the look, and the way the boy's long lashes smudged his dark eyes in the same way that . . .

With a look of concentration as stern as Joaquim's she turned towards the picture in the silver frame, towards the little boy caught there in that one arrested moment of time, Andrew safely there in the silver frame between the two long windows, Andrew invulnerable there, time stopped, arrested, defeated.

She did not hear Antonio and Joaquim playing Violet's arrangement of the Two Part Invention, the theme moving back and forth from guitar to guitar, from the low voice to the high, questioning, answering, moving in time, in space; but when it was over she applauded, and Antonio and Joaquim bowed, first to Violet, then to Charlotte, as though to a large audience.

"We should play some fado for you," Antonio said.

She brought herself back into time, to winter in Beja, to Violet's villa, and asked with formal courtesy, "What is fado?"

"A special kind of Portuguese—I don't know—Dame Violet, what would you call it? Folk song? Ballad?"

"I would call it only fado," Violet said. "It is always full of *saudades*. And don't ask us to translate that for you, Charlotte, because it is a Portuguese word which is utterly untranslatable. It means, in part, passion, unrequited love, nostalgia, tristesse, but none of these or even all of them gives you a really adequate idea. Only the music itself can do that. One of your own songs, please, Tonio."

Antonio nodded submissively, but Charlotte suspected that he was delighted at being asked to show off. Joaquim yawned, looking younger than he was, looking not more than five, a wide, pink, kitten's yawn, then shook the tangled dark hair out of his eyes.

"Jacopo doesn't like fado," Violet said.

"This one," Antonio announced, "is, of course, a love song, specifically for Mariana." He spoke briefly to Joaquim in Portuguese, and the little boy struck a series of minor chords. "I have translated this into both French and English—German is not good for fado—and though I shall sing you the English version I think I am coming to prefer the French."

His tenor voice was amazingly simple, clear and rather light. Charlotte leaned back, looking at Violet who still sat upright on the bench of the harpsichord, listening with the usual severe consideration she gave to music that was not her own.

If I could know
If I could tell
How love can grow
And thrive in hell,
How heaven is caught
And held in sin
And a soul that fell
Has God within
I'd turn back time,
Enact again
A heavenly crime
Paid for in pain.

"But it's beautiful!" Charlotte cried. "It's lovely, Tonio!"
Antonio shrugged. "It's not much. Remember, Dr. Ferreira says there's a poet on every street corner. I'm just on one corner."
Why had that stuck so in Antonio's craw?
"Play it again, please do," Charlotte urged.

. . . a heavenly crime,
Paid for in pain.

She must have paid for it, Sister Mariana. The payment would have started long before she knew of it. It would have started the moment she replaced God with Noël, but, more tangibly, it would have started the moment the affair stopped being private, the moment that the watching nun saw Noël climb up to the balcony, the moment his friends realized that his visits to the convent were not the innocent times he tried to make them believe.

Was it simply that they knew him too well? That what had broken Mariana's life in two had not basically changed the Frenchman at all? That he was still one of them, hunting, drinking, going to the wine cellars in Mertola and Beja, where he would have, in the end, been unable to refrain from boasting . . .

"How could they ever have thought it could be kept secret?" Antonio asked as Joaquim curled up once again on the rug, though still holding his guitar in readiness, and Violet walked the length of the room to sit across from Charlotte. "I don't imagine he really wanted to."

Violet drawled, leaning down and touching Joaquim's tangle of curls, "Yes, it would have been quite something to brag about. Give him a bit too much wine, a few friends wanting to know why he was always riding off in the direction of Beja, and I imagine it would have leaked out."

"What is there," Antonio asked, "about a nun? Charl—Mrs. Napier has somewhat the same quality."

She cut him off sharply. "You make generalities about my being an American, you make generalities about my having been in convent schools. That's not how you write poetry. Poetry comes from particulars."

"I'm quite aware of that," Antonio flashed back, "and sometimes from seeing in a particular something particular that nobody else sees." Then he turned from anger to his quick, confident smile. "And of course that's when the trouble would have come. When this very particular romance began to leak out. If one of the sisters at one of your convents had an affair with a soldier, do you think she could keep it a secret for long?"

"You keep saying how different things were then," Charlotte said. "It's not the kind of thing that happens in convents today."

"But a group of people living together—any group of people—doesn't change that much. Don't you think it would have leaked out in Mariana's convent?"

"Yes," Charlotte agreed. "I suppose it would have, sooner or later."

Antonio said, "They'd have tried to hush it up, of course, to convince people nothing was happening, that it was just the usual unfounded gossip. But certainly sooner or later someone would have enjoyed making Baltazar suspicious. And then I see him as a clever one, that Noël Saint-Leger. I can just hear him pouring it on Baltazar."

Antonio's voice became smooth, frighteningly plausible. "As for my physical pleasures, dear Baltazar, I find they are sufficiently satisfied by the more acceptable local means. Even if your aunt's convent weren't different from the picture we've been given of Portuguese convents, I could hardly afford to get involved with a Portuguese noblewoman, nun or no. You ought to know that. I have my career ahead of me and you must be aware that I have no intention of jeopardizing it. I believe you told me—or your father may have—that your sister is being trained to become next abbess. She undoubtedly has the same sense of family obligation that I do."

Antonio leaned forward, poured a glass of wine, absently offered it to Violet, and continued, "You know that I am already betrothed, that my family has arranged a most profitable alliance for me, one that will be invaluable in furthering my career. As a matter of fact, I was going to tell you tonight, anyhow, I'll be returning to France any day. My father has sent for me, and I'll be going up to Lisbon or down to Sagres, wherever I can catch a ship at the earliest opportunity. Now do you understand? Are you satisfied?"

Violet sipped at her wine. "Absolutely. You've missed your vocation, Tonio. Go to Lisbon and try the stage. Meanwhile that candle on the mantelpiece is guttering. See if you can fix it. Or maybe there's a draft. Charlotte shouldn't sit in a draft."

. . . The candles, the two candles that were always lit in the chapel, flickered and the thin smoke rose from them, as tenuous as Mariana's prayers. She knelt with her arms stretched out as though on a crucifix, as though embracing the entire world. Her lips moved:

"I confess to Almighty God, to blessed Mary, ever Virgin, to blessed Michael the Archangel, to blessed John the Baptist, to the holy Apostles Peter and Paul, and to all the Saints, that I have sinned exceedingly in thought, word, and deed, through my fault, through my fault, through my most grievous fault. Therefore I beseech blessed Mary, ever Virgin—

"No, Lord, it's no use. I can't say these words to you alone any more than I can when I'm with Father Duarte. I can't say them. Not here with the blessed Mother. No, no, my dearest Lady, I can no longer pray to thee, not now that—

"Oh, my God, I am heartily sorry for having offended thee: and I detest my sins above every other evil—no, I don't detest them, because I feel no sin! How can I ask to be forgiven for what has opened me to light? My heart was closed in before, shut like a bud in early spring. And I didn't even know it.

"Oh, God, O my Christ, now that I know how to love Noël, I know how to love you better, too! Dear my Lord, our faith is a joyous one, and yet I am only beginning to know what joy means! If I have been wrong in my vocation—that is what I must ask forgiveness for, isn't it? The sins of pride in my vocation I've committed up to now. *They* are my sins. To think that I had a vocation was my sin. Oh, God, O gentle Father, I ask you humbly, isn't it right for me to go to my spiritual mother, to my aunt? If I have your permission first, then shouldn't I get the permission of the church? For I must leave here, mustn't I? I must show my love of you through love of him . . . I am right, I know that I'm right . . ."

. . . Antonio sang,

By the rood
And by the rod
What is good
And what is God?
Vast as water,
Bright as fire,
What is God
But man's desire?
Deep as earth
Soft as breath
Sharper than birth
Stronger than death
Is the vast God

Whose wrath is taught
Aught but the fear
Of being naught?

As Antonio stood, strong and beautiful, singing, Joaquim let the Portuguese guitar slip from his hands and drop onto the rug beside him. He gave his kitten's yawn. Violet picked up the guitar. Antonio continued,

Old as Adam
Is the cry
Since I think
Then I am I!
By the rod
And by the rood
I am God
And I am good.

Violet said with deliberate cruelty, "You could get a job in some night club. Your voice is not unpleasant."

Charlotte looked at her, startled at the ice in the voice, the rage in the light blue eyes.

Antonio shrugged sulkily. "You used to like that one."

"Never," Violet said. "Go home now, Tonio. It is much too late for Jacopo to be up. Be careful of him. *He* will be an important artist one day."

Antonio's words were brittle. "If you would be kind enough to have my horse brought around, I will be delighted to take Jacopo home."

"That damned black horse," Violet said. "It won't take you back into the seventeenth century. I would have sent you home in the car." But she rang and asked for the horse. "Just see that Jacopo doesn't fall off. Take care of him."

Antonio pulled Joaquim to his feet, not ungently, and without further adieux limped from the room. Charlotte and Violet stood watching in the wide doorway as he climbed up onto the horse's back, then leaned down and picked Joaquim up and set him before him, circling the boy with his left arm.

"He would like to be Noël Saint-Leger," Violet said as Charlotte followed her back to the great room, "but he lacks the real flair. He will never quite make it. Just as he will never quite make it as a poet. He is *manqué,* all the way down the line."

"Why do you say that?" Charlotte asked. "You were awful to him. Why?"

"Because he maddens me. He will never finish his book on Mariana. He will never pull it together and so he will never pull it off. If he could he might have something. But it is just a collection of hodgepodge lyrics and a confusion of history. Some of his lyrics are better than he knows; he cannot separate his poems from his blasphemies. He cannot tell the difference. In his work or in his life."

Charlotte said, "I found his songs very moving. They made me want to cry."

Suddenly the rigidity of Violet's voice and manner relaxed; warmth flowed back. "Charlotte, when did you cry last? I mean really cry?"

Charlotte did not answer.

"Cotty, I asked you. When did you last cry?"

"I almost cried this afternoon," Charlotte said. "And again tonight."

"But you didn't?"

"No. I don't know what happens. I was all ready. But the tears won't come."

"Are you sleeping properly?"

"No."

"Cotty—" Violet's voice was low, gentle, with the tenderness that came through her music but seldom in her spoken words and that certainly had been singularly absent during the evening. "Have you cried, really cried, since Andrew died?"

Again Charlotte did not answer.

"You have to, you know. For your sake. And Patrick's."

She stood with her back to the fireplace, twirling the enormous spectacles she wore only when she was reading, either words or music. Charlotte sat on the fur rug, where Joaquim had been, Joaquim who seemed to be in Violet's heart where Andrew might have been.

"Violet, it's not that easy!"

"Who said it was?"

"Good night, Violet. I'm going to bed now," Charlotte said, as she had said it once to Patrick.

Violet was, as usual, probably right.

But she could not cry for herself or for Patrick until she could accept those minutes of holding the small, broken, bloody body, and the child still alive

no God no no no

She had to accept it herself as everything, ultimately, must be accepted.

Can't we comfort each other? Ever?

The long French windows in her room were slightly open, but a fire had been lit and was blazing, warming the room with flickering light. Outside on the lawn Orlando Gibbons was barking, chasing a shadow.

She undressed, numb as from Novocain, and got into bed. The three books were as she had left them on the bed table, with the letters on top. She did not want the unhappiness, the naked anguish of the letters. The ordered life of the convent, where everything was structured, all questions answered, the safe world of childhood, yes. Even the mystical poems to the heavenly bridegroom, even the language in which she had at first thought the letters were couched, even this would be analgesia, anesthesia.

But the patient always comes out from under, doesn't he? That is, unless he dies.

The operation was a success, but the patient died.

Mariana, too, had been wakened from anesthesia, from the dream, not gently, as the Sleeping Beauty, by a kiss, for it was the kiss that had put her to sleep.

. . . So that everything in this dark spell meant something else.

Even the psalms.

Have I not remembered thee in my bed? And thought upon thee when I was waking?

Meaning within meaning.

Even in the midst of her dreaming it frightened her.

She went to Mother Escolastica. Her hands were trembling. "Please, Mother, I cannot hold a paintbrush today . . ."

The old nun looked at her, silent, searching. "What is it, child? What has happened?"

"I can't tell you."

Mother Escolastica stood at the tall desk in her tiny office. With her rheumatic joints, her painful back, it was slightly easier for her to stand than to sit, though nothing was easy any more. She looked from Mariana's trembling hands to her own gnarled and distorted fingers. "Have you spoken to Father Duarte?"

"Yes, Mother."

"Fully?"

"Yes, Mother."

"Then what is it you want of me now, child?"

"Permission to go to the chapel. I cannot work this afternoon. I—please let me go to the chapel."

Mother Escolastica studied the girl's clouded eyes. Usually she could read Mariana by those eyes. Now there was a darkness moving up from the depths through which nothing could be seen; it was like silt swirling in the disturbed waters of a pool. She could see nothing.

"For half an hour, then," she said. "After that you must join your Sisters in the attic. You must not shirk your assigned duties. Even for prayer."

"No, Mother. I—thank you."

In the convent attic, under the rather ineffectual supervision of Sister Isabella, the younger nuns worked on altar linens and vestments. Beatriz, Joaquina, and Michaela were mending the frayed gold thread on a heavy brocade cope. It was a feast day and they were allowed to talk. The attic was hot and crowded and musty, filled with candelabra, prie-dieus, unwanted gifts, all the paraphernalia of a large convent, as well as the magnificent linens and brocades of gold, purple, scarlet, blue, white, violet, black, many heavily embroidered and encrusted with jewels; these could not be taken out into the gardens to be gone over in the fresh air for fear that they might fade in the brilliance of the sun. Yellow light filtered in through small, high windows.

"Why," Sister Joaquina asked, her face damp and white from the heat, "is Sister Mariana staying in the chapel?"

"To pray, presumably," Beatriz answered dryly.

Joaquina asked, "Did her Grace give permission?"

Sister Isabella spoke with her usual mildness. "Sister Mariana's not in the habit of doing things without the Most Reverend Mother's permission," and moved across the attic to help another group of sisters fold a great linen altar cloth.

Joaquina murmured, her voice low so that it would not carry across the dusty room to Sister Isabella, "It seems to me that Sister Mariana's in the habit of doing pretty much anything she wants to."

Across the attic one of the sisters tried to muffle a dust-provoked sneeze and came out with a strangling coughing. Under cover of this, Beatriz said, "We're all tired of this kind of talk."

The dust made Joaquina's nose stuffy and her voice was unusually nasal. "I suppose someone always has to be the scapegoat. And I'm the one."

Little Michaela raised a shocked face from her work. "Sister, what's the matter with you today?"

Sister Isabella, whose ears were as sharp as her eyes were dim, returned and said with unusual asperity, "Sister Joaquina, if you do not feel well you will please report to the infirmarian."

"I'm perfectly well, Sister. I'm just very tired."

The dust and heat of the attic was irritating them all. Beatriz blew her nose, asking, "Why? We haven't done anything out of the ordinary lately. Nothing but our usual duties."

"No? None of us?"

Sister Isabella's face was distressed. "I know you took the lock-up for me this week, Sister. I'm sorry it tired you so. I won't ask it of you again."

"But Sister!" Joaquina cried. "You misunderstand! I wasn't thinking of myself when I said that perhaps one of us was doing something other than her ordinary duties. I was glad to help you for a few nights. We all know your headaches—"

Michaela, who more than once had bathed the old nun's pain-tensed brows with cooling lotions, asked earnestly, "Is it really quite gone now, Sister?"

"Quite, thank you," Sister Isabella said, and could not leave well enough alone. Her insatiable streak of curiosity made her turn back to Joaquina. "What *were* you thinking about, then?"

"Nothing. Nobody. I'm upset."

"But why are you upset?"

Michaela, her pliable face anticipating trouble, said, "We can see that something's bothering you, Sister dear."

With unusual acumen Sister Isabella asked, "Did something happen last night when you locked up?"

"Not last night."

"When, then?"

"The first night."

Were all the sisters in the attic listening? Sister Isabella drew in closer to the little group, almost whispering. "Then perhaps you'd feel better if you talked to us about it."

"Perhaps I would. Perhaps it's my duty to tell you."

At the word *duty* Beatriz looked up sharply. "Tell us what?"

"What I saw when I took the lock-up."

"What did you see?"

The four veiled heads were close. "I know you think I take my duties too seriously. Even doing the lock-up for Sister Isabella."

The air, too, was close. "No," Sister Isabella said, "our duties *are* serious. Even the most minor, like mine. Go on."

"After I'd finished locking up I couldn't sleep. I felt responsible. And then I heard—" Joaquina gave an ugly gasp.

"Heard what?" Beatriz asked testily.

The tension in the group was heavier, more stifling than the air. Sister Isabella tried to draw back from what she had started. "If you are telling us something of gravity, and I can tell by your voice that you are, you must be sure that it is true. Perhaps you should go to her Grace instead of talking to us."

Beatriz was suddenly irrational with anxiety. "We're always disturbing her Grace about nothings, and she's very tired right now. Let Sister Joaquina tell us what's on her mind and then if it's really serious enough she can go to her Grace."

Even through her fear Beatriz spoke with authority, but with such courtesy that it could not seem that she was usurping the prerogatives of the older nun.

"It's serious enough," Joaquina said.

Michaela dropped her hands, with the needle and heavy gold

thread, onto the cloth on her lap. "Oh, Sister, it sounds as though it were going to be something unpleasant."

"It is."

"Come on, come on," Beatriz said impatiently. "What did you hear?"

Sister Isabella reproved, "Let her tell it in her own way, in her own time, and with God's help. If she feels it is something that should be told at all." Perhaps if Sister Isabella had been able to see Joaquina's face, even now she would have stopped her.

"I would rather tell you first, then if you think—what happened was—I thought—I was sure—I heard something out in the garden. And I remembered how sometimes the soldiers—so I went and opened the door to the cloister. I didn't want to disturb you, Sister Isabella, or her Grace, unless I was sure there was somebody there."

"Quite proper," Sister Isabella murmured automatically. "Go on."

"I went out and looked around the garden. The moon was high and very bright. At first I didn't see anything, and I thought I must have been mistaken, that it must have been the wind in the trees or somebody going by outside the walls. But now I feel that I must have been sent out into the garden at that particular moment because—" Again the ugly gasp.

"Because *what?*" Beatriz demanded.

"Hush, Beatriz." Sister Isabella was as unrealistically romantic as Michaela.

Joaquina filled each word with portent. "I saw a man climbing over the garden wall."

Again Beatriz cut in. "What's so terrible about that? Drunken soldiers have tried it before."

"This wasn't a drunken soldier. But it was a soldier."

"So?" Beatriz masked her apprehension with scorn.

"You're trying to stop me from telling it, because you know what I'm going to say."

"No." Beatriz's voice was heavy with defeat. "I'm afraid, but I don't know. I apologize for interrupting you. Please go on."

"It's difficult for me. I don't like telling it any more than you like hearing it. But it's my duty. He climbed over the garden wall. Like someone who knew where he was going."

Sister Isabella asked, "Did he see you?"

"I stepped back into the shadows."

Beatriz's voice came clear and cold. "And spied?"

"What would you have done?"

"The same thing, I suppose."

At last Sister Isabella realized that she should never have allowed Joaquina to start. She realized, also, that if she sent Joaquina to the abbess now, she would never hear the whole story. She peered dimly around the attic. She saw a dark blur of discreetly bowed heads. Pulling more closely towards the three young sisters she whispered, Since you have gone so far you had better continue."

"He went to the balcony. He climbed up. He went across it and into Sister Mariana's cell."

"Stop!" Beatriz's voice rang across the attic.

Sister Isabella knew that she had let things go too far. "Come," she said, and shuffled across the attic and out the door and stood breathing painfully on the tiny landing that led to the steep, circular stairs. Joaquina, Beatriz, and Michaela followed. Beatriz closed the door, shutting them off from the others. Sister Isabella said, "Joaquina, you don't know what you're saying."

Joaquina stepped down two steps, bowing her head, muttering, "I told you that it was as hard for me to tell you as it is for you to hear it. I didn't want to tell you. You made me."

"You couldn't wait to tell us!" Beatriz, looming over her, cried.

Sister Isabella, wringing her hands beneath her scapular, tried to keep calm. "Please be quiet. Whether or not Sister Joaquina wanted to tell us or is doing a disagreeable duty is now beside the point."

Michaela sank down on the top step, crouching over, her head down on her knees. "I don't believe it."

Beatriz said, "Of course not."

Sister Isabella tried, too late, to mend matters. "You saw shadows, Sister Joaquina dear. You were mistaken, I'm sure. I've been out in the cloister on a moonlit night and I've seen shadows in the garden I thought were real, and then they turned out to be shadows. I've even disturbed her Grace for what turned out to be nothing but wind and moonlight."

"You saw what you wanted to see," Beatriz said, ruthlessly.

"No!"

"Sister Isabella is right. You saw shadows, and your mind distorted them and turned them into the image of a soldier."

"I know a shadow from the French officer who's been here in broad sunlight and spent so much time with Sister Mariana in the locutario."

She stepped down another step, as though fearful Beatriz would pursue her. "I spoke to him once myself when I was called to the locutario by mistake. The moonlight was as bright as day. Why would I invent such a thing?"

If Michaela had not been blocking the stairs Beatriz might indeed have gone for Joaquina. "Because you're jealous of Mariana!"

"I, jealous?"

"Yes, you jealous. She's everything you've always wanted to be and never will. She's always had everything you've wanted to have and never will. Gaiety and beauty and intelligence. *And* the French officer. If you dreamed you saw him going to her it was because you wanted him to come to you!"

Joaquina gave a harsh cry.

"We cannot have a lie like this spread about one of our Sisters, a lie born out of sick jealousy."

"I know what I saw—"

"You know what you thought you saw! What you went out to see! What you wanted to see!"

"Wanted!"

"You wanted to see a flaw in perfection! You wanted to see a stain on purity!"

Joaquina gave a strangled cry of denial and Sister Isabella's voice at last rose above Beatriz's. "Sister, you must stop this."

But Beatriz was beside herself. "I tried to stop it earlier."

"Sister Joaquina," Sister Isabella said, "are you very sure of what you have just told us?"

"You must hate me very much if you think I'd invent something like that."

Beatriz pulled herself under control. "Nobody hates you. We love you and want to help you. We know that you aren't inventing your story. We believe that you are mistaken."

"I was not mistaken."

"You felt responsible for us all because of Sister Isabella's headache, and sometimes a strong feeling of responsibility can excite the imagination. There was a breeze from the plains and the branches of the trees were moving. There were many shadows and sounds. It would have been easy for you to be confused."

At last Michaela raised her head, her face blurred with heat and consternation. "That is what we believe."

"Sister Joaquina," Beatriz continued, "you are asking something impossible. You want us to be absolutely perfect. And when someone shows the human qualities that all of us, being fallen creatures in a fallen world, must show, then you want her to be absolutely sinful."

Michaela's soft hands fluttered like small birds. "Dear Sister Joaquina, I talked to Sister Mariana once when *I* was upset. Why don't you ask permission to talk to her now?"

"She's the last person I could talk to."

"What she said that helped me most was to remind me that I'm human. Sometimes I think we expect too much of ourselves. We expect to be angels, now, here on earth. And isn't that pride? What do we have confession for if it isn't that we're supposed to have something to confess?"

Sister Isabella leaned against the wall, waves of dizziness rolling over her. She thought that she was going to faint.

Joaquina asked, "Are you trying to excuse what Mariana has done?"

"No," Michaela said with unusual firmness. "I'm trying to excuse what *you* have done. I don't believe you saw anybody. I believe you only thought you did."

Sister Isabella spoke through a sea of vertigo, her voice slurred. "Sister Michaela is right."

Joaquina came up a step, not noticing that Sister Isabella could hardly stand. "Sister Isabella, you are our senior here. What is your advice to me? Do you think I should ignore what I saw?"

"Thought you saw," Beatriz corrected.

Sister Isabella pulled herself away from the wall. She pressed her hands against her stomach as though to hold nausea at bay. She spoke slowly to try to control the blurring of her words. "No, Sister Joaquina. I do not think you should ignore it. But I think you must be very sure. And even then I think there should be an acceptance that there may be some confusion in your mind. But I think we must go to the Most Reverend Mother."

"Thank you, Sister. If I found the courage to tell you, I can find it to tell her Grace."

"And the humility."

Joaquina nodded. "May I go now?"

"I will go with you," Sister Isabella said. "You will have to help me down the stairs. Sisters, I think it best if you do not discuss what Sister Joaquina has told us, so I would prefer you not to go back into the attic, even in silence. Please go to Sister Maria da Assunção and tell her that I have asked her to assign you to something else for the next hour."

As they descended the attic stairs, Mariana was rising slowly from her knees in the chapel. She moved stiffly, for she had been holding one posture for a long time; she left the shifting facets of sun falling through colored glass and walked into the square chapter room where the Infanta Dona Brites lay in marble on her sarcophagus.

Michaela came running in from the opposite direction, having left the others to look for Mariana so that Joaquina's words could be denied. Both Mariana, in her dream of ecstasy, and Michaela, in her spasm of fear, moved without looking, and the two sisters almost collided.

"Michaela!" Mariana said. Jolted out of herself she looked into Michaela's wild, troubled face. "What's wrong?"

"Oh, Mariana, Mariana, please, please—"

"What is it?"

"Sister Joaquina—"

"What now?"

"She's been saying things—"

It was apparent that Michaela was trembling on the verge of hysterics and Mariana tried to shake off her annoyance. She made her voice calm and low. "Sister Joaquina has a habit of saying things. What is it now, to upset you so?"

"It's about you."

"Then forget it."

"But—"

"Sister Joaquina doesn't—approve of me. Don't let it upset you."

"It was far more than just disapproving. It was lies. Horrible lies. She said—"

Although Michaela paused, as though questioning, it was obvious that nothing could stop her. Mariana sighed. "Said what?"

"We didn't believe her, none of us did, but—"

"But you're not sure you don't believe her after all. Is that it?"

"No—no—but Mariana, you *have* seemed different."

Mariana was arrested. "I've seemed different to you?"

"It's just that—oh, you've always seemed happy before, so gay and full of enthusiasm—but now it's different—"

"Sister," Mariana asked, "what did Joaquina say?"

"That you and—you and the French officer—"

"What about us?"

"That he—Oh, Sister, I know it isn't true!"

"Sister Joaquina said *what* about Noël and me?"

Michaela's eyes widened at the use of the first name. "That he—that he climbed over the wall—and then up to the balcony—and then—You must tell her that it isn't true."

"I can't."

"But—"

"It is true."

"Oh, no, Sister, no, no, no—"

Mariana bent and took Michaela's face in her hands. "Sweet little Sister, let me tell you in my own words, not Joaquina's. Somehow or other she's made up a half truth."

Michaela drew away. "She says she saw him when she took the lock-up for Sister Isabella."

"Poor Sister Joaquina. Yes, it would have to be Sister Joaquina, wouldn't it? It doesn't matter."

"Doesn't—"

"I was on my way to her Grace when you ran into me and almost knocked me down."

"To *tell* her?"

"Yes, of course. To tell her. And to ask her to go to the bishop on my behalf."

Slowly the inner door to the chapter room was pushed open by Peregrina, who was closely followed by Urraca, Ampara, and Sofia. Peregrina, seeing the two sisters, turned swiftly, finger to lips, to silence the other girls.

Mariana said in her clear voice, "I want to be released from my vows here at Nossa Senhora da Conceição so that I may marry Noël."

Michaela gasped. "But Mariana, Sister, I don't—you—you're already married."

Mariana looked at her in astonishment that anybody could fail to comprehend her love. "You don't understand."

"But even if— Sister, you can't divorce Christ!"

With a peremptory gesture Peregrina shoved the other three avidly listening girls out of the chapter room and banged the door on them. Mariana and Michaela swung around as Peregrina demanded, "Does Noël want to marry you?"

The two Sisters turned in surprise.

"Does he?" Peregrina repeated.

There was a fraction's hesitation, then Mariana said, "Yes."

"Peregrina," Michaela said, "you should not be here."

Ignoring Michaela, Peregrina went up to Mariana. "Has he said that he wants to marry you?"

"There are some things that don't need saying."

Peregrina's voice, clear as Mariana's, echoed in the chapter room, "Mariana, I know you think I'm still a child. But I go home. I've seen how Noël behaves at home. I've listened to the way Dom Alipio and papa talk. I know that maybe there are things a woman doesn't need to say, but it's different with a man. Especially a soldier."

"Sister is right," Mariana said. "You shouldn't be here."

"But I am here."

Mariana turned from one to the other of them. "Peregrina. Sister, darling. Since I see now that it's going to come out—and it's inevitable that it should, though I hadn't meant it to be this way—I'm glad you can hear it from me, and not from anybody else. Don't worry. It's all right."

"All right?" Michaela cried. "But how?"

"I *know.* I know in a way that I've never known anything in my whole life before. Peregrina, you're right. You do know more about the world than I do. How on earth could I even have guessed? The knowledge of what a man is like, a whole man, is carefully kept from us. And why? If you could only know Noël as I do, the purity, the nobility of his soul! I had no idea— What men have I ever seen, here in the convent? Who, besides Baltazar?"

Love Letters

223

She turned to Michaela. "Sister, how can I tell you?—the blessed archangel Michael! A man can be like that, and worthy of worship. That's how I want to spend my life. Serving him and caring for him. Can't that be a vocation as noble as—can't it?"

Michaela's face was blurred with confusion, like a painting that has run.

Peregrina looked suddenly old. She said, as if to herself, "Papa shouldn't have—Aunt Brites—oh, I hate them both."

Mariana turned to her. "Darling, please be happy for me. Please want it for me. I'm so full of joy that I tingle with it from the tips of my fingers to the tips of my toes. I had a body before, but I never realized it. Oh, I thought I knew. But I knew nothing. Nothing. It was as though my body were blind. And now I can see. And I feel the rapture of a blind woman opening her eyes and seeing for the first time. Peregrina—Michaela—I know I am right because otherwise I couldn't talk to you like this without running full tilt against the word *shame*. What is shame?"

The door behind them opened and the abbess, unobserved, entered and listened until Peregrina turned away from Mariana in helpless anger and saw her aunt. The two of them, abbess and niece, stared at each other as Michaela faltered in answer, "It's what you feel when you've done something wrong."

"No," Mariana said. "That's guilt, and it's a very different thing. Shame is what you feel when you're afraid. When you're afraid to open yourself up to be a complete human being. The word *shame* and the word *love* seem to get mixed up together, and the word *shame* destroys the word *love*. And I won't let it happen!"

Michaela whispered, "You're different—"

"Yes, I'm different. I've just been born!"

"Be quiet!" The abbess stepped forward.

"Your Grace!"

"Sister Michaela," the abbess commanded, "go to your cell at once and wait for me there."

Michaela dropped a frightened curtsy and scurried out. The abbess turned to Peregrina. "Go to your dormitory. Urraca, Ampara, and Sofia will be there. The four of you are to remain in complete silence until I send for you. You, as an Alcoforado, are to see that silence is kept."

"Yes, your Grace," Peregrina said, and followed Michaela out.

The abbess turned to Mariana. "That was the most shameful display of carnality it has ever been my misfortune to—"

Mariana cut in. "If you can use the word *carnality*, either your ears deceived you or you misunderstood me completely."

"Have you no shame?" Her words dropped into the chapter room like marble.

Mariana turned a radiant face towards her. "Shame? For what is the greatest glory I have ever known?"

"Child, don't you realize what you have done?"

"Your Grace, you don't understand," Mariana said swiftly. "You don't know what it's about. I was just on my way to tell you—"

"I'm afraid I do know what it's about. I've just learned from three children in our school who overheard your wild words to Sister Michaela."

"They can't have heard me say that I was on my way to ask you to go to the bishop for me, to use your influence with him, so that I may be free to marry Noël Saint-Leger."

The abbess's eyes were pale and cold with bitterness and rage. "Sleeping with a man was a sin. Marrying him would be a catastrophe."

Mariana stepped back in horror.

"I *must* make you understand!" the abbess said.

"I understand for the first time," Mariana cried. "It's as though I went out on the balcony and saw the sun rise out of the east and the day break over the hills for the first time. For the first time I have seen day, I know light."

"Perhaps," the abbess said, "for him there have been other sunrises."

"He's a man! He's a soldier!"

"Precisely. You don't have the faintest idea what he's like. How many times have you seen him?"

"I don't know. Enough."

"Out of the locutario?"

Mariana nodded.

"In your cell?"

She nodded again.

"You admit it?"

"Your Grace, I told you I was on my way to you. I love him. I want to spend my life with him."

"Did you know what you were doing?"

"How can anybody know about—that—"

"Are you aware that you have sinned?"

Mariana raised her face. "God has not told me so."

"—that you're exposing your soul to eternal damnation?"

"You don't consider Ana's marriage a sin, yet she married Rui de Melo purely for prestige and property and there's never been any love between them. I love the man I want to marry. And you consider that sin?"

"Did your vows mean nothing to you?" Dona Brites asked hoarsely. "Nothing at all?"

There was a knock on the chapter-room door, and Sister Isabella came in, gropingly. "Your Grace—"

"Yes. Here."

Sister Isabella went to her and whispered. Mariana heard only the word *Joaquina,* saw the ripple of annoyance, but the abbess's voice was back in control as she spoke. "Very well, Sister Isabella. I will come now. Sister Mariana, wait for me in your cell."

226

In the abbess's study Joaquina was groveling and in tears. "Why are you so angry with me? I *did* see him."

The abbess spoke hissingly. "Your behavior has been beneath contempt. If you had the faintest glimmering of what the religious life is about, you could never maliciously have poisoned your Sisters' minds with vicious tales."

In an agony of sobs Joaquina fell to the floor; the shadow of the crucifix struck harshly across her as though with a blow.

The abbess stepped contemptuously around her and swept out of the room.

There are things that are unbearable.

. . . But the unbearable has to be borne. Is there anybody who has ever lived who has not been asked to bear more than is possible? And we do it. Most of the time we do it. Occasionally we go mad. We break under the unbearable.

We fill the mental hospitals. We shriek and scream the blasphemy of our horror. Or we retreat into silence, loss of movement, the rigidity of the catatonic. Or we regress to the slobbering, self-soiling, mewling of infancy.

—I didn't, Charlotte told herself. —In a sense I bore it. Someone sent my clothes to the cleaner's and the blood was removed. In a few weeks I was even able to go out whenever Patrick wanted me to. I stopped waking up in the middle of the night screaming. I cooked the things Patrick liked to eat. I bore it.

—So why is it still to be borne?

They had friends in to dinner. Sometimes when Patrick stayed at the hospital she went to the theater or a concert. Alone. Or with Ursula and her husband. Or with Gus Gregory who had the office next to Patrick's.

They stood, Gus and Charlotte, in the crowded lobby of a theater during intermission.

"You're nuts, Lottie," Gus said. "Both you and Patrick were given lousy deals by your parents."

"I wasn't!" Charlotte started.

Gus patted her gently between the shoulder blades. "I grow more grateful every moment for my nice, safe youth in Indiana," he said. "I'm glad I'm in New York now, I love this filthy, stinking place, but if I ever get married and have kids I'll be in a quandary, because I wouldn't change my childhood in my frame house and big back yard for any penthouse on Park Avenue."

"I don't think I'd change my hotels and convent schools, either," Charlotte said. "I think we like best whatever we've had."

"You're nuts," he repeated. "Most people spend the rest of their lives resenting their childhood and blaming all their problems on it. I thought I was unique in being satisfied with my parents and my youth."

"Do you think you're lucky, Gus?"

He smiled at her. "Yes. Yes, I do."

"Are you happy, Gus? I mean, now?"

People were bumping into them, jostling them, shoving out onto the sidewalk to smoke, pushing back into the lobby to get out of the cold. But Gus answered as though they were alone. "In a sense, yes. I'm happy in my work. I believe in it. It provides a creative satisfaction for me, as well as the fleshpots, which I also enjoy. But personally: I'm not unhappy, Charlotte, but if I'm happy it's a rather sterile happiness. My work is not enough. I'm not married to it. I, like you, need to be married to a human being."

Her voice was low, almost inaudible under the roar in the lobby. He bent his awkward, rangy body so that his ear was near her lips. "But you do have your work, Gus. You do have it."

"An operating table is hardly a bridal couch."

"But it's something. It's a focus for you. It keeps your life from being blurred."

"What blurs yours for you, Charlotte?"

She turned away. Without words she had already told him too much.

But he was good. He didn't force himself. He accepted it with awkward kindness when she said, "No, Gus. Please. Maybe I seemed to be asking for it, but it's not what I was asking for."

"For what, then, Charlotte?"

"To understand."

"What?"

"Anything. To understand anything. If I could understand just one thing . . ."

For the first and only time with her he sounded angry. "You little fool, you mean you're still looking for the meaning of life? You'd better grow up."

"How?"

"Stop looking for rational explanations of the absurd. That is what maturity means. Accepting the absurd. Not with resignation, but with love."

Gus continued, in his own loneliness, to take her that bitterly cold winter after Andrew's death to the theater, to concerts, to the opera. He was gentle with her. He was concerned. He watched for drafts. He walked on the outside of the sidewalk. He offered her cigarettes, knowing that even though she would refuse she liked to be asked.

He tried once to talk to her about Andrew. As she went rigid he took her firmly by the elbows. "I know it hurts you, Charlotte, but you cannot deny five years of a life. They were good years. They are part of what has gone to make Charlotte Napier." She shook her head. "I'm only a surgeon," he said, "but I know there are certain things that can't be cut out. You can't cut Andrew out."

Love Letters

228

"I'm not," she said. "Could we go somewhere and have a drink, please?"

They sat at a bar, sipping scotch and soda. At the end of the dark, narrow room a jukebox blared.

"I'm not cutting Andrew out," she said. "I couldn't do that. But all I see is what I saw when the superintendent called me and I ran downstairs. When I try to think of the rest of it—and I've made myself look at his baby pictures, and all the snapshots we took to send to Violet—the other—the other image—superimposes—"

His hand again held her elbow, his grip warm, strong. "It will go, Charlotte, and the rest of Andrew will come back."

It had been Gus who had met her at the hospital, who had done what had to be done, knowing that there was nothing to be done. It was Gus, not Patrick, who had shared.

"It was bad, Charlotte," Gus said. "It was as bad as anything can be. But you are alive and you have to heal. For Patrick. He cannot until you do."

❖

. . .—No, Charlotte thought. Not yet. I've done what Gus said and I've looked at Andrew, but I cannot look at this. Not yet.

She turned out the light in the large lovely room in Violet's villa and lay there in the enormous four-poster bed. The dog had stopped barking. Had Violet let him in?

For Violet had probably not yet gone to bed. She would have returned to the enormous room, to the harpsichord. She would be practicing, as she always practiced at night, as she always practiced when she was upset, and Antonio had upset her. Charlotte wished that the sound of the music would reach to this room in the wing where Violet had planned silence. It would help if she could hear Bach now: it would hold chaos at bay.

. . . But even the structure of the Divine Office could not hold chaos at bay in the convent. Who could silence Urraca and Ampara? Sofia's fat face was puffy from weeping. The sisters all moved warily through their silence, as though listening for something to break it. In the shadows of the gatehouse old Sister Portress sat and blinked, for once roused from her ancient apathy. She sat upright when Baltazar, on his white mount, galloped along the road in a cloud of thick dust, swerving to avoid running down a wagonload of gobbling, gabbling turkeys. He reined up abruptly at the convent gates, jumped down from his sweating horse and hitched him to the post. When old Sister Portress came hobbling out to let him in he brushed by her, hardly seeing her.

"Here, here, young man," she cackled after him, "where do you think you're going? Who is it you've come to see?"

In the wagon one of the turkeys lifted its head on its long skinny neck, and gabbled in accurate echo of the ancient nun.

Baltazar hurried along the path and into the covered walk of the cloister. With his head down, as though against the wind, he slammed through the convent until he reached the abbess's study. It was empty. So she was still in the chapel. He paced impatiently.

Morning prayer was ending. The chapel emptied in routine order, with the children leading the procession, the littlest ones first. At the back of the line Peregrina whispered fiercely to Urraca, Ampara, and Sofia, "If any of you says a word I'll kill you. I have her Grace's permission."

After the children came the postulants, then the novices, then the professed nuns according to rank. The abbess was last, walking with Mother Escolastica.

At this first hour of the teaching day Mariana was gathering the littlest children around her in the garden when Mother Escolastica approached. "Her Reverence wishes to see you in her study, Sister. I will stay with the children."

Several of the little ones ran to Mariana, clinging to her. She picked up one small girl who was clutching her robes, kissed her, and put her down. "I'll be back as soon as I can. I promise." She moved slowly to the study, delaying the moment of meeting, though hope was still stronger within her than fear.

She flinched as she saw Baltazar standing beside the abbess. She had not expected this.

"Here is your brother," the abbess said. "Go home with him."

Baltazar spoke with angry patience. "Aunt. If you would allow me a word."

"I do not see that we will gain anything by conversation. I cannot keep talk out of my convent while Sist—while Mariana is in it."

"Aunt!" Baltazar shouted. "Our father will not have her!"

"He will have to."

They were both ignoring Mariana. "Listen to me: papa asked me to come to you this morning—"

"He was too busy to come himself? After the letter I had delivered to him last night?"

Baltazar held up his hand in an impatient gesture. "Papa said, and I am forced to agree with him, that the best way to keep scandal from spreading is for Mariana to remain quietly in the convent. We have discussed the entire situation with Noël Saint-Leger. He is leaving for Sagres today and will sail for France from there. The less we ourselves make of this whole business the less it will be talked about."

Mariana had been looking in a bewildered fashion from one to the other. "Talked about?"

Baltazar asked, harshly, "Are you naïve enough to think that anything like this can be kept secret?"

"Well, I don't suppose it matters any more."

"Doesn't matter!"

"I have asked her Grace to go to the bishop for me. I want permission to be released from my vows so that I may marry Noël."

Baltazar groaned, "Oh, my God, Mariana."

She spoke with curious dignity. "Noël and I love each other. For us there are no vows except our vows to each other."

"Noël isn't going to marry you!" Baltazar shouted.

"You sound like her Grace," she said with a half smile.

"Mariana, how do you think I come to know about this?"

She looked at him trustingly. "Did Noël tell you?"

"Oh, yes, he told me and everybody else at the gaming tables too."

"No!"

Dona Brites snapped at Baltazar, "You knew before?"

"I knew but I refused to believe it. I imagine I was one of the last to hear. It's a little more difficult to brag about it to the nun's brother than to the others."

The fragile shell of Mariana's calm began to crack. "Brag—"

"Conquest of a virgin nun," Baltazar said bitterly. "This is really the grandest of all his considerable record of seductions."

With a cry Mariana fell to the low stool.

The abbess spoke brutally, as though the young nun were not in the room. "You have talked with this—man—about Mariana?"

"Yes."

"And?"

"I told you. He's leaving."

"Nevertheless I cannot keep Mariana here."

Baltazar flung his arms out. "Aunt! Papa doesn't give a rap if Mariana sleeps with the entire French army as long as she is discreet about it. She has not been discreet. If any word of this scandal gets out it will endanger papa's position at court. Therefore Mariana must be kept here and the whole thing hushed up."

"And you agree with this?"

"Whether I agree or not doesn't matter. The fact that Mariana may have feelings about this is as much beyond papa's comprehension as it is beyond his monkey's."

"Nevertheless, I want to know how you feel."

"If I knew perhaps I could tell you. Last night all I wanted was to kill Noël."

"Why didn't you?" The words came out before she could stop them.

"As a matter of fact, I had to be held back. Now, in the cold light of day, I think papa may be right for once, and that defending Mariana's honour is unrealistic nonsense. The only solution is for her to stay here in the convent."

"She has broken her vows."

"Aunt, I know that. But you know that she is innocent."

"Innocent!"

"As a child."

There was a knock on the door and Mother Escolastica looked in, nodded to the abbess. "Wait," Dona Brites said, and left, shutting the door on the brother and sister.

Slowly Mariana raised her head. "Baltazar, it's not true. Nothing you've said is true."

"God knows at this point I don't know what's true and what's false."

"I love Noël. He is my life. And he loves me."

"Noël doesn't know what love is. The breaking of a heart is his casual occupation."

"No—"

"And what about *your* vows? Do you break them as casually? What about your responsibilities here? Your responsibility as an Alcoforado to follow Dona Brites as abbess? Or, if you won't think of that, what about Noël? He has a career opening out before him, and a fiancée waiting for him in France."

Mariana cried out in uncontrolled anguish. The door opened. Noël stood there beside the abbess. Mariana flung herself towards him and he caught her.

"Wait, my darling."

The abbess held the door open. "You may have only a few minutes. I will be waiting."

"Very well. But I want these few minutes alone."

"Baltazar." The abbess jerked her head toward the open door.

As they left, Noël disengaged himself from Mariana and shut the door after them.

"Noël!" she cried, "what are they trying to do?"

He held her, caressing her, murmuring quiet endearments.

Her breathing began to come more regularly. "How could they have found out?"

"One of your Sisters here at the convent—"

"Baltazar thinks that you—"

"That I told?"

"Yes."

"What do you think?"

"That you'd never tell. Not at sword's point."

There was a dark sadness in Noël's voice. "Have you such faith in me?" For response she clung to him. "For me it was like being in heaven," he said, with the same deep sadness. "And now I'm plunged back into the world. And I have to think of what's best for you."

"You. You're the best for me."

"No," Noël said. "I should never— I understand that now. And the only thing left for me to do is to leave you."

"No!" It was the anguished scream of the bird shot in midflight.

Noël spoke through the cry. "The only thing—"

Mariana stumbled through his words. "Please—listen—I was going to her Grace anyhow. Even if nothing had happened. And I've asked her to get permission for me to break my vows so that I will be free to marry you."

"Dear Lord," Noël said.

"Don't you love me?"

"You know that I do."

"Then don't you want to be with me always, as I want to be with you?"

Noël pulled carefully away from her, took both her hands in his, and gently forced her to sit. "Mariana. Even if it weren't for—for what has happened, I'd have had to leave Portugal anyhow. My family has sent for me. Baltazar . . . , your father . . . , damn all of them. I could have told you so that it wouldn't have hurt you."

"Told me—"

"Sweet love, I'm a soldier and you're a nun. We both have duties to a rule that is more important than either of us."

"Nothing is more important to me than you are."

"That's not true. I feel as though I were being torn limb from limb. But I know that nevertheless I must go."

"You—you don't want to marry me?"

A note of despair crept into Noël's sadness. "I love you. You know that I love you. There has never been anything like this before in my whole life. There never will be again. But we both knew it couldn't last."

"Everybody acts as though marriage were a dreadful thing!"

"Marriage is a political necessity."

"It's a sacrament! A promise before God that our love is pure and holy, that it's not a sin."

"Our love has been outside the world," Noël said slowly. "That's the only reason it's been possible. Because it's something apart. Separate. More lovely than anything in the world could ever be. For me it's the only glimpse of heaven I ever hope to have. But Mariana, we must face the fact that I live in the world."

"Then I must come into the world to be with you. We'll bring our heaven into the world."

"Sweet child," Noël said in desperation, "I have commitments in the world that cannot be ignored."

Baltazar's words came back to her. "You mean you—are already betrothed?"

"Yes."

"Jesu—"

"It has nothing to do with us."

"Then it's like—Ana and Rui de Melo—isn't it—a political convenience—you don't love her—"

"Love and marriage have nothing to do with each other. You have duties to God that you can't avoid. I have duties to my king and my country and my family. My marriage arrangements are part of these duties. It's a question of honor. The arrangements are legal and binding."

"More so than my vows? I'm willing to break my vows."

"I must go," Noël said, flatly, "and you must let me go."

"And then?"

"You must go back to the life that I should never have interrupted."

"You think I can do that?"

He stood, looking expressionlessly at her, making no response.

"My God, Noël, no I can't! I can't go back! You've wakened me! I can't go back to sleep again! You've shown me the light! I can't go back to the dark!"

Noël spoke with desperate quietness. "I can't help what I'm doing. I have no choice."

Mariana's cries echoed through the vaulted room, seeming to hit against the clouds and cherubs of the ceiling, the intricate design of the floor. "Then promise me that you'll send for me! Or that you'll come back to me! Don't leave me without hope! You can't bring me to life and then throw me away to die! I love you! I can't live without you!" She fell on her knees at his feet.

"Get up," he said harshly. "Don't kneel to me."

"I don't care about Brites, about the bishop, about the rules. Take me with you on the ship! Don't leave me here!"

She was beyond reason, but still he tried. "You know that is impossible. It's a ship for fighting men."

"I don't care! All I want is to be with you. I don't care about anything else."

"If you were my wife you couldn't be on the ship with me."

She cried out again. "Noël! Don't leave me. My love will kill me. Take me with you. I'll die without you." She clung desperately to his knees.

He pushed her away from him and she fell to the patterned floor. He crossed to the door, turned back as though to speak again, then, with a helpless gesture, left.

She cried after him, once, "Noël!" Then she lay, face downward, stretched out in despair, her habit like a dark stain against the pattern of the mosaic.

The door opened and the abbess came in. She walked rapidly over to Mariana. She looked down at her, said, "Get up."

Mariana did not move, and the abbess bent over and started hitting her. "Get up. Get up. Get up!"

. . . "Wake up. Wake up," Violet said.

Charlotte sat up in bed, roused with a jerk from the deep pit of sleep into which she had fallen. "What—"

"Sorry," Violet said. "I knocked. I didn't think you'd be asleep so soon. I want to talk to you." She came across the room, carrying a dusty wine bottle and two glasses, Orlando Gibbons ambling amiably at her heels, and stretched out on the chaise longue.

"I couldn't practice," Violet said. "You and Patrick kept cutting across the music. So did my own thoughts."

Orlando Gibbons again investigated the bed and Charlotte in it, then returned to his mistress. Violet pulled a large handkerchief—one of the doctor's?—out of her pocket and spread it on her lap, but the dog flopped down on the floor beside her. For a moment Violet pulled affectionately at his ear, then she took the wine bottle and uncorked it, slowly, professionally, silently, poured, and handed a glass to Charlotte.

"You have no idea," she said, "you have absolutely no conception of what marriage is. And I find that I have to have rather more wine than usual before I can bring myself to tell you. What are you looking for, Charlotte? What do you want?"

Charlotte replied in a low voice. "I suppose I think there should be love."

"Love is a four-letter word. And you, having been wrapped in the cotton wool of those damn convent schools all your life, know nothing about four-letter words. Love is the wildest one of them all. We take it and we separate it and we are too cowardly to accept the violence of the union of all its parts. And a marriage that is a marriage has to accept this fusion. It has to be done, Charlotte. It cannot be evaded. I have been a coward all my life about love. You might as well face that about me. I do not like admitting it, but it is a fact. All I have been willing to accept in my relations with men is passion. Passion is a part of marriage, and a necessary part, but it does not endure unless it is sustained by a foundation of love that is—"

"That is what?"

Violet sighed, deeply, sadly, took a long draught of wine. "Endurance, for one thing. Acceptance. All people are impossible to live with, don't you know that? You are impossible—"

"I know—"

"Hush. Patrick is impossible. So what a marriage is founded on is a commitment to this impossible. You make promises when you get married and you stand by them. You stand by them no matter what. You stand by them even if you have broken them. And you break them over and over again, in intention, if not in act. And it doesn't matter. You still stand by them. I did not do this, Charlotte. Ever. I come closer to love now, with João—who refuses me passion, despite Antonio's insinuations—than I ever have before. We are not in love, you know, Charlotte; not in the sense in which gossipers would understand it. So perhaps I will not short-change him as I have everybody else I have pretended to love. I have loved nobody but Violet Napier."

"No—," Charlotte started to protest.

But Violet cut her off with an imperious gesture. "Love me for what I am, Charlotte, not for what you would like me to be. That is how you must love Patrick. You must love him for what he is. And you must love him for no reason. You must love him simply because you love him. It is an act of commitment. You have committed yourself to it. And you can do it. Where I could not, where I refused."

Violet paused. "You have a strange sort of virginal innocence, Charlotte, and this is irresistible to most men."

"But that's idiotic."

"It's not a physical quality. The fact that men confuse it with this is what makes the problem."

"I'm sorry," Charlotte said. "I still don't understand."

Violet leaned back against the chaise longue, looking up at the ceiling, her empty glass on the floor beside her. The dog raised his head and rested his chin in her lap and she stroked one of his ears, not noticing that he had carefully pushed the handkerchief aside.

"No, of course you don't. I'm speaking in vague generalities, am I not? Just to hear the sound of words. Any words. Because we're still leaving the important ones unspoken. Let us be silent until we can bring ourselves to say something."

Charlotte finally broke the silence. "After Andrew died—"

Violet did not move but she opened her eyes. "Yes?"

"Then I learned something about my father."

"What did you learn about Clement?"

"Before you came—before you knew him—he used to lie on the black leather couch in the library and go away."

"Away?"

"Yes. You never saw it. But I think you could have understood it. Better than I did. He used to lie there and—well, what I said: go away. I tried for a while to make myself think it was like the great Eastern fakirs who could lie down and leave their bodies and travel about among the stars. He was as far away as that. He was so far away that sometimes it was very hard for him to come back. But it wasn't out among the stars or anywhere glorious. I know where it was now because I have been going there."

"Where?" Violet's voice was gentle. "Where, Cotty?"

"Nowhere. The abyss of nothingness. You go there when there are things you can't bear. You go into the abyss so deeply that you barely exist. You go into nonbeing. And this is far more of a sin than getting drunk would be, or adultery, even. I wanted Patrick to bring me back to life. And when he didn't—wouldn't—then I was like—I don't know, Violet, somebody in a dream, not real. I laughed and dressed carefully and was charming when we entertained because I was afraid to be real. So he accused me of adultery. But you cannot do anything as real as sinning when you are in a dream."

"Wake up, Cotty," Violet said, still very gently.

"I am going to have to. But it is going to hurt, the way your foot hurts when it's been asleep for much too long and the blood starts flowing again. I don't want to hurt."

"All life hurts," Violet said.

"But it is glorious," Violet said. "It is filled with a wild and brilliant joy."

Outside the villa the moon shone on the white sand of the driveway. The poplars stood in dark contrast on either side.

. . . It was a night of wind and clouds and the moon occasionally flickering in a naked black patch of sky. A carriage rolled wildly up the driveway. In the carriage sat the abbess, her features cold and rigid. Beside her was Mariana, white, withdrawn, blind, like one dead.

She whispered faintly, "Where are you taking me?"

"To your father. Did you think I could keep you at Beja? For your information, I run a convent, not a whorehouse."

If Mariana heard she gave no indication.

As they approached the villa the lights were snuffed out, as though at a signal, one by one.

Dona Brites gave an angry murmur. "What does he think he's doing?"

The coachman climbed down from his high seat and rang the bell to the great front door. Darkness. Silence. The abbess leaned out the carriage window. "Ring again. Keep ringing until you're answered."

It was time outside time that they waited. There was no counting the minutes. The coachman rang. Rang.

When the door was opened an elderly servant, holding a torch, shook his head angrily, waving his hands in excited gestures of rejection. The abbess flung open the carriage door and stalked up the steps. "Let me in."

"I'm sorry, madam. As you can see the household has retired for the night."

"Then they will have to be roused."

"I'm sorry, madam. The master has given me orders—"

"Do you know who I am?"

"Yes, madam, the Most Reverend Mother, the abbess Brites, the master's sister."

"And you still will not let me in?"

"The master has ordered—"

She pulled out money. "And will you now obey my order? I tell you to open."

The old man took the money. "Well, if I didn't open to you, seeing as you're the holy abbess, it would be—"

"A black spot on your record. See that we have some light." She turned on her heel and went back to the carriage, beckoning to Mariana. The girl did not move or react in any way. The abbess reached into the carriage and dragged her out. Going up the steps Mariana fell, but Dona Brites pulled her to her feet.

Francisco Alcoforado's valet hurried down to them as they went into the great hall, saying, "Dom Francisco begs to be excused. He is indisposed and cannot see anyone." The monkey appeared chattering at the top of the stairs, slid down the banister, then ran back up the stairs on all fours, looking back at the two nuns.

Dona Brites ignored the valet and pulled Mariana up the stairs and along the wide, portrait-hung gallery, with the monkey dancing ahead of them until he reached a heavy door which he tried unsuccessfully to open, giving little mewling sounds of frustration. The abbess pushed the monkey away and flung open the door without knocking. Francisco and a chambermaid sprang apart.

"You may go now, Catalina," Dom Francisco said. "I'll call when I need you." The girl gave a nervous giggle, dropped a curtsy, and scurried out.

Dom Francisco turned angrily to his sister. "What is the meaning of this?"

The abbess pushed Mariana in front of her. "Your daughter."

Dom Francisco put out his hand in rejection. "I gave her up to God a long time ago. She no longer belongs to me, as you've so often reminded me."

"God, then, if you like, is giving her back to you."

He gave a grimace of sheer rage. "Oh, no, sister dear, neither you nor your God can get out of your responsibility that easily. You let the man into your sacred walls. I didn't. Now you have to stand the consequences. I don't. And I won't."

"You reject your daughter?"

"You think I'll open myself to be a laughingstock at court for this whore? Do you think I'll jeopardize my position because you can't make your nuns behave?" He gave a snarling laugh. "You're really very amusing, Brites."

"You don't care what happens to her?"

"I care enough to know that she has to stay in the convent. The only way to avoid a scandal is for you to keep things quiet and pretend that nothing has happened."

"So what she has done makes no difference? I'm to forget about it?"

"I don't care whether you forget or remember. That, like the girl, is your problem."

He moved deliberately to Mariana and struck her across the face. "You've made me look like a fool, you whore. Get out and never let me see you again."

She reeled. Dom Francisco raised his arm as though to strike her once more, but the monkey, gibbering, clawed at his hand, and he turned his wrath on the little beast, who fled, screeching, up the bedpost.

Dona Brites pushed the unresisting Mariana from the room, down the stairs, out of the villa, and into the carriage.

The carriage rolled back down the dust of the drive and into the heat of the night. Sheet lightning flickered behind the hills, the trees. The abbess thrust her face close to Mariana's. "For tonight only, do you understand? I will keep you for tonight only."

But if Mariana heard, if she understood, she gave no sign.

She was in the abyss of nonbeing.

The others could not, would not, so withdraw.

The convent, under the structure of order and regularity, tottered as the one night turned into days and weeks.

The lay sisters buzzed over the pots and pans, the laundry. The choir sisters were acutely aware of Mariana's empty stall. The children ran everywhere, listening, whispering.

"She wasn't in chapel this morning," Ampara hissed.

"She's been confined to her cell," Urraca whispered back.

"My father said," Ampara's sibilance continued, "that Baltazar

Love Letters

241

Alcoforado wanted to fight a duel with the Frenchman but his friends held him back."

"Stop it!" If Peregrina could speak loudly enough Mother Escolastica would come and stop them; but her throat was so tight that her words were barely audible.

"My father came," Ampara said with relish. "You should have heard him. He threatened to take me out of school if she stays. 'Who do you think this convent is for,' he asked her Grace, 'the scum that nobody else will have?' And her Grace said—you should have been there, you should have heard her, I've never been so frightened in my life—her Grace said, 'Yes!' and my father said, 'Get her out of here—'"

"Stop—" Peregrina whispered.

But Ampara went ruthlessly on. "And her Grace said—I was there, I heard it, I'm not making it up—'My dear sir,' she said, 'where do you think she'll go if I don't keep her? Out on the streets. Because there's no place else for her to go. Would you have that?' And my father said, 'If Alcoforado won't have her, he is putting her on the streets, not I!'"

At last Peregrina's voice rang clear. "Be quiet!"

At the harsh sound that shattered the quiet, Mother Escolastica at last looked up from Sofia's work. Why had she been paying so much attention to Sofia's needlework which everybody knew was impossible? Ampara and Urraca bent diligently over their sewing. Mother Escolastica started sharply, "Peregrina, if you can't—" Then she saw Peregrina's face and moved quickly to her, putting a gnarled hand on the girl's shoulder, "—see well there, come sit by me where there's more light."

"My father came this afternoon," Urraca told the girls at bedtime. They were supposed to be in Silence, but no one had come to them, no one had put out their lights. They had evidently been forgotten and they took full advantage of this. "He told her Grace to get things under control. He said of course Sister Mariana should stay. He said everybody's taking it much too seriously. He has no idea of taking me out of school, worse luck. He says now maybe Sister Mariana will be worth something to them as a teacher. He has no patience with virgins."

One of the floating wicks flickered and went out. At last Sister Maria da Assunção came in. "Girls! Why are you still up? What is the meaning of this?"

The convent slept.
The abbess knelt in prayer.
Lord. God.
O holy Spirit, penetrate me now.
Let me know thee.
Break through my darkness.
Fill me.
Let me not remain closed against thee.
Tell me thy will.
Help me to obey.

All duties were rearranged by the abbess. Rules were made, were broken, by the nuns, by the children. A day of Great Silence was ordered. There was the sibilance of whispering hanging on the air.

Be quiet.

Mariana stayed in her cell.

Joaquina took Mariana's place with the younger children in the morning. The children cried, misbehaved.
Where is Sister Mariana? We want Sister Mariana. Why is she in her cell? When is she coming back to us?
Joaquina had to call Mother Escolastica to restore order.

Beatriz taught the French classes.

Sister Maria da Assunção was called in to help with Mariana's little ones. They cried but they did what she told them to. They played in the garden like little birds with clipped wings.

Old Sister Portress fell and was sent to the infirmary. Mariana took her place at the gate.

"How's *that* for a grand Alcoforado?" Ampara asked.

Urraca snickered. "Only a lay sister is ever Sister Portress. Never a choir sister. It's a servant's job."

Peregrina's face was white. She spoke through clenched teeth. "Be quiet. All nuns are servants of Christ. There is nothing that is too lowly. It is part of the obedience. Be quiet."

Ampara, smiling, asked, "But who will be next abbess now?"

Urraca purred, "Peregrina, I suppose."

All laughter had an edge.

All silence was noisy, like the insect-filled air about the compost heap behind the kitchen gardens.

"Mariana will be the next abbess," Peregrina said. "Be quiet."

The abbess spoke to the nuns. Her blue eyes were so pale they were almost white. Like diamonds, they could cut glass. "I am still abbess here. I shall see to it that my rules are enforced. Your behavior is execrable. Without exception. What do you take the Religious life to be? There is to be no more whispering. Silence is to be kept. Gossip in the mouth of a Religious is sacrilege. Don't you realize what you are doing?"

"It is not what we are doing," Sister Joaquina said during recreation, speaking loudly to nobody. "It is what she is doing to us."

But who was she?

. . . "Be quiet. I want to talk about myself," Violet said. Her spectacles lay on her two-day-old London *Times*. "I've bent over backwards in order not to manipulate people but it was really a shield to keep me from being involved. Whenever I've been involved I've been hurt. I was involved with Clement. And he died. Because I love you and Patrick I wanted to stay clear of your pain. If you're in pain now, Charlotte, at least you're alive and there's hope for you." She picked up the paper. Put it down. "I dreamed about your nun last night. What a fool she was."

"A fool?" Charlotte asked. "Yes, I suppose she was. But she was involved, at any rate. Maybe that's why I'm drawn to her."

"Remember, then, that she did end up being abbess of the convent."

Charlotte looked across the table in surprise. "She did!"

A deep voice said, "We know it from her death notice," and both women turned as the doctor came through the dusk of Violet's room and into the sunlight of the balcony. "Do you have a cup for me, Violet? I would like some coffee."

Violet rang for Julia, and Charlotte sat, eating croissant and apricot jam, while the doctor persuaded Julia that he had breakfasted, that he wanted coffee, nothing more. With his cup finally in front of him he leaned back in his wicker chair, stretching his great body comfortably. "She was an old woman when she died. In her eighties. Abbess of the convent after thirty years' penance. That's all the death notice tells us."

"From the letters, even the last one," Charlotte said, "there seems to be no penitence."

He shrugged. "What do you expect? It is sin that makes news, not repentance."

"But it seems so strange," Charlotte persisted, "that she would have been allowed to stay there, even demoted to portress. I don't see how the abbess could have let her stay. If anything like that had happened when I was at school it would have made an awful stink."

"Stink?" The doctor laughed. "What a graphic way of putting it, Charlotte. I imagine that is precisely what did happen. The convent must, indeed, have been in very bad odor. And I imagine the abbess must have been sorely tempted to throw Sister Mariana out into the streets."

"Why didn't she?" Charlotte asked.

Violet reached across the table for the butter. "What would you have done?"

"I don't know. I don't see myself as an abbess type. It's far easier for me to identify with Mariana."

"Then don't forget that Mariana became abbess, and that she was probably an excellent one. But first she would have had to do a lot of growing." Violet looked at Charlotte, then at the doctor, then buttered a bite of croissant.

"What would *you* have done, Violet?" Charlotte asked. "Would you have let her stay? What about its effect on everybody else?"

"I imagine that must have been considered," Violet said.

"Was it because she was the abbess's niece? Because she was an Alcoforado?"

"No." The doctor was positive. "Dona Brites, *because* of her family pride, would have considered that beneath contempt." He reached across the table, drew Violet's plate towards him, and helped himself to croissant, butter, and jam. "Remember that Dona Brites was struggling against all kinds of odds to run a reformed convent. Keeping Mariana would have made things exceedingly difficult for her."

Charlotte leaned back and watched him with affection. The sun warmed her shoulders. The hot coffee and milk, the croissants and homemade jam, were comforting. The fever was leaving her, but more than this it was the doctor himself who was part of her comfort; there was something safe in his very physical solidity.

He would always give his patients a feeling that he had everything under control, that he would never give way to alarm. (How different a doctor he was from Patrick, part of whose success came from his giving his Park Avenue patients a sense of urgency, of the dramatic, of the extreme importance of their most minor aches and pains.)

"Well, then, why did the abbess keep her?" Charlotte asked.

"Think about it. Think of the setup. She had every kind of woman there under her care, from the poorest peasant to the richest noblewoman. The rich were undoubtedly more of a problem to her than the poor, but she needed them. It must have been no trouble for her to understand why it's easier for a camel to pass through a needle's eye than for a rich man to enter the kingdom of heaven. Why do you suppose most of her boarding students became nuns? She'd have been lucky if half of them had vocations."

. . . "So what's to become of the girls who get sent to me, for whom the world has no place?" the abbess demanded. "Mariana was the one I thought had a true vocation. She had the gift of silence, the ability to be alone. Most important, she had joy. And she has destroyed it all. She has closed herself off entirely. Either she won't talk, or she talks wildly."

"This has been a devastating experience for her," Father Duarte said.

"For us all. That this could happen in my convent—"

"Are you thinking more about the reputation of your convent than you are about the soul under your charge?" They walked along one of the paths that led them away from the white buildings.

The abbess looked at him starkly. "Yes. I suppose it was pride, to think that sin could not come into this convent, where I had tried so to protect my Sisters from evil—" She looked around her at the peace of the garden, beautiful even under the tumid skies.

Father Duarte looked around, too. "Don't forget that the angels fell from heaven. Or that Adam and Eve sinned in Paradise. You cannot keep evil out of a *place*. Evil is born in the heart."

"And God hurled Satan out of heaven, did he not?" Brites demanded. "Nor did he allow Eve to remain in Eden."

The great gruff voice sharpened. "Take care, Mother Brites."

She bowed her head. "No, Father. I am not confusing myself with God. Nor my will with his. I only beg to know what God's will is." The priest did not speak. They paced the patterned path in silence. Then she continued. "Yes. I admit it. I have been proud. And I have allowed Mariana to be proud. In my own arrogance I have raised her too high. It is for my sin now, more than hers, that I must strike her down. *They that did feed delicately are desolate in the streets. They that were brought up in scarlet embrace dunghills.* For the salvation of us all I must strip her."

"And Mariana's salvation?"

"Isn't she already beyond salvation?"

"You don't mean that."

"I cannot keep her."

"Is the decision up to you?"

"No, thank God. It's up to the bishop."

"I did not have the bishop in mind."

"No, Father, forgive me."

Father Duarte said quietly, "You didn't really plan to go to the bishop, did you?"

"No. I cannot go to a Spaniard whose very presence here is an insult. And when I think that he supports his personal excesses by demanding concubinage money from his priests—No, I cannot go to him, Father, even if you were to command me to."

"Then I shall not endanger you by doing so," the priest said. "The responsibility for Sister Mariana is yours."

"You want me to ignore what she has done?"

The warm voice steeled again. "Not at all. Unless we can make what has happened have meaning for her, then indeed it will be our responsibility to send her away."

The abbess took several steps in silence. "I don't see how we can avoid it, either out of fear of scandal, or willingness to condone wrong."

"You're willing to risk her eternal damnation?"

Anger edged the abbess's voice. "She's already sold her soul to the devil."

"No, Mother. She's rejected the devil as much as she's rejected God. She's keeping her soul to herself, which is the most deadly sin of all."

"Then why do you want her to remain in the community?"

"Because I think her redemption is possible. The father did not turn away the prodigal son."

"After he had repented."

"You want to deny Mariana her chance to repent? What will her repentance be worth if we throw her out into the streets? Who are we to throw the first stone?"

The abbess said angrily, "More wrong has been excused in the name of Mary Magdalene than—"

"Magdalene died to her sins. She was born again. Unless there is repentance the stain of sin will not be washed away."

A slow, steaming drizzle began to mist their heads. The starched white of the abbess's coif began to wilt.

"If I let her stay they will say it is because she is an Alcoforado, because I am her aunt. There is no right thing I can do. If I keep her or if I turn her out I sin. If I turn her out I hurt fewer people than if I keep her."

"That is not the point. A soul is at stake here." Again the abbess raised and dropped her arms helplessly. Father Duarte continued, "In our search for God we can often proceed only by searching for the meaning of life. This is so important that we must be very slow to condemn any means that will bring us close to it."

"You're willing to excuse any kind of debauchery, by saying that it's a search for the meaning of life?"

He answered in an angry growl. "Mother, you are deliberately misunderstanding. People interested in debauchery aren't searching for the meaning of anything."

"Very well, what *is* the meaning of life? Do you know the meaning? I had thought that it was to love and praise God, but all I see is the reputation of my convent damaged and my own slender faith further shaken. And my child, my Mariana, has turned from a beautiful, vibrant girl into a ravaged whore. Does it have meaning, any of it? I manage the outward offices, the barren forms, while within me my soul withers in a world without meaning."

Now he replied gently, "This strange world in which you and I try to serve God often seems to have little meaning. Without him it would have no meaning at all."

She folded her hands again under her scapular, bowed her head. "Yes. Forgive me."

"Who do you magnify, Mother Brites?" he asked her. "Do you magnify your work? Or do you magnify the One who has called you to your work? Sometimes we Christians tend to magnify men's sins whereas we should magnify God's forgiveness."

"Yes," she said, her head still bowed. "It is difficult for me to accept that he can and does forgive where we can't."

"Let us go into the chapel," he said. "Alone, we can do nothing. But with God's help—"

The abbess's words were a prayer. "God knows we need it."

Mariana herself almost spared them a decision by trying to run away, to cross the ocean . . .

She hurried along a deserted road that wound through rocky hills; occasionally she glanced behind her as though afraid of being followed. She stopped in an agony of impatience as an old shepherd crossed the road with a large flock of sheep and she had to wait as they went by, the sheep *baa*ing, the big old sheep dog running after the younger sheep who tended to stray and herding them back into the flock. When she was able to proceed she ran until she was exhausted, then slowed to a stumbling walk. She was so tired that she no longer looked behind her for pursuers, nor realized that a peasant had drawn up to her in his mule cart until he stopped, tipping his cap and asking courteously, "Give you a ride, Sister?"

She looked up at him, smiled painfully, and nodded, climbing up onto the wagon without speech.

"Where are you going, Sister? Perhaps I could take you there."

Briefly she raised her downcast eyes. "I'm afraid not. I have business in Sagres."

"Sagres? That's a long way, Sister. You'll be spending the night somewhere, then."

She nodded, and began moving her fingers on her rosary to discourage further conversation.

The road left the windings of the rocky hills and cut across a vast plain. The peasant stopped his wagon by two stone gateposts marking the entrance to a long drive that led to a large yellow house. He looked at her shrewdly. "If you would care to spend the night here, Sister, my master is a devout man, and would be glad to care for you."

She shook her head. "Thank you. I must try to get a little farther."

"You needn't worry about my master, Sister. He's not like some with women, even nuns. He has a sister who is a Religious herself, and his mother would tend to your needs."

"No," she said. "Thank you." She climbed down from the wagon and started walking. The peasant stared after her for a moment, then got back into his cart and turned it up the drive.

The road narrowed, became a path, became at last a field of waving grain. She waded into it, and the grain moved like water about the dark folds of her habit. She could scarcely move, but she pushed through the tall, clinging grasses until she came to what must be the road she sought, but which was no more than a narrow path winding southwards. She stood at the start of the path, then fell to her knees and rolled over and lay down in the sharp grass at the side of the path, her vulnerable face exposed to the blinding sun.

A merciful cloud moved across the sky.

She fell asleep, moaning softly from time to time, a small, animal whimper. The clouds gathered, massed. Rain began to fall, in great soft drops, glistening against her face, her robes. The drops came more quickly, sharply, stinging her face, waking her. She sat up, not knowing at first where she was. Then she stood and started to walk again, lurching along the path. The rain progressed to a drenching downpour, whipping her wet robes against her body.

The sound of horse's hooves was muffled by the wet ground. Even when she heard she did not turn to look. The horse drew up beside her, and the rider bent down to her. It was the small, delicate French officer, Noël and Baltazar's friend, Mathieu de Berenger. "Sister!" he cried.

She raised her arm as though to ward off a blow.

"I won't hurt you," he said gently. "You're Baltazar Alcoforado's sister, aren't you?" She nodded. "You shouldn't be alone here so far from the convent, and in this storm. It's not safe."

"It doesn't matter."

"Where are you going? May I take you somewhere?"

"I was going—I was going—"

Realizing her distraught state he bent down closer to her. "Where, Sister?"

"To Sagres—"

"Sagres?"

"Somebody who might be there—"

He spoke to her kindly, but with firmness. "The ship has gone, Sister, and he with it." She shook her head, rejecting his words. "Let me take you back to the convent." She shook her head again. "Do they know you're gone?" Again she shook her head. "There's nobody for you in Sagres, Sister. The ship has gone. He has gone. He will not return. It's a long journey from here to Sagres for nothing. I'll get you back to the convent without anybody's seeing you. Nobody'll ever know. I promise you."

She let him help her up onto the horse before him, and they turned back, the horse moving swiftly through the rain.

So they had to make a decision after all.

. . . "Whatever I do now it is going to be wrong. Anything I decide will be wrong. Does that ever happen to you? that you get involved in wrongness so deeply that everything is part of it?"

"Daily," Violet said dryly.

"But I mean in the large things."

"Those, too."

"I came away to get perspective, to try to understand. But I seem to get more and more deeply into confusion. If I understand anything at all it's only by paradox."

"How else?"

"I wish I knew more about paradox, but I suppose if one did then it wouldn't be paradox. And yet I'm coming more and more to feel that this is the only way one ever understands anything at all. Never directly."

She looked apologetically first to Violet, then to the doctor. Since neither of them looked disapproving she continued, "If I'm to understand Patrick it will have to be this way, obliquely, by paradox and contradiction." She smiled unsurely at the doctor. "The way it is about your Portuguese nun."

"She's not my Portuguese nun," the doctor said.

"Tonio's then."

"Not Tonio's, either. He understands her least of all."

She pushed the thought of Antonio away with a shoving movement of one hand. "I guess I'm pretty simple if you compare me to Patrick, but even Mariana can be seen more clearly glimpsed out of the corner of my eye than if I try to look at her directly. We count so much on the looks of things, and yet what we actually see isn't really the object we're looking at, but just the minute part of it that our inadequate vision can cope with, and even that little bit we see upside down, and then our brain has to turn it right side up, to translate, as it were, for us. Since everything is upside down anyhow I don't see why it should bother me."

"I find it rather fascinating," Violet murmured.

Charlotte watched the gardener carefully watering the little row of seedlings—water, after all that rain? —and Orlando Gibbons chasing his tail in the sun and looking suddenly undignified. "Except," she said, "that I do want to see right side up and I haven't anything except my own inadequate understanding to do it with."

"That's all any of us has, Cotty," Violet said.

"But you always seem to know exactly what you have to do and how to do it."

"Perhaps the times I seem most sure are the times I am most unsure. A good deal of the time I simply act, with great positiveness and very little assurance. I have all the arrogance of utter insecurity."

"But you do act—"

"Don't try to imitate me. I have made as many mistakes as it is possible to make, and a few more besides. And Cotty, dear Cotty, you must stop making the error of thinking that the people you love can't do wrong. We can. I, in particular, have."

The doctor got up from his chair and picked up the breakfast tray around which bees were beginning to buzz. He moved quietly through the long open windows into the cool darkness of the house, leaving Violet and Charlotte alone.

"I do not go back on saying that I did what I had to do," Violet continued, looking not at Charlotte but at the withdrawing figure of the doctor. "But in doing it, I did wrong. To put it bluntly, I sinned. In a sense you are paying for my sin now. I am partly responsible for what Patrick is. Not entirely. I don't overestimate myself to that extent. Charlotte, tell me, what do you want for Patrick?"

"I want him to be happy and alive. And I haven't been making him happy. That's obvious."

"Do you think leaving him will help?"

"That's one of the things I came to Beja to find out."

"If you leave him do you think he'll get things in their right perspective again? Or will it be just one more betrayal in human relationships? First me, his mother. Then his father putting the South American aborigines before his son, though who am I to say he was wrong? I haven't the faintest notion. And then Andrew, Cotty. Just the fact that Andrew was killed must have seemed to Patrick another betrayal. And now you."

"You're putting too much on me," Charlotte said desperately.

"I, who of all people have no right to?"

"It's not that, it's—"

—if I could understand anything. Anything at all. Father said once that to love is to listen. I haven't listened to Patrick, but only to my own cries. Like Mariana.

If I could laugh again, God. That's what's wrong. I've forgotten joy. And it's the only thing. . . . How do I move back into joy? Sometimes Patrick and I in the middle of the night . . . what's happened to the fun? the wild glorious laughter? If we were still able to laugh he could never have said . . .

So I came to Beja in the middle of the winter

where Mariana

The winter is long. Joy is nipped by the cold, washed away by the rain.

But there are flowers. All winter long, beside the black wet branches of the fig trees, the naked crawling of the grapevines, there are the winter flowers. They are there, thrusting into bloom, opening to a sun that never seems to shine.

In the winter the children wouldn't have been able to work in the gardens, though it couldn't have been much colder out of doors than within the raw damp of those thick walls. But at least they would have been protected from the rain.

The older ones, the ones who would soon have to return to the world or accept the cloister for the rest of their lives, who would soon become someone's bride, man's or God's, were sometimes allowed to work in the library, taking over Mariana's task of copying and illuminating manuscripts.

. . . Ampara looked nastily at Peregrina. "You needn't sound so grand. Her Grace may be called before the Inquisition for keeping a certain sister here."

Peregrina rolled her brush carefully against gold leaf (Ampara was not allowed to use the gold). "You keep quiet."

Urraca purred, "Ampara's silly. My father says no Alcoforado's peccadilloes are important enough for the Inquisition to notice."

Ampara spat across the table at Peregrina, "Perhaps. But in any case my father says they're laughing at your father in court."

Peregrina rose, leaned across the table, and struck Ampara.

"Sister! Sister!" Ampara called. "Peregrina Alcoforado hit me!"

Sister Maria da Assunção came over to the table where the girls were working. "What's the matter, Ampara?"

"Peregrina hit me."

Sofia looked up from her copying. If her fat fingers could not cope with needle and thread they were meticulous with a paintbrush. "It was Ampara's fault. She asked for it."

"I didn't do a thing!" Ampara cried with injured innocence.

Sofia looked at Sister Maria da Assunção, wishing it were Mother Escolastica. "Ampara was talking about Sister Mariana."

Still full of innocence, Ampara cried, "I never mentioned her name."

"Was that necessary?" Urraca leered.

Sister Maria da Assunção drew in her thin lips. "Ampara, you know that we do not talk about Sister Mariana, even indirectly. Peregrina, you know that the Most Reverend Mother Brites does not allow any pinching or slapping. There have been too many complaints about you lately."

Peregrina looked down at her work, muttering under her breath, "I don't care."

Before Sister Maria da Assunção could come in with a reprimand, Sofia took a breath and plunged in. "It's not Peregrina's fault. People tease her about Sister Mariana's being locked in her cell when she's not in the gatehouse, and about her not being allowed to see us or teach us any more. Everybody thinks it's strange."

"It's not strange at all," Sister Maria da Assunção almost shouted. "Sister Mariana's not well, and her Grace wants her to rest all she can. That is why she has been relieved of her duties."

"If Sister Mariana's not well," Urraca asked slyly, "then why does her Grace make her be Sister Portress and sit at the gates?"

"Because it's quiet, easy work," Sister Maria da Assunção said, her voice still unusually loud. "I am ashamed of all of you. What would you think of the sisters if we gossiped the way you girls do? If you can't talk without upsetting each other and making up wild tales about one of the sisters, then I think you had better be in silence until Sister Beatriz comes to give you your French lesson."

In her cell Mariana lay face down on her bed. Her hard bed. The straw pallet on the narrow slab of wood was unkind to her bones. She lay not moving, not breathing. On her face. If she opened her eyes she saw only the rough blanket. Not the window. Not the cross.

A key turned in the lock and Mother Escolastica entered with a bowl of fish soup. She put it down on the floor by Mariana, stood looking at her. Then she sat down on the narrow pallet beside the girl and took her into her arms, holding her and rocking her as though she were a very small child. Mariana lay in the old nun's arms, rigid, her blue eyes vacant, the gold flecks dulled, almost lost. Suddenly she burst into a wild torrent of sobbing. The old nun continued to rock her. At last the sobs spent themselves and Mariana lay limply against the old woman. When Mother Escolastica saw that the girl was relaxed, she laid her gently down on the pallet and left the cell, turning the key in the lock.

When she was not in her cell, Mariana sat in the gatehouse. Old Sister Portress, retired, like an old horse put out to pasture, warmed herself by the kitchen fire and the kitchen gossip. Visitors to the gate were no longer welcomed by her toothless grin, her cackling laugh. She was missed. The only pleasure anyone had in coming through the gates now was in seeing a great Alcoforado brought so low, though the new Sister Portress herself seemed unaware of either who she was or what she was. Her face was indifferent. She did not speak unless it was absolutely necessary.

Beatriz went to the abbess. Her cheeks were flushed; she had lost her usual marble dignity. In the serenity of chiseled stone she was beautiful, but now life pulsed through the marble so that the abbess caught her breath, checked her sharp words, and listened with infinite sadness. It was Beatriz, she knew now, who would be the next abbess instead of Mariana.

"I do not believe that this is what is asked of us," Beatriz said, "to behave as though we were dead. It is in the first place arrogance to think that we can in human life—even the Religious life—attain this degree of beatitude, disinterestedness. I am alive and I am flawed and I am interested, I am passionately interested. What is happening to Mariana concerns us all. I do not believe that we are not intended to suffer from it, or that we ought to withhold our love. All we can

Love Letters

do is discipline our interests, all we can do is control it by the structure of the sacraments."

"And your vows," the abbess reminded. "You have promised obedience."

"I have not forgotten, your Grace," Beatriz said. "That is why I am here."

Michaela sought Beatriz out as she had once sought Mariana. "I can't find God anywhere." Her voice trembled, as it nearly always did now. "All I see and hear is the devil and I am afraid."

Beatriz sighed. "You are not afraid of God?"

"God is love," Michaela said.

"You are not afraid of love?"

"Love is supposed to be kind."

"Is it?" Beatriz asked.

Michaela would wander out to the gatehouse when she should have been helping Sister Isabella. She would stand looking at Mariana sitting in the shadows, but though Mariana seemed to be staring directly at her she did not in any way acknowledge her presence, and Michaela would flee back to the safety of work and rule.

Baltazar, too, went to see Mariana at the gatehouse. Sometimes she would speak to him, but usually she turned away her face.

Spring and the heat of the sun returned.

Baltazar stood with Peregrina on the dusty road outside the wrought-iron gates. The walls that surrounded the convent threw the glare back at them. In the thickening excrescence of wall that was the gatehouse the heat was fierce in summer, the cold bitter in winter. Old Sister Portress had kept the shutters almost closed against the glare of sun, the blast of wind, but Mariana simply sat there. The wind blew from the Alentejo plains, leaving a fine grey film of dust on her coif, her veil. She herself seemed as grey and lifeless as the dust.

Peregrina looked helplessly at Baltazar. "Where does she go?"

He shook his head, staring down at his feet, watching the bright polish of his boots dim with dust.

"She sits there and she is not there." Peregrina looked into the dark of the gatehouse. The open half door was like a gaping mouth in the white of wall. "It's like the saints when they're at prayer. They move so deeply into the mind of God that they are hardly in their bodies at all."

"She is not at prayer," Baltazar said sharply.

Peregrina wrinkled her face in distressed acknowledgment. "I know. But I don't know where she is. She just sits there, and she isn't there at all."

With an impatient movement Baltazar turned away.

"When she cries," Peregrina said, "I can understand that, Baltazar. I can understand it when she cries. She is alive. She is suffering. She—she wants something. But when she just sits there at the gates, the way she's doing now, and isn't there—I'm afraid."

"I have to leave," Baltazar said. "Go on in, Peregrina. You'll get in trouble with Aunt if you stay out here. I'll come back tomorrow."

The next day he returned, but not alone.

She sat there. It was not that she sat and endured. It was simply, as Peregrina said, that she sat there.

Two soldiers approached the gates but she was staring away from them, not into the dark shadows of the gatehouse, not, at this moment, into nothingness, but back into herself, as though she were looking down into the darkness of a well, the walls slimy, the water black and stagnant in the depths.

One of the soldiers was in Portuguese uniform, was Baltazar. The other was French. They dismounted and hitched their horses, and still she did not turn. Baltazar rang the bell.

She roused slowly at its clangor. She did, somehow or other, the habit of obedience not entirely broken, manage to perform the minimal duties of the portress. She turned. With a glad cry she rushed towards the Frenchman.

"Noël!"

But it was not Noël. It was little Mathieu de Berenger, who replied, sadly, "No, Sister."

She retreated into herself, into the shadows of the gatehouse. Where for moment there had been a strange and stormy glow, there was dark-

Love Letters

ness again. Baltazar moved into the shadows towards her. "Mariana."

She bowed her head in a mockery of greeting. "Baltazar."

"Will you talk to me today?"

"What about?"

"Please, Mariana, I have a suggestion."

"Brites will be delighted."

"Not for Aunt. She mustn't know. Will you listen at least?"

"I always listen."

"It may not be the right thing; I may be compounding the sin that has already been done. But I thought it might make you a little happier if—Mariana, if you want to write a letter to Noël, the Marquis de Berenger—" he indicated the Frenchman, "—will see that it reaches him."

Mariana whispered, "A letter?"

"If you want to write." Baltazar spoke loudly, clearly, as though she were standing far away. "If you think it would help."

Mariana turned slowly to Berenger. "You're going to France?"

"Not yet. But a battalion is leaving for Lisbon tomorrow and I'll see to it that anything you write gets into the hands of one of the officers I know to be reliable and discreet."

She murmured, half comprehending. "Yes. Discreet."

"And if there is an answer I will see that it gets to you."

"An answer. Yes. Yes. Thank you."

"Mariana." Baltazar's voice was urgent. "You must not let our aunt know that you are writing."

Her voice was scornful, almost careless. "What business is it of hers?"

"She is your abbess. She is your Mother Superior."

"I have no mother, natural, superior, or inferior."

Baltazar looked around, but Berenger had withdrawn to a discreet distance and was contemplating a clump of overgrown flowers at the side of the road. "I can't bear to see you like this."

"Then go away."

Stung, he replied, "I only came because—"

"To tell me that I might write a letter. Yes. I'm sorry. I'm grateful to you. And to you, monsieur," she called.

Berenger looked up, came back towards them. "It's nothing. If I can help—"

"Thank you. And now if you—"

"Yes." Berenger's smile was full of compassion. "I know you want to be alone to write. I'll go down the road and wait out of sight."

"I have to write now?"

"I'm afraid this is my only chance to come to Beja before—"

"Of course. I see. I'll be as quick as I can." With an abrupt movement, with no farewell or further thanks, she turned her back on them and went into the gatehouse.

Oh, my darling, if only you had known when you first came to me what was going to happen! You expected so much joy from our love, and all that is left is the pain of our parting. Will this separation keep me from ever looking into your eyes again, those eyes in which I saw so much love, which taught me so much, which filled me with joy, which replaced everything else in the world for me, which became my entire world?

❖

. . . "Still at those letters?" Dr. Ferreira asked, coming back out to the balcony. Violet had gone in to the harpsichord, leaving Charlotte sitting in the winter sun and relaxing in the framework of a pattern of four notes, repeated and repeated, tirelessly, rising to the balcony in the clear air. "Charlotte," the doctor said. "You had no business getting up and going downstairs last night, but it does not seem to have done you any harm. How is my patient today?"

She put the book of letters down on the soft linen of the tablecloth. "Thoroughly impatient."

"Good. So you will not be a patient much longer. Your temperature was subnormal this morning, but do not be surprised if there is a slight elevation this evening. It will not be as much as yesterday. Let us go inside so that I can listen to your chest again."

During the examination she watched him, studying the kind, tired face. His was not a vague, general good will that could fall apart under stress, but a specific, disciplined compassion. It would not alter, though it might alteration find.

As he put away his stethoscope she said, "I wish you were a priest."

"I am not."

"I would like to talk to you as though you were."

His great laugh boomed through Violet's room. "My sweet child, I am only an obscure medical man."

"I know, but—" Her voice trailed off.

He sounded gruff. "Are you still looking for that famous point of reference of yours?"

"Not the way I was yesterday. I just want to know—if you would tell me—I just want to know what yours is."

He answered simply, "For me it is God."

"Is it still?"

"Yes."

"What kind of God?"

"Have you ever read Plato's *Republic?*"

"Yes."

"You may perhaps remember, then, what Socrates said: *God is single and true in word and deed, and neither changes himself nor deceives others.*"

She nodded for a moment in silence. "If I can't find God I suppose it's more my fault than his, isn't it?"

He smiled. "It usually is. However, I do not ever presume to define God."

"But Plato—"

"Did not define him either, Charlotte."

"To give yourself wholly to someone—" Charlotte said. "It doesn't mean to drown him with you, does it?"

"No." He turned from her and sat down at Violet's desk, its inlaid top almost hidden by a disordered mass of papers and music manuscripts.

"I don't know what's right and what's wrong any more," Charlotte said. "Aren't there unalterable standards, doctor? Is it all right for anyone, even people like Violet and my father, to live apart from the laws that are supposed to bind the rest of us?"

(Mariana did. Wasn't that the trouble? She wanted it to be right for her to do wrong with Noël. She wanted special rules to be made for her. And when they weren't she got mad at God.)

"To give yourself wholly," she said. "What does giving yourself wholly mean? Did Mariana give herself wholly to God before Noël came to the convent? And then did she give herself wholly to Noël?"

"What do you think?"

"To neither. Not in the way you're talking about it. So how, in the end, could she learn what giving wholly means?"

"The same way Charlotte is learning it."

"Is Charlotte learning it?"

He sucked at his pipe. "Forgive me if I seem to generalize about Americans—"

"You too?"

"I have a reason for this, Charlotte."

Smiling, at last she pulled herself up to a sitting position, leaning back against the pillows of Violet's bed. "Go on."

"Two people are never equal in the outward needs of a relationship. There is always one who is more physical, less cerebral, or perhaps only more insecure, who wants the constant reassurance of affection. But marriage is acceptance of this discrepancy. Of saying, I would like more of the outward demonstration of love, but this is the way I am and not the way my spouse is. He loves me in his own way to his own capacity. And I love him in mine. And you are quite right, Charlotte child. If you are the one whose love flows most freely you must be careful not to drown him. Not unless he is very well able to swim. I think, Charlotte, that if you will grow up, you will be an excellent swimmer. I think that is your vocation: to do the loving. But with discipline. Not with demands."

"You sound like a priest after all," she said. And then, quickly, "You're right. Everything you've said is right. So I wanted to hit you. I'm sorry."

He smiled at her, his great bear's body perfectly capable of accepting any number of blows. "It's a lovely day, Charlotte. Walk out in the garden for a bit. It will do you good."

"Yes." She picked up the letters.

He looked at them, raising his shaggy brows. "You must understand, Charlotte, that it is perfectly possible that these letters are a fraud."

"But what do *you* think?" Charlotte asked. "Do you think it all happened? There *was* a nun in the convent called Sister Mariana, wasn't there?"

"Yes. But there are many people who think that the name was

stolen, that she has been maligned, that the religious vocation has been smirched."

"And you?"

"There have always been people who cannot understand the meaning of vocation and therefore would like to see it belittled. As for Soror Mariana, yes, I happen to think it probably happened, but that is hunch and personal opinion, not authentication."

"Do you think the letters are shocking?"

"If they are real, no. If they are a literary fraud, yes."

"Why?"

"They aren't good enough art. If they aren't a true outcry, they were written purely for sensationalism. It is not that as a subject I find it shocking. I don't feel that in art there is any subject that is taboo. It is how it is handled that matters. A study of nudes is a simple enough example. Some are art; others are nothing more than pornography. Your father, Charlotte, wrote of shocking enough matters in *Piero's Giraffe,* but I think it is his greatest book. Do you remember the setting of *Piero's Giraffe* when 'domestic animals had already been tamed and wild animals were not yet shy?' In a sense Mariana lived in Piero's world." He looked at Charlotte's fingers loosely holding the book of letters and said, "And so did Andrew, didn't he?"

"Violet told you about Andrew?"

"It was a grief for Violet, too, you know, which I shared with her as best I could. She had a concert in Madrid that night. After the concert Julia called me to come to her. But I had a patient I couldn't leave in the hospital here. I couldn't go to Violet any more than she could to you."

"I didn't expect her," Charlotte said. "I understood."

He made a strange, angry face. "We're both protecting her, aren't we? She could have come. Violet can do anything she wants to. She didn't want to. She was afraid."

"It's all right," Charlotte said. "I knew that, too. It didn't matter." Then, "Andrew and the other little boys in the park used to play horrible games. At least they seemed horrible to me. Sticks for guns or swords, stones for bombs. Always some weapon of death. And somebody had to be killed. I didn't want to give Andrew guns to play with. I thought it was parents teaching death and war. So in the park they used sticks. Children are more intelligent about death than we are, aren't they? We're afraid of it because we believe in it, and we're afraid to mention it for fear death will hear us and come. But children aren't afraid because they don't believe in it. Not as something permanent and dark and enduring. It's just going somewhere else, down the street, around the corner, to the grocery store. It isn't any further away for them than that. So they can play games and shoot themselves without fear. Bang. I shot you. Bang. I'm dead. Now I'll get up and let's start again. Let's play another game."

She held her arms tightly across her chest as though for protection.

"Andrew used to go completely *in* to his games. The way Violet does into music. That's why she couldn't come. She'd have gone into pain the same way. Andrew's pain. And Patrick's and mine. It isn't because Violet is dispassionate that she stays away from things. It's because she's much too passionate. It's that her awareness of suffering, like all her other senses, is more acute than the ordinary person's. She can sustain the peaks of emotion and pain; she can stay impaled on them. It's only her music that orders this and makes it bearable. I think it's really only artists and saints who know the meaning of compassion."

To her surprise the doctor came over to her and folded her in his arms, holding her in a great, warm hug.

"Oh, Charlotte," he said. "Sweet, beautiful little idiot." He held her close to him, rubbing the warm fur of his beard against the pale gold of her head. Then he released her.

"Go out in the garden, child. I'll be along later."

In the garden the sun was warm, touching her head and making her remember, as sometimes a tactile sensation or an odor will do, a day when she had walked with Andrew in the park, and he had trotted along beside her, talking, while she had been preoccupied with her own thoughts.

"What makes people be robbers?" he asked.

Charlotte, only half listening, answered, "They don't have mothers to help show them how to behave."

Andrew, disbelieving, asked, "They don't have mothers?"

"No."

"But if they don't have mothers, how did they get inside there so they could be borned?"

Charlotte then absentmindedly, still with only half her attention on the child, explained how they had mothers once but either lost them or lost track of them.

Andrew, trustingly, satisfied, said, "Robbers on television aren't real, right mummie? They aren't real robbers. They're just pretending to be, because they really have mothers."

Later, when she was writing Violet, Charlotte had remembered enough of this conversation to record it for Violet's amusement, as she had when Andrew, out of the blue, had asked her, "We're human animals, aren't we, mummie? But we're made differently, without tails or barks or meows. Only with talks."

Andrew.

She shivered, in spite of the warmth of the sun, the remembered warmth of the doctor's hug, and stretched out on one of Violet's lawn chairs. Her fingers held the book of letters too tightly. She could look at Andrew's picture. She could listen to his words. But Patrick's words were still to be faced. But she could, she knew now, face them. As her father had always risen from the black leather couch and turned back to his typewriter.

"... why should I try not to remember all the wonderful ways in which you showed your love? How can such beautiful memories have become so cruel? It's unnatural that they should hurt me ..."

Memories. Was it unnatural for them to hurt? She had sat with Patrick, that wild glorious winter after he had come back to her, in the kitchen of the house on East Seventy-fourth Street. Essie and Reuben had gone to bed; her father was tapping away on the typewriter in the library. Violet was in Boston for a concert. Charlotte and Patrick were eating; how much they ate in those days, their appetites ravenous in all directions.

"Eat your crusts, Cotty," Patrick said. "It will make your hair curl."

"*You* make my hair curl," Charlotte said. "You make it stand on end." She threw her crusts across the table at him.

In response he pulled her from her chair, held her, searching for her mouth.

How little she knew.

There was nothing she knew anything about, except, perhaps, martinis.

But she felt more grown up than ever before. Or since. Adult. Sophisticated. Worldly wise.

"Patrick, do you believe in free love?"

His arms tightened about her. "Honey," he said, his lips brushing close against her ear, "there is no such thing as free love. All love is extremely expensive." He brushed her pale hair back from her face. "Actually, I'm quoting Violet, who has a reputation for being rather free about it. But she's right, you know, Cotty. You pays your money and you takes your choice. You get what you pay for. Or one might rather reverse it and say, you pay for what you get."

It's true that in loving you I felt a joy I hadn't known was possible, but I'm paying for it with a pain I didn't know was possible, either.

Even granting that nothing, even love, is free, Charlotte still would have been willing to be free with Patrick.

But, "No, Cotty," he said. "We may have unconventional parents. Our first meeting may have been unconventional. But our marriage is not going to be."

Another time, with an edge of anger, "Once we are married, Cotty, there will be no more baths in strange young men's bathtubs in rooms without shades at the windows. Once we are married you belong to me, understand? And I will not tolerate your behaving with anybody the way you behaved with me."

"You said we were going to forget that evening."

"We will. As long as you don't remind me of it."

Did she remind him of it? Often? Then how could she expect him to trust her?

You made me completely yours with your violence. It was your love that made mine burst into flame; your tenderness melted me, and then your promises completely reassured me. My own awakening passion undid me, and the result of what started with such happiness is tears, and deathly despair, and I see no help anywhere.

That first letter, half-crazed with misery; it must have burned in Mathieu de Berenger's pocket.

There were only five letters in all. Five too many.

                                                    . . . How did
Urraca and Ampara find out?
They would; of course they would.
"She's writing letters to him. Someone's sneaking them out."
"And in. He's writing to her. They both write every day."
"Hush. Somebody's coming."

You weren't blinded by love as I was; why did you let all this happen to me? . . . Why do you want to be so cruel to a heart that belongs to you utterly? . . . I couldn't ever forget you . . . Would I be able to overcome the thoughts that fill me and go back to a life of dull tranquillity? No, I couldn't bear to be empty and unaware . . .

Urraca whispered to Ampara in the dark of the hall, "They say it's an Italian soldier who's delivering the letters and that he's madly in love with Sister Mariana . . ."

Mariana, writing, waiting, waiting for responses, was aware of nothing but the ocean of water, the ocean of time, the ocean of silence between her and Noël.

Beatriz came to Mariana in her cell: how did she get the key? Did Mother Escolastica—
"Mariana."
Mariana did not look up to see who was speaking. "Go away."
"Mariana, it's Beatriz."
"You're not supposed to come in. Brites has forbidden—"
"I know that. I have a letter for you."
Mariana rolled over onto her back. She looked up at the ceiling.

She lay there as still as the sarcophagus of Dona Brites in the chapter room. Then with a sudden animal leap she was off the bed and had snatched the letter. She tore it open and read it. It was not long, and when she had finished she crumpled it and stood holding the ball of paper in her clenched fist. "How did you get this?"

"I was at the market today with Sister Procuratrix, and while I was waiting for her I saw your brother, Baltazar. He asked me to give it to you."

"How did you know who it was from?" Mariana sat on the edge of the bed. "The envelope's plain."

Beatriz shrugged. "Baltazar's guilt."

"The poor fool." Mariana put her elbows on her knees, her chin in her hands. "Now I suppose you'll go to Brites."

Beatriz leaned against the closed door to the cell. "I've known you've been writing to him."

"Known?"

"Don't write him again. It doesn't do any good."

At last Mariana looked at her. "But it *has* to do good! I have to write to him!"

"His letters make you cry. *When* they come."

"When I cry, at least I'm alive."

"You call that being alive?"

Mariana rose and went to the long window that led to the balcony. "I'm nothing without him. He's my life. If I couldn't hope— When he comes back I'll be—"

"You think he'll come back to you?"

"It's all that sustains me."

"You pray for it?"

Mariana looked out the window, out across the balcony to the gardens. "I don't pray anymore."

Beatriz asked, her voice carefully impersonal, light. "Why not?"

"Why pray when God has forsaken me?"

"He has forsaken *you?"*

"Hasn't he? Would I still be here if he hadn't? If he cared?"

Beatriz's voice deepened with intensity. "You think he doesn't love you anymore just because you've stopped loving him? You think he doesn't care? You think he sits up in heaven and sees you suffering and is indifferent?"

Mariana put her hands over her ears. "Go away, Beatriz. Leave me with my letter."

With a helpless motion Beatriz left. Mariana rolled face downward on her cot, stuffing the rough blanket in her mouth to stifle her cries.

"Where did you get the key?" the abbess asked Beatriz.

"From Sister Isabella."

"She gave it to you?"

"No, your Grace. I took it."

"Without permission?"

"Yes, your Grace."

"This is not like you."

Beatriz bowed her head, a stubborn expression on her beautiful face.

"I know about the letters," the abbess said, abruptly.

"I'm glad, your Grace."

"You wonder why I don't stop them?"

"No, your Grace."

"You took a letter either to or from Mariana this afternoon?"

"Yes, your Grace. That is why I do not wonder."

"We are all involved in the guilt. But I want as little of it to be on the sisters as possible. You are not to take such an action upon yourself again. Do you understand?"

"Yes, your Grace."

"It is one thing for me not to stop the letters. It is another for anyone within the walls of Nossa Senhora da Conceição to participate in their delivery. I know that you love Mariana."

"Yes, your Grace. I do."

"You must be careful not to love her too much. You know that I do not allow special friendships."

"I know, your Grace. But it would seem I have little control over the feelings of love in my heart."

The abbess's voice was sharp. "This is not reasonable of you, Sister. Of course you do. This is what Sister Mariana might say about her actions with the French soldier."

"But I do not let the feelings of my heart dictate my actions, your Grace."

"And stealing the keys from Sister Isabella? Going against my orders to Sister Mariana's cell? You don't call that your heart dictating your actions?"

Beatriz said steadily, "I would have done the same thing for any one of the sisters who was in the same situation. For any one of them. Even Sister Joaquina."

"That is hardly likely, and I do not think you are being completely honest with yourself, and this, too, is unlike you."

"I am very sorry, your Grace."

"Are you?"

Beatriz was silent for what seemed an interminable time, standing motionless before the abbess's desk. "I feel very far from God, your Grace."

"There are times when this happens to us all. Is it because of Sister Mariana?"

"No. I think it would be weakness to blame it on anybody else's action, or on our response as a community to that action. Why has it shaken us so, your Grace? Why has her blindness thrown the whole convent into darkness so that we are completely unable to see to help her—or ourselves? I used the letter as an excuse to try to see her alone, because I thought I might be able to break through to her. I see now that this was pride."

She paused again, and the abbess sat, head bent, at her desk, her brooding face half hidden by her veil. At last Beatriz continued, "I suppose one reason I feel so alienated from God is that I want him to love me, I want him to give me signs of his love, and yet I don't love him. I don't know how to love him. How can I expect God to show me his love if I do not love him?"

"You are not alone, Sister," the abbess said, softly. "You know that many Religious, even saints, have gone through periods of drought, even of despair."

Beatriz leaned toward the desk. "And you, your Grace? Are you out of yours?"

The voice cracked like a whip. "Sister Beatriz, you presume."

Beatriz dropped swiftly to her knees. "I beg your pardon."

"I have given you too much intellectual freedom, but I need your mind. It is a necessary curb to the religious emotionalism that is currently sweeping our convents. I need to counter it with reason. But you must not take advantage of this."

"No, your Grace. I did not mean to. It was not meant as presumption. It was only a cry in the dark. But I had no right to make it."

"You may go to the chapel," the abbess said. "There the candles are lit if you need tangible evidence of light. I have your obedience about the letters?"

"Yes, your Grace. You have my obedience. And I will make my confession to Father Duarte tomorrow."

In the chapel, in the classrooms, the corridors, Joaquina made herself a self-appointed watchdog, reporting the smallest infraction of a rule by sister or child, the raising of a glance, the turn of a head. Mother Escolastica confronted her. "You take too much upon yourself, Sister."

Joaquina stared with hostility at the shriveled little nun. "I don't demand any more of my Sisters than I do of myself. But when I demand a great deal of myself it always seems to be pride."

"Demanding of oneself is not pride, child. It is being disappointed in oneself that is pride."

"But how can one help being disappointed in oneself?"

"One can't," Mother Escolastica said, and left Joaquina standing in the darkness just outside the chapel.

In the tight confines of the confessional Mariana turned so that she could not see Father Duarte through the grille. "Father, I cannot come to confession again."

"You must."

"I've come and I've come because you've made me promise and because I've hoped that perhaps something—but nothing has happened, Father, and it's no good. I don't even want to be absolved."

"You will."

"Why? Why did he leave me? Why did he stop loving me? If you could only tell me that . . ."

"Perhaps you gave yourself so completely that your very gift became a demand."

"But I asked nothing of him, except—"

"Except everything. Mariana, my child, you can destroy with a love that is possessive and demanding." Leaning her forehead against the rough wood of the box, she moaned. "You overwhelmed him with love, Mariana. You drowned him in it. Perhaps this is why he turned and fled."

She dropped to her knees facing the grille, but it was not in order to see Father Duarte's face, it was not to put herself in the posture of prayer. "But if I loved him, how could I help showing my love? Love isn't to be hid, is it? Father, what am I to do?"

"Move through time until you can turn to God again."

"Time! Every day another speck of time has been lost into Eternity, and I with it."

"God will wait."

"It seems that everybody is willing to wait!" she cried. "Brites was going to throw me out. Why didn't she? Why did she let me stay? I oughtn't to be allowed to stay!"

"That is not a decision for you to make, my daughter."

"But I have broken my vows. I have sinned."

"You realize this?" the priest asked her. "You understand it?"

"I have sinned in *your* eyes."

"And in God's?"

She shook her head, rejecting his words. "If you think I'm in a state of sin, how can you let me stay here where I can contaminate the other sisters? I *can* contaminate them."

"We are aware of this."

"So?"

"Once the plague came to Beja, and the sisters helped care for the ill. When the first sister herself was stricken with the plague she was not thrown out of the convent onto the streets in order that the others might perhaps be spared, and more than half the women in Nossa Senhora da Conceição died."

"Father! If only you'd stop trying to save me, and throw me out. I don't want to be saved."

"I realize that."

"I don't want to stay here. I don't want to be Sister Mariana. I don't want to be Sister anything."

"But you are Sister Mariana."

"I don't want God, I don't want my soul, I don't want anything but Noël. Don't you understand? I'm being eaten alive with love."

The gentleness left the priest's voice. "You have yet to learn the meaning of love."

"I'm tired of words!" she shouted at him, ignoring his hand raised to silence her. "If I can't have Noël I don't want anything else."

He waited until the echo of her words had died against the small confines of the confessional. Then he said, "Mariana, hold out your hand. What does this gold ring on your third finger mean?"

"It means that I'm the Bride of Christ, and I don't want to be married to God! I want my lover to be a human being." She looked directly at the priest; even the expression in his eyes could not stop her. "How can being the Bride of Christ be like being the bride of man when he has so many brides?"

In the world in which Father Duarte worked and struggled with his priesthood many things disturbed and grieved him, but little shocked him. The very quietness of his reply undercut her cry. "You don't understand the nature of God."

She grabbed the grille with both hands and shook the bars. She was like a beast tormented behind the bars of the cage. "He doesn't want me! Christ or however you want to call him doesn't want me! He's abandoned me! At the time when I need him most desperately he's left me completely alone."

Father Duarte's voice cut through her hysteria. "You are not talking about Christ. You are talking about Noël."

. . . "I lose sympathy for Mariana," Charlotte told the doctor when he joined her in the garden. "The more I read these letters the more I see she wallowed in self-pity. And this shakes me. I've done it too. But at least now I've lost sympathy for myself. So maybe that's something. I do apologize. I've trumpeted my anguish aloud like—a wounded elephant trampling blindly through the jungle. Usually when I'm unhappy my single effort is that nobody see it, that I endure my pain alone so that I bore nobody with it. Nobody wants anybody else's suffering. But I've been pouring it out all over, on you, on Violet, even on Tonio. *Is* it the fever?"

"Yes, partly. Although I think you'd about reached the overflowing point anyhow. Tell me, Charlotte—I don't probe this wound for

—when Andrew died did you go all stiff upper-lip? Did you hide your grief from Patrick?"

"No. From everybody *except* Patrick. It was our grief together, Patrick's and mine. But we couldn't share it because my guilt came between us."

"Was it your fault, Charlotte?"

"I don't know. In a sense everything is everybody's fault. We all share in a corporate guilt."

"That's much too abstract an answer."

Her face was strained, very white. "I know. But I've needed abstractions. I've needed to share the blame."

"Patrick wouldn't?"

"He tried. But I still—I still felt that it was all mine."

"Isn't that because he needed you to carry it for him? Because of the two of you you're the strong one? Because he needed you to comfort him?"

"But I needed him, Dr. Ferreira. I needed comfort, too."

It did not matter how many times Patrick told her that she was in no way to blame. The truck could have gone out of control while she was walking Andrew to the park. It was not her fault. It was not anybody's fault. It did not matter how many times he told her. All she could hear was his first bitter accusation: "Why did you let him go out alone? You should have kept him in the house or taken him to the park."

But you cannot always take a child to the park. There are things that have to be done about a house. And the child needs to be out of doors. He cannot sit on the kitchen floor hanging around with pots and pans and getting in your way. He needs to be outdoors. And Andrew was always careful. She knew she didn't need to worry about his going out into the street. She knew she could trust him to stay on the sidewalk.

I told him to get out from under my feet while I was trying to clean the kitchen.

But all mothers tell their children to get out from under their feet. No matter how much we love them, there are always times when

I told him to go out and play and leave me alone for five minutes
But I didn't mean it.

No mother ever means it.

But it's what I did. It's what I said.

Gus said, "You must stop blaming yourself, Charlotte. It wasn't in any way your fault."

But Patrick said, "Why did you let him go out alone?"

He didn't mean it, any more than Charlotte meant "leave me alone for five minutes."

But I did mean it. I said it and I did it. I sent him out. And I have this knowledge to live with for the rest of my life.

It isn't that I think God can't forgive me. It's that I can't forgive myself.

. . . Father Duarte said, "Before you can accept God's forgiveness you have to forgive yourself. It is arrogance not to forgive yourself."

Mariana replied coldly, looking at him through the grille, "I feel no need to be forgiven. As to forgiving myself, I will never forgive myself for having lost him."

"For having lost God?"

"No, Father. You know who I am talking about."

"Is there, for you, a difference?"

She shrugged.

He said, "Sister Mariana. I want you to go into the chapel and kneel before the altar. I do not forget that you say you cannot pray any more. I don't even ask you to try to pray. Simply kneel there."

He did not miss the weary insolence in her voice. "How long?"

"Until your knees are sore. Until you start to fall."

How could she pray?

She had forgotten what prayer was.

Staying on her knees was no more than a physical posture. She was not on her knees before God. Nevertheless she knelt there.

While Father Duarte talked with the abbess in her study. His great hulk seemed shrunken; the deep brown eyes had retreated with age and fatigue. He spoke almost as though to himself, his voice a low rumble. "One of the most difficult things we have to do with those we love most is to love them enough to let them do it themselves. We have to believe in their capacity—or God's—to do it themselves. I know that it hurts you to see poor foolish Sister Isabella bump into things, to see her spill food on her habit as her eyesight grows dimmer. But you are letting her do as much as she can for herself. It would be far easier for everybody if you assigned various sisters to lead her around, to feed her, to help her dress and undress. Because Sister Isabella is childish and ignorant it is what she longs for. She thinks that you are cruel to let her blunder about alone in her increasing darkness. And so do some of the other sisters who rush to help her when they think you aren't looking. But if you did what she wants, if you did the easiest thing, if you didn't snap at the sisters when they do too much for her, you would be diminishing her, you would be helping to destroy God's image in her."

The abbess leaned against the back of her carved chair. "I have never quite put it this way, Father. But yes: I suppose what you say is true. What does it have to do with Mariana?"

"We have to love her enough to let her find her way in her own darkness. We have to love her enough to let her crash, as it were, into furniture in her way, to fall downstairs. Sister Isabella's sight is going to continue to fade, but for Mariana we must never lose hope that she will move into the light again. Can you imagine Mariana if she were physically blinded, thrust into absolute visual darkness as she is now into spiritual? She would perhaps go through a period of this same kind of wild resentment, of anguished rebellion. But the time would come when she would start to fight through it, when we would hear her say to any offer of help, 'Leave me alone. I can do it myself.' And she *would* do it herself. And we would have to love her enough to let her."

"Yes, Father," Dona Brites said. "I see the analogy. But she cannot start doing it herself, as you call it, until she has repented."

"Do you think I'm not aware of that? Do you think I'm not aware that doing it herself means doing it with her hand in the hand of God? But we cannot repent for her. We can only repent with her, and for ourselves."

"Yes," the abbess said. "But I am tired. We are all tired."

After her French class (which had been Mariana's) Beatriz was so tired that she remained at her desk in the damp schoolroom, ostensibly looking through papers, although actually she was not seeing the penned translations she had asked the older girls to do for her.

"Sister."

She did not hear.

"Sister. Sister Beatriz."

She looked up. It was Peregrina Alcoforado. Beatriz said coldly, "You are supposed to go to sewing now."

Peregrina stared back, equally coldly. Her voice was faintly contemptuous. "I am tired of being treated like a child. I want to talk about Mariana."

Beatriz shuffled her papers. "I have nothing to say."

"You loved her," Peregrina persisted. "Not idiotically, like the rest of them, like—like dogs snuffling around a scent they can't understand. You loved her enough to go on loving her now, didn't you?"

Beatriz looked down at her long white fingers holding Ampara's messily penned paper. "Yes."

Peregrina continued, standing, her legs slightly apart, braced. "Enough not to blame her for everything that is wrong with you, yourself, the way everybody else is doing."

Now Beatriz looked up at the girl. Peregrina had lost weight. Her eyes were dark and smudged with fatigue. Her hair was unkempt. She looked ugly and old.

"It's not all her fault," Peregrina said. "That's nonsense. The atmosphere of an entire convent shouldn't depend on one sister. And yet, while she's here, at the gates or in her cell, it's as though we had a wild beast in our midst who might break the chains at any time and kill us all."

"Sit down," Beatriz said peremptorily.

Suddenly a child again, Peregrina moved obediently to her chair and sat. "I am being driven mad. Her Grace, the sisters, everybody treats me like a child. I cannot stand Urraca or Ampara or any of them any longer. My father frightens me. When he is drunk he forgets that I am his daughter. I have to have somebody to talk to. Don't tell me to go to my confessor. I have. Father Pessanha's penances don't help. I have to talk to somebody who doesn't have to be wise, who doesn't have to know God's will. Do you know God's will?"

"No."

"Thank you," Peregrina said.

Beatriz put the papers down. There were three books on the desk and she pulled out the bottom one. Without opening it or looking at it, but with her long steady fingers holding it closely, she said, "If I have learned anything from all this sorry business it is that I can learn nothing, I can understand nothing. I had thought of God as a God of reason. My vocation was to a God of reason. I see now that I was wrong. That he is not. Why should he be?"

"What is he, then?" Peregrina asked.

Now Beatriz opened the book, looked silently and unhurriedly until she found the portion she wanted, then said, "St. Chrysostom," and read, *"It is an impertinence to say that He who is beyond the apprehension of even the higher Powers can be comprehended by us earthworms, or compassed and compromised by the weak forces of our understanding."*

She looked up from the book and across the row of empty chairs to Peregrina, the picture of a meek and dutiful schoolgirl, her hands obediently folded. "You have a mind, so I think you can understand that. And then, after that, we fall into the mistake of thinking that because we cannot comprehend God we can escape him."

Peregrina made a grimace that might have passed for a smile. "Like my father. My poor papa who is so afraid of being laughed at. He doesn't understand God so he doesn't believe in him. He's afraid God might laugh."

"It isn't only your father," Beatriz said quietly. "I've just begun to come up out of the destruction of faith that followed my own misconception of God. Now I know that I have no conception of God at all. All I know is that he won't let me alone."

"Then you think that perhaps—"

Beatriz nodded. "I think he won't let Mariana alone, either." She began looking through the book again. "We've all been too busy trying to understand with our minds, as though our minds were capable of— And Mariana never did this." She read aloud again, *"What do we hear from the Angels? Do they inquire and reason meticulously among themselves about God's nature? By no means. What do they do? They praise him."*

She shut the book. "That is what Mariana did. Her life was a song of praise. So perhaps we made the mistake of thinking that she was an angel—or at least angelic. But she is a human being, and she has spoken only with fallen angels for a long time."

"Do you think," Peregrina asked, "that she will ever praise God again?"

"Oh, yes," Beatriz said definitely. "When she gives up worshipping man."

"Noël?"

"Perhaps it was Noël at first. Now it is only herself."

The thing that is impossible for me to bear is your indifference. . . .
The heart makes a god of the one who wakens it . . .

. . . "I made a god out of my point of reference," Charlotte said. Julia had brought bouillon out to the garden, and she sat with the doctor, sipping the warm liquid. "The idea was all right. I just pushed it over into—a kind of sacrilege, I suppose. Wanting from people what I should want only from God."

"You are talking now as though you believed in him." With his usual relish the doctor picked up the lemon slice from his soup bowl and ate it.

"Oh, that—," she said vaguely.

"I think you're missing the point," the doctor said, stretching his big body out to the sun, "the point to your life. You condemn yourself for your love of people, even your love of Patrick. You don't need to justify being Patrick's wife, being a mother, as your career. It has been a true passion with you, as it is not to all women, and it is as creative a passion as Violet's fugues, or your father's strange and brilliant books. Or as Patrick's surgeon's knife. Don't underestimate it. Don't underestimate yourself."

She said in a low voice, "I hardly think that would be possible."

"If you want to speak foolishly I am not going to flatter you."

Quick to flush under reproof, she said, "It must have been hard on her, too."

He sighed in exasperation, "On whom?"

"His wife."

"Whose wife?"

She looked up in surprise at his not knowing. "Noël's."

"I dare say it was. Although these things were looked on differently then."

"Even so, it must have hurt her to read those letters."

"Many things hurt, Charlotte. You must stop paying so much attention to pain."

"How could he have let them be published? That was a vile thing to do. Even if he didn't take them seriously, still to let them be published was unpardonable."

"We all do unpardonable things. Some people think they were stolen from him."

"How could they have been stolen?"

The doctor smiled at her vehemence. "Just as Noël couldn't quite keep from talking about Mariana when he was in Portugal, so probably, when he'd had too much to drink, he showed her letters to one or two of his friends. It wouldn't have been difficult for someone to 'borrow' the letters long enough to get them copied. And once they were published they were evidently a staggering success. They were, you might say, the first best-seller."

"It was still unforgivable of him," she said. She stood up and walked away from him, toward the driveway. At a distance, almost hidden in the deep shadows of the poplars, she saw a figure on a bicycle. It was the child Joaquim whom Violet called Jacopo after Dante's son . . .

Behind the child came a truck, stirring up a cloud of dust. Had the road dried so quickly from all that rain? The child on the bicycle swerved. There was a scream of brakes.

God.

No!

Not again!

She ran gasping down the road.

When she reached the truck Joaquim was untangling himself from the fallen bicycle. The truck had stopped safely behind him. Blood was trickling down his leg from a long scratch. Otherwise he was unhurt.

"You idiot!" she screamed at him through the blind fury of her pounding heartbeats. "You could have been killed! You ought not to be allowed out this way if you can't be more careful!" She went on shouting at him as he stood there, straightening out the handlebars of his bicycle and looking at her in a completely uncomprehending way.

She could not stop. The little boy stood and stared. The truck driver honked at them and Joaquim pulled his bicycle over to the side of the road, so that the truck, with a load of earthen wine bottles, could drive on up to the house.

She was unaware that she was crying until she was caught and held from behind. She turned around and pressed her face against the rough tweed of the doctor's vest. The sobs shook her so that if he had not held her with the strength of his great arms it seemed that she would have been torn apart. He spoke over her head to the little boy, who wheeled his bicycle down the road to the house in a subdued manner. When the tears had abated somewhat the doctor led her back to the garden.

"It's all right, Charlotte. It is all right. Let it go. Don't try to hold it back."

But she could not have held back.

At last the sobbing spent itself. She lay back in one of Violet's garden chairs, breathing deeply, slowly.

He sat down across from her. "Charlotte."

"You could call me Cotty if you felt like it," she said. "Violet does. Joaquim—it made me—" She paused, swallowed. "Joaquim—"

"It's all right, Cotty. I understand."

"Dr. Ferreira, I'm pregnant."

He looked at her quietly, without surprise. "Yes. I suspected that you might be."

"How? I didn't say anything, did I?"

"No. I'm a doctor, Cotty. And you have a rather extraordinary way of telling people things without words. It is very good that you will have another baby. Violet will be very happy."

But it was not Violet's happiness that was at stake here. There was something else. She had to take it out and look at it now. It had to be faced.

"I'm glad someone will be happy," she said.

"Are you not? And isn't Patrick?"

"We ought to be, oughtn't we?"

Now, Charlotte. Now. Look at it with open eyes. You can't go running across oceans indefinitely. There are not that many oceans.

She picked up her bouillon cup and drained it compulsively. Without thinking, as she always handed her cherries to Patrick, she took her lemon slice from her cup and handed it to the doctor. "I will have the baby," she said, "but I will not go back to Patrick."

Chewing the lemon, he asked, "Is the choice up to you? Do you have a right to make it?"

"Don't I?"

When she had told Patrick about the baby, he had looked at her coldly and said, "By whom?"

"But he didn't mean it," the doctor said.

"Patrick is not in the habit of saying things he doesn't mean."

The doctor took her hands in the gentle strength of his grasp. "Then why did he say it?"

"Because I'm a fool."

"Are you telling me that he had cause?"

"No. It is Patrick's child."

The doctor's grip tightened. "Then it was an unpardonable thing to say."

She shook her head. "No. No. It's not that easy." Her voice shook. She looked at him, opening her eyes wide to stop fresh tears. When she was back in control she said, "I flew to Portugal because Patrick had done something unforgivable. But it doesn't mean anything, forgiveness. I don't understand it. It doesn't even enter into it. The pardonable things: forgiveness doesn't even come into those, they're so easy. And the unpardonable things: forgiveness can't come into them, can it? So it isn't forgiveness that's the problem, ever, is it?"

"What is, then, Cotty?"

She spoke with great formality. "I have never in the Mosaic sense of the word been unfaithful to Patrick. I have never legally committed adultery. But in Jesus' sense of the word I have been unfaithful over and over again. This is worse—I do know this—than the casual adultery that has become almost accepted among most of the people we know. I wanted to sleep with Gus when I couldn't get near Patrick. And with other men, too. I was filled with feelings of—isn't the word concupiscence? As for Patrick, I don't know. I didn't even ask myself what he'd done or hadn't done or with whom. When the relationship between two people is broken as ours was broken, the outward act of infidelity is only the smallest part of it."

Her voice trembled again, and she raised the empty bouillon cup to her lips. Putting it back on the cracked green paint of the garden table, she said, "Yes, it was unpardonable. But we all do things that are unpardonable. Over and over again." She turned away from him, looking down at the fresh grass.

In an even, emotionless voice she told him about how the child she was now carrying had been conceived.

She had gone to the ballet with Gus, all Tchaikovsky, so that she felt drowned in the lushness of the music, in velvet and gold, in the unsubstantial dream of gauze tutus, in the vacant passion in the eyes of the ballerinas. Afterwards Gus took her over to Beekman Place where he had just bought an apartment.

"I want you to see it, Charlotte, to grace it with your presence."

They were walking across town and as he spoke she tripped and only his steadying arm kept her from falling. She laughed. "If it's grace you're looking for—"

"The place is full of fresh paint," he said, keeping his arm around her, "and emptiness. I don't move in until next week. And I want to see you in the rooms so that I will know where things need to go. You will walk through rooms that are unfilled, unfulfilled, and your presence will bring them to life."

They turned into the building and she gave him a startled glance. He laughed angrily. "Doesn't sound like rough Gus, does it? Didn't know I was a poet, did you? I used to write reams of poetry when I was in college. I used to—" He snapped his jaw shut and they rode up in the elevator in silence.

He opened the door to the apartment and the odor of paint was almost suffocating. He strode across the large, empty living room and opened one of the windows that looked out over the river, and a gust of damp air came in. She followed him as he began moving back and forth between living room and aseptic kitchen, bringing in first a red and white checked tablecloth, which he spread carefully in the exact center of the bare, polished floor, then a bottle of wine, glasses, a breadboard, a long loaf of French bread, and a chunk of cheese. He sat down and held out his hand to pull Charlotte down to the floor beside him. Raising one eyebrow as though to denigrate himself he said, "'A loaf of bread, a jug of wine, and thou singing beside me in the wilderness.' It *is* a wilderness, Charlotte. You are all that makes it bearable for me."

"You're nice, Gus," she said softly, embarrassed, "to build me up this way."

"I don't build you up. Why does Patrick tear you down?"

"He doesn't."

"He does, and he always has. I've watched him do it, and I've watched your terrible efforts to please him. You hop and dance to his bidding like a little dog going through all its tricks so that its master won't whip it. You cringe like a beaten puppy."

She turned away, staring down at the checked tablecloth on the floor. "That's not true! Patrick doesn't—" She reached for the bread and broke it.

Gus took a piece from her, turned it in his strong and tender hands. "To break bread with you, Charlotte, is an act of such intimacy—"

"Don't," she said. "I'd better go, Gus. This isn't a good idea."

"It's the best idea I ever had," he said. "And you're not going yet. Not until—" He poured the wine, handed her a glass, then sat looking at her over the rim of his, motionless, silent. She held her fingers about her glass to steady them. "Drink," Gus said. She raised her glass and drank. "Drink it all," he commanded, and she drained the glass. He refilled it. "It is time," he said, "that you stop subordinating yourself to other people. You've always done it. First your father. I'll accept it that he was a misunderstood genius, but he devoured you."

"No—," she protested, but he silenced her with an authoritative wave of his hand.

"And the nuns in those repressive convent schools terrifying you with God so all you could see was an imaginary sinfulness and a needless guilt."

"No—," she started again.

"Drink your wine. You are not inadequate, Charlotte. You are everything I could hope for in a woman. Stop trying to compete with that bitch Violet. Be Charlotte."

She looked at him bleakly over her wineglass.

He took the glass from her hand, put it down on the cloth, then turned and kissed her. Her body's response was so violent that she was able to use the wave of passion that shook her to pull away, to stand, to turn from Gus to the door. Her flesh rebelled at the interruption so that she thought she would be sick there in the emptiness of Gus's room before she could get to the door.

She wrenched it open and ran down the corridor to the elevator, leaving Gus there, leaving her coat and bag, and ran out into the black and shocking air. There at the curb a taxi stood, waiting for her, it seemed, and she climbed in and leaned back against the cold leather. When the cab drew up in the front of her apartment she realized that she had no money, but the doorman paid the driver and she hurried upstairs.

Patrick was sitting up, reading a medical magazine. "Where the hell have you been?"

"To the ballet with Gus. You knew that."

She went past him and into the bathroom where she splashed cold water over and over again on her face. She did not know Patrick had followed her in until he said, "Did he give you what you want?"

Numbly she shook her head.

"Come here." His voice was harsh. "You want it, you can have it."

They lay there, spent.

"Andrew," she said. "Oh, Patrick, Andrew."

Patrick shoved her words away with a pushing gesture of one hand, and a strange, negative sound deep in his throat.

Until both she and Patrick accepted Andrew's death, how could there be new life?

She had had a long and hard labor with Andrew. She did not do it well. It took over forty-eight hours. The longer it took, the angrier Patrick got. He kept appearing with ill-concealed impatience. When Gus ordered exercise he walked Charlotte up and down. Then, when Gus said she was too tired, when Gus sent her to bed, Patrick kept stalking in and out of the small room where she was knotted with pain. He was furious with her and he made no attempt to hide his rage and contempt. She looked at him in a brief pause between pains and started to ask him to help her, but the pain caught her again.

Her legs cramped, muscles knotting against the pain. She clenched her fists so tightly through the peaks that her palms were bloody. One of the nurses cleaned her hands with alcohol during a moment of respite and it was a relief to feel the sharp sting, to know that she *could* feel something through the tight web of agony within which she was bound. The nurse cut her fingernails and gave her the roughness of a towel to clutch. "It doesn't matter if you tear it, Mrs. Napier." It was obvious from the concern of the nurses that things were not supposed to happen like this; it was not supposed to hurt this much. Gus had prepared her well, but not for anything like this.

"Sorry, Charlotte, love," he said. "This is a rough one."

Patrick stood at the foot of the bed and glared at her and at the great drops of sweat that beaded her upper lip as a fresh pain started. "You're doing it abominably," he shouted. "Can't you even have a baby like anybody else?"

Gus said sharply, "Shut up, Patrick, or get out." Then he put his hand gently on Charlotte's belly. "Try to hold on," he said, his hand firm, tender, somehow by the authority of its touch holding the pain at bay. "If I give you anything against the pain now it will just slow things down even more and be bad for the baby. You're dilating too slowly, but you are dilating, and once that's done you'll start working, pushing pains, and you won't mind those."

She was blinded by pain.

"Don't be so bloody brave," Patrick said. "Go ahead and yell, goddam it, Cotty."

She had been trained not to yell. All her life she had been trained not to yell (why had James Clement sent her to those convent schools?), and the pain had become, in any case, beyond yelling.

There was a consultation. Should they do a Caesarian? How much more could she bear? They kept checking her heart. The heavy grey bandage of the blood-pressure machine was left on her arm. The consulting doctor said something about danger to the baby.

"I don't give a goddam about the baby," Patrick said. "You've got to stop this. I can't stand it."

Gus, his hand again gentle on her belly, said, "Charlotte, love, we've decided—"

She interrupted him, gasping, "Gus, I've got to push—"

"No, Charlotte, you haven't dilated—"

"Can't help it—pushing—Gus—"

There was a rush of activity and suddenly she was at work. Now her voice sounded in a deep "a-a-a-h!" It was, as Gus had explained to her early during her pregnancy, like the work noise sailors make pulling on a rope. One, two, three, heave, a-a-a-h! There was no need to be ashamed of or to fight this noise. There was no need to brace herself against this pain. She could, instead, throw herself into it. One, two, three, push, a-a-a-h!

A rush, and a ripping, and a splitting, and then there was Gus holding the tiny wet thing up by its heels and a new cry came into the world. Andrew's first healthy, indignant yell.

And she was filled with glory.

Gus had been tender and gentle and strong and Patrick had behaved abominably.

Can you be tender and comforting as Gus was only if you are not really involved?

Patrick.

You cannot behave this abominably to anyone unless you are sharing the pain beyond the point of reason.

"I'm pregnant." Her hands trembled as she reached out to Patrick. "We're going to have a baby."

His face was hard. "No."

"Patrick, yes—"

"It will be Andrew all over again."

"No, Patrick, no—"

"Don't do this to me," he said. "I can't take it. Get the hell out."

So she left. She packed her bags and left.

This was what she had to face now, not Patrick's words, but her own flight, her refusal to accept, to bear, to endure.

She had tried to flee from Patrick

from Andrew
from the responsibility of being either mother or wife
from the responsibility of the new life within her

She looked across the garden table in surprise. She said wonderingly to the doctor, "I came here to reject. But what I have to do is accept, isn't it?"
to accept
to accept Patrick
Patrick not as I would like him to be, but Patrick as he is
to accept myself, not as I would like to be but as I am
to move from the noisiness of my own demands into love

For Mariana it was a different acceptance, but she must have come to it in the end. In the end she had faced her sin, she had repented, but first there had to be an acceptance of what had happened, as it had happened, that it was what it was and not what Mariana would have liked it to be.

I have discovered that you yourself were less important to me than my own passion.

Yes.

Did she know what she was saying when she wrote this? For this one sentence the letters might have been read. All the things that made their fame, all the scandal, everything else could be forgotten. But that one sentence would stay.

And in the end Mariana became the abbess.

But first?

The unpardonable, as usual.

The publication of the letters was unpardonable.

And then, once that was done, once their fame, or infamy, had swept through France, it was inevitable that they would get to Portugal, to Lisbon, to . . .

. . . In Lisbon a fat priest walked up to a small, rather disreputable bookstall. He looked through the books as though searching for something special, picked one out of a pile and was eagerly leafing through it when a plainly dressed woman came up to him.

"Good morning, Father."

Surreptitiously the priest slipped the book back into the pile, took in its stead a religious tract. "Good morning, my daughter."

Was it he who had taken the letters to the bishop, who in his turn had . . .

In the Convento de Nossa Senhora da Conceição the abbess stood very still in the center of the room, holding a book in her hands, looking at it with a face that was stern and pure in its complete control of visible emotion. She put the book down on the table and walked slowly, heavily, as though the rheumatism that crippled Mother Escolastica had crept into her bones, to her prie-dieu, where she knelt, the look of stern concentration never changing.

In the Alcoforado villa Francisco Alcoforado, in a beruffled nightshirt, was chasing a giggling chambermaid about his enormous four-poster bed. Sitting on top of one of the carved posts and gibbering excited comment was Pinto, the monkey. The maid fell onto Dom Francisco's prie-dieu (it was a much more ornate one than the abbess's) shrieking with laughter. "I'm safe here! You can't catch me here!"

The light glinted on the gilded crucifix above the prie-dieu as the door opened simultaneously with a sharp knock, and Baltazar precipitated himself into the room and thrust a book into his father's hand, then turned to the chambermaid with deadly calm. "Get out."

She turned to Dom Francisco, but he was looking at the book, his mouth slightly open in shock, a vein pulsing dangerously at the side of his forehead. Baltazar pulled the girl up off the prie-dieu and she scuttled out of the room, the monkey at her heels looking back in chattering terror.

"My God," Francisco said, "what will this do to my position at court?"

It was inevitable that the abbess would be unable to keep it from the sisters. There was too much going back and forth between the lay sisters in the kitchen and the tradesmen from the town, between the schoolchildren and their parents. The choir sisters themselves were often sent to the market where they were given vegetables and eggs.

Beatriz went with Joaquina, each carrying one of the large convent marketing baskets, moving from stall to stall where the farmers gave them squashes, melons, heavily salted meat and fish. A group of French foot soldiers, drunk, came rolling through the narrow street that ran the length of the market. Two of them broke away from their companions and swaggered after the two nuns. One of the group called after them, "That's right, good luck to you; a nun's the tastiest morsel of all."

One of the men thrust his reeking face close to Joaquina's. "How about it, Sister mine? Shall I climb up to the balcony tonight?"

Blanching, Joaquina tried to shove him away.

The second soldier thrust a volume of the letters into Beatriz's basket. "Present for you, sweeting." He tried to kiss her, but a farmer came out from his booth and grabbed the two soldiers by the collars. "Move along now and leave the sisters alone or I'll have you turned in." As the Frenchmen rejoined their companions, laughing noisily and shouting lewd suggestions back at the sisters, the farmer cleared his throat in embarrassment. "Don't listen to those foreigners, Sisters. They've had too much wine. They don't mean anything by it. Sorry they disturbed you."

Beatriz bowed her head in acknowledgment. "Thank you for helping us. I will tell the Most Reverend Mother the Abbess Brites of your kindness. Come, Sister." Moving swiftly, she led Joaquina out of the market.

"It's insufferable," Joaquina said.

Beatriz did not slow her long, swinging stride. "Apparently not, since we seem to be suffering it."

They walked on in silence, moving to the side of the road as a carriage with galloping horses came up in a cloud of choking dust and passed them.

In the carriage was Francisco Alcoforado. He did not see the two nuns. He saw nothing but his own anger and humiliation. When the carriage drew up at the convent gates he leaped out without waiting for his man to open the door for him and rang the bell violently.

Mariana opened the gate, and when she saw who it was, she cried out softly, "Papa!"

He struck her across the mouth, shoved her aside, and strode through the garden and into the convent, unannounced.

Beatriz took the baskets of food to the kitchen. As she put them down on the table she remembered the book and pulled it out, glancing at the title: *Letters of a Portuguese Nun*. She caught her breath and opened the book. Yes. There was no evading it. The letters were those Mariana had written to Noël. Turning with quick decision, Beatriz moved to one of the fireplaces where a caldron of soup was stewing and threw the book into the flames. No one had seen. No one must ever see.

In her study the abbess was praying and did not turn around when her door was banged open. Her brother went up to her and held the book in front of her eyes. When her eyes closed as she attempted to continue her prayer he deliberately pulled open one of her lids. She stood up, stiffly.

"To what do I owe this most unusual honor?"

Dom Francisco flung the book down on her desk.

The abbess glanced at it. "I have already seen it." Her suffering over Mariana, and her own disciplines, had carried her beyond the point of showing shock.

His eyes bulging, Dom Francisco shouted, "Am I to be spared no humiliation, no disgrace? When Baltazar was sent a copy of this—this—filth—from France, I thought it could be suppressed, but no, *Jesus Christus* no, well enough could not be left alone. Can you guess the kind of jokes I'm made the butt of? No, of course you can't, you pious idiot; and your bishop, the sniveling hypocrite, has the gall to twit me about it. It's entirely your fault. If you had been more careful this would never have happened."

The abbess sat wearily at her desk during this tirade, her hands loosely on the book, her eyes closed.

"Damn you, do something about it! That's what I came to tell you, *do something!*" On this note of hysteria he rushed out.

He passed Baltazar on the road, but, as he had not seen the two nuns, he did not see his son.

❖

Baltazar was not in a carriage, nor on his white stallion. He walked slowly on foot, not quickening his step when a dank, dreary rain began to fall, spattering the dust. He was not in his bright Portuguese army officer's uniform, but in dark garments as somber as the lowering day. When he reached the lodge and the convent gates he did not ring, but stood staring at Mariana as she sat at her place in the small room until, feeling the brooding intensity of his gaze, she turned and looked over the barrier at him.

"Mariana."

She continued to look, but did not speak.

"Sister, I wanted to tell you myself." She did not react and he was not sure that she was listening. "I am leaving the army. I am taking Holy Orders." Now her look held questioning, but still she did not speak. "Mariana, you know why I am doing this?"

Her voice was the dead voice that he had become used to. "If you say it is because of me I shall not believe you. Or I shall say it is nonsense. You are doing it because of yourself. Very well. Go ahead and do it. But don't come to me for approval."

"All I want is your love, Mariana."

"Don't come here looking for love, either."

"Where God is, shouldn't love be?"

"God? You won't find God here either. And in any case love has nothing to do with God."

"Mariana, your turning away from God doesn't mean that he can't love you. Love doesn't always flow in two directions. It takes only one to love."

Without answering she turned and left the gatehouse, left the gates unattended, and wandered to the lily pond.

She went there often, so often that the abbess declared it out of bounds, forbidden to both sisters and children.

So Joaquina, in the damp of an early morning, finding Mariana's cell empty, knew where to look for her. She hurried along the cloister and out of its shadows. She had at last been trusted again with the key. The early morning mist lay wispily about garden and grounds, its tenuous streamers still undispersed by the sun. Her heart beating heavily, she crossed the rose garden and ran along the forbidden path to the pond. Mariana was standing there, her clothes a sodden mass clinging to her body. It had rained during the night. How long had she been there? How had she left her locked cell? She, like Noël, must have used the balcony for a door.

When she saw Joaquina she turned her face away.

Joaquina approached her, speaking with an urgency beyond her usual nervous tenseness. "Sister. Sister Mariana. I know I'm breaking rules to come here. But I must talk to you." Mariana turned slowly to look at her. Joaquina spoke in too loud a voice. "I forgive you."

Mariana gave a wild and startled laugh, and turned away again. Joaquina bit her lip for self-control, then said more quietly, "We know you're not yourself. We're all unhappy for you."

"Leave my unhappiness to me."

"But we all share it."

"It seems my life is public property."

"A nun has no private life."

Mariana smiled at Joaquina, an unamused grimace. "Don't talk to me. I'll corrupt you."

There was no doubting Joaquina's unwelcome, unlovable sincerity. "I only want to pray for you."

Mariana turned on her furiously. "I forbid you to—"

Fury met fury. Joaquina's slender control snapped. "You still think you're better than anybody else, don't you? You're even too good to be prayed for. And what would be sin for the rest of us must be excused in you. But you *have* sinned. All your special privileges can't change your sin. You've betrayed our Lord, and the man you have betrayed him for has betrayed you."

Their faces had come close together.

"You lie," Mariana whispered.

Joaquina's voice was still too loud. "You don't understand anything about being the Bride of Christ! You never did. You know nothing about loving him. Don't you see what you've done to us? Don't you see what you're doing to us all?"

Mariana whispered, her face as white and mottled as Joaquina's, "Go away. Leave me alone in hell."

"You're dragging us into it with you!"

By the closeness of Joaquina's face, her wild eyes, her sheer volume as much as her words, Mariana was brought up short. "What?"

"You're destroying us all!" Joaquina cried. "We never laugh any-

more. Beatriz does nothing but pace. We no longer hear the sound
of the Angelus in our ears. We hear your sobs."

"But I—"

"Oh, I know, you cover your head, you stuff your fingers into
your mouth to try to stifle your cries. But we hear. We see your eyes
rimmed in red. Oh, God! My God! I wanted to help you, I wanted
to pray for you! And then as usual I got angry and spoiled everything.
And even my praying wasn't selfless. It wasn't only for the rest of
us. It was for me."

"But—"

"You think you can suffer in private? You think you can keep it
to yourself? You think it hasn't eaten through the whole convent like
a cancer? And even the little children: they're devoured by it, too.
They play quietly, with grave faces, instead of running and shouting."

"They know—"

"How can they help knowing? I cannot tell you when a laugh was
last heard in this place. I have learned now that one cannot worship
God in a place where there is no laughter. Peregrina cries like an
old woman. Others who were always happy and gay can't eat for
homesickness, and that's just as well, because there's never enough
food. Dolores and several others have been taken away."

"Taken away—"

"Because we're not fit to care for them, we sisters who are in the
same convent that you are! And we're *not* fit anymore, it's true!
Sister Michaela wants to leave the convent—"

"To leave—"

"She's lost her vocation."

"Why?"

"Why do you think?" Joaquina accused.

Mariana moved away, leaning against the rough trunk of a tree to
steady herself. Joaquina went up to her and said loudly, "You could
see if you'd just look! If you'd think for one moment of something
other than your own misery." Joaquina's flood of words stopped as
she looked at Mariana's face. "No. No, Sister. I'm sorry."

Mariana stretched out one hand as though reaching for something. Her voice was very quiet, very low. Joaquina had to strain
to listen. "Don't be sorry, Sister. You're quite right. I should have
realized."

Joaquina's voice trembled; her eyes filled. "I've hurt you again. I didn't want to hurt you—" Her tears spilled over.

Mariana reached out toward her, then drew back. "No, you've helped me. I thank you, Sister. I thank you very much."

She walked, as though in her sleep, through the garden and into the cloister. She went into the chapter room, through it, along the silent corridor, up the stairs, and into her cell. There she walked round and round in her cage.

The rising bell rang.

The bell for Matins, Lauds, Prime.

From her cell she could hear the antiphonal sound of grace from the refectory below.

She went out onto the balcony, walked across it, and looked down on the cloister. There she saw the abbess and Michaela not at breakfast with the community but walking up and down the arched walk, up and down, as Mariana had walked in the smaller confine of her cell, walking up and down and talking.

With a quick turn of decision Mariana went back into her cell, dropped for a fraction of a moment onto her knees on the prie-dieu, then she rose and hurried through the convent, cutting across the square to the abbess and Sister Michaela. She went directly to the little nun.

"Sister Michaela, you must not leave."

There was no emotion in her voice. It was cold and clear, like a voice coming from a marble statue.

"Who gave you permission—," the abbess started.

Mariana ignored her. "You're leaving because of what I've done. Because of what I've said to you. Because of Noël and me."

Michaela said, "Please stop, Sister."

"You overestimate yourself," the abbess said icily. "I am handling this. It is not your concern."

In the center of the cloistered square the fountain splashed with charming indifference.

Mariana continued to ignore the abbess, speaking to Michaela as though they were alone, her words tender but her voice still marble.

"Sister Michaela, dear sweet little Michaela, I love you, and all I've done is hurt you. Don't destroy yourself because of me."

For a moment Michaela forgot the formidable presence of the

abbess. "But if you've destroyed yourself—"

The two words came with the impassive indifference of stone. "Have I?"

"You must have, because I don't love you anymore."

Mariana did not flinch. "What is important is you, little Sister, what you're doing to yourself. Please listen to me. Stay here where you belong."

Michaela wrung her hands, the thin, delicate fingers white and tense against her dark habit. "How can I turn back now when the love is gone from my heart?"

Mariana said, "I love you."

The abbess, not comprehending, accused: "You know nothing about love."

Mariana turned to the abbess, her words careful, controlled. She was no longer the ravaged nun, wild with grief, moving like an animal between cell, gatehouse, and pond; but neither was she Mariana. "I know that love isn't love as long as I care whether or not my love is accepted. Unless I can love without asking anything in return, it isn't love."

"But you *are* asking!" Michaela cried. "You're asking me to stay!"

"I won't ask any more, then," Mariana said, still too calm. "Instead I'll make you a promise." The abbess looked at her searchingly. Mariana's steady voice continued. "I will send him back his letters. Noël's letters. And his medal."

She ripped the medal from her neck and dropped it in front of Michaela on the grass. "I will never write to him again. I will open my hands and my heart and let him go."

Michaela seemed suspended on the pale blue point of Mariana's gaze. She broke away from it, reached down at her feet for the medal, picked it up, dropped it again, and looked at it as it lay on the grass.

"You will—you will do that?"

Mariana's face was white and blind and emotionless. "Yes."

Michaela made a small, confused moan and dropped to one knee, again touching the medal with trembling, tentative fingers. The abbess spoke softly, carefully, as though afraid her words would destroy something. "Sister Michaela finds it difficult to learn that nothing we can do or say is irrevocable. Perhaps what you have just said— Do you realize what you have said, Sister Mariana?"

"Yes, your Reverence."

The abbess winced. It was the first time Mariana had called her by this title since the abbess had struck her. "You can do this?"

There was a faint crack in the marble. One of Mariana's hands moved gropingly toward the abbess, then returned to its place in the wide, dark sleeve of her habit. "If you will help me. If you will take his things and send them back to him."

"Before you have time to think? If this is done without thought it means nothing."

Mariana looked at the abbess steadily. Behind her eyes a small light of life began delicately to flicker: could the gold perhaps return? "It is not done without thought."

"You will never write to him again? Sending back his old letters doesn't mean that you will have the strength not to write again."

"I will not write." She stretched her hand out toward the abbess, though she did not touch her, nor did the abbess dare to reach out for her hand in return. "And if I should ever ask you for anything of his, even if I come to you sobbing and begging and groveling, then you must deny me."

The abbess commanded Michaela, "Give me the medal."

At last Michaela picked it up. She held it out to the abbess, who took it, in turn offering it to Mariana. "I do not want you to do this unless—"

Mariana recoiled. "I don't want to touch it again."

Michaela, like a small child needing comfort, spoke to Mariana but moved closer to the abbess. "Mariana, how can you do this?"

Mariana's words came clear, but there was still the strange coldness to them. They were understood, but they were not felt; they were not alive. The sun broke through the clouds and moved across the convent roof, the cloistered walk, falling on the three of them standing there, but Mariana seemed untouched by its warmth. She said, "Her Grace told me once that there is no virtue in loving the lovable. There's no virtue in loving where it's easy. Maybe I will learn to love Noël now. When I want nothing from him. When I don't even want him."

Michaela hid her head against the abbess like one of the smaller children. The abbess drew her hand lightly over Michaela's coif almost as though she had been going to smooth a child's hair. Michaela said, "I don't understand. You don't—you don't love the Frenchman any more?"

"Oh, yes, I love him," Mariana said clearly. "Or I will. I *can* love him now that I see Christ in him. Before, I saw only myself, only the gratification of my own self will. Now I can love him within God's will. If God will."

Dona Brites looked at Mariana. Mariana returned her gaze; the abbess's voice strengthened. "It is not necessary that we understand everything, Sister Michaela." She put the back of her hand for a moment gently against the young nun's flushed cheek. "Would you like to be excused to go to your cell and pray?"

Michaela nodded mutely, looked at Mariana, at the abbess, back at Mariana, tried to speak, could not, and ran off, disappearing into the shadows of the arched walk and then into the convent.

The abbess looked long and searchingly at Mariana, then held out her arms, and Mariana moved slowly into them, but still like one dead, like one in a dream. The abbess was afraid, but she asked, her voice harsh, demanding, "You are going to give me his letters?"

"Yes, your Grace."

"All of them?"

"All. There aren't very many."

"You will not ask for them back?"

Mariana looked steadily at her aunt. "This isn't only because of Michaela, your Grace. Perhaps she was what made—but the time had come."

The iron was back in the abbess. "It had come a long time ago." Then she asked, sharply, "You are ready to make your confession?"

Mariana shook her head.

"You will not confess?"

"No, your Grace. I cannot do that."

"Why?"

"I have gone too far away for that. But at least I can stop dragging others into the pit with me."

The abbess looked into the cold, unmoving face; she hit the back of one hand into the palm of the other in sudden decision. "You could begin now to make use of your suffering."

"No, your Grace," Mariana said. "Suffering has no use. No use at all."

The abbess turned away from the girl; her voice was harsh. "You *shall* suffer," she said. "Come with me."

She led the way to her study. She took the book of letters from a drawer and thrust it at Mariana. Mariana looked at it, opened it. It was a moment before she realized what it was. She gasped. Her pupils dilated until they were enormous, swallowing up the pale cold blue. It was as though she had been struck a violent blow. But she was stunned, rather than in pain. She handed the book back to the abbess and turned away. She walked to the door.

The abbess shouted, "Where are you going?"

Mariana did not answer. The abbess moved as though to follow her, but Mariana said, "No," just the one word, but in such a way that the abbess stopped. When Mariana was out of sight the abbess hurled across the room to the window and stood, watching, until the dark form appeared in the sunlight of the cloister and moved, like a shade, a phantasm, to the gatehouse.

In the refectory the sisters were still eating breakfast.

In the gatehouse Mariana sat in the shadows and stared, not within herself now, dulled eyes turned in to some vast dark chasm within her skull, but out the gates and down the road.

She seemed to be looking for something.

Was she looking for someone to approach the convent?

Surely not a black charger?

In the distance, at the turn of the road, a small figure moved, limped, toward the gates. Through narrowed eyes, against the sun, Mariana watched.

The figure, whoever it was, was carrying something, cuddled tight like a baby (was it a baby?) against the breast.

The early sunlight hit the white of convent walls and was thrown back upon the road, upon the figure.

It was Peregrina.

It was Peregrina carrying Pinto, the monkey, her own face wizened, distorted, simian, the monkey's placid, in repose, like a sleeping infant's.

The monkey was dead.

Peregrina saw Mariana and began to scream.

Mariana was out of the gatehouse, out of the gates, on her knees on the dirt before the child, holding the child and the dead stiffening body of the monkey in her embrace.

Peregrina screamed. Screamed.

Then, as Mariana did not loosen her embrace, the screams thinned, became a whimper.

She sounded frighteningly like the monkey.

Mariana said nothing. Waited.

The strange, animal moans continued.

"God," Mariana said. "God."

In the tight circle of her sister's arms Peregrina began to shudder. Her mewling stopped. She pulled back so that she could see Mariana's face, opened her mouth to try to speak, opened it again, again. Finally: "Mariana—"

"Yes, my darling?"

"Mariana, it was papa—"

"Yes."

"You know?"

"I can guess."

"I don't have to tell you?"

"No."

"I screamed. Pinto came in. He jumped on papa and pulled at him. And papa killed him. He flung him across the room and Pinto hit the prie-dieu and I think it broke his neck—"

"Hush," Mariana said. "Hush. It will be all right."

"I wanted God," Peregrina said, "and he didn't come."

"He has come," Mariana said. "He is here. Give me the monkey."

"Where are you going? What are you going to do?"

"We will bury him in the garden. But first we must go to the chapel." She rose from her knees and took the dead animal. She held him in one arm. With the other she still protected Peregrina. The shuddering had stopped now, and Peregrina's voice once again came steady, the voice of an Alcoforado.

"He was drunk, of course," she said. "He didn't know what he was doing or who I was. When he threw Pinto I got away. I picked

Pinto up and ran upstairs to my room and locked myself in. I was afraid in the dark. I didn't dare leave until daylight. Then I slipped out of the house. No one saw me. And then I ran. And ran."

"All this way?" Mariana asked gently. "All this way by yourself?"

"I needed you," Peregrina said. And then, in a surprised voice, "You're back."

Mariana spoke through a great wave of pain. "Yes. I'm back."

The abbess had wanted her to suffer.

Peregrina asked, "Are you praising God again?"

The question did not seem strange. Mariana answered, "Yes. I am praising God."

"I never have," Peregrina said. "But if you can, perhaps one day I will be able to, too."

Outside the chapel they wrapped the monkey in Peregrina's cloak and placed him gently on a marble bench. Then they went in, to the scarlet and the gold, and the stone floor beneath their knees.

In the afternoon, when Father Duarte came, Mariana was waiting for him.

"Her Reverence would like to see you, if you please, Father. But she has given me permission to ask you first if you will hear my confession."

"Gladly, my child," Father Duarte said.

They walked in silence from the gatehouse through the cloister and into the chapel. The priest went quickly to the sacristy and returned, wearing his stole, then went into his side of the confessional. Mariana genuflected toward the altar, then entered the confession box, knelt, and made the sign of the cross. She held her face up and the light struck against the gold flecks in her eyes.

"In the name of the Father, and of the Son, and of the Holy Ghost. Pray, Father, give me your blessing, for I have sinned." Then, "I confess to Almighty God, to blessed Mary, ever Virgin, to blessed Michael the Archangel, to blessed John the Baptist, to the holy Apostles Peter and Paul, to all the Saints, and to you, Father, that I have sinned exceedingly in thought, word, and deed, through my fault, through my most grievous fault . . ."

In his place behind the grille the priest bowed his great, shaggy head. Tears filled his eyes. The spring sun streamed into the chapel. Now there was no darkness in Mariana's face, only light.

. . . The light was gentle in the garden. Charlotte closed her eyes, opened them as she heard Violet's voice calling her, imperious, demanding. Charlotte hurried across the lawn to the house. Violet pulled her into the shadows of the hall, gesturing to the phone. "Answer it."

Unthinking, Charlotte picked up the old-fashioned black receiver. "Hello?"

From the other end of the line, from far, far away, she heard a choking sound.

"Charlotte—love—" and then a sob.

Patrick. Patrick was crying. At last, with hundreds of thousands of miles between them, they were together.

When she went back to the garden, the doctor was waiting, holding his empty cup. The book of love letters was lying on the table.

"Mariana was, I suppose, a saint," Charlotte said. "Or at least she may have become one. I am only Charlotte and I am called neither to suffer nor to rejoice as she must have done."

The doctor merely raised his brows. The warm sun flowed over them. Julia stalked out to the garden and took away their bouillon cups.

Charlotte said, "Mariana had to turn away from Noël and back to God. I think that all that is wanted of me is to be willing to live again, without blame or guilt." She looked at the doctor and smiled.

Author's Note

The Letters of a Portuguese Nun do, of course, exist, and the quotations from them are not inventions of the author, nor are the members of Mariana's family. However, the text of the novel indicates how little is known, how much is problematic, about Mariana. The letters, then, have been used only as a springboard for a work of the imagination, and that part of the narrative which speaks of Mariana is in no sense an attempt at biographical or historical reconstruction.

M. L'E.